# low-fat no-fat
# ITALIAN

The authentic healthy taste of Italy in 160 recipes

LORENZ BOOKS

This edition is published by Lorenz Books, an imprint of Anness Publishing Ltd,
Hermes House, 88–89 Blackfriars Road, London SE1 8HA; tel. 020 7401 2077; fax 020 7633 9499
www.lorenzbooks.com; www.annesspublishing.com

If you like the images in this book and would like to investigate using them for publishing, promotions or advertising,
please visit our website www.practicalpictures.com for more information.

UK agent: The Manning Partnership Ltd; tel. 01225 478444; fax 01225 478440; sales@manning-partnership.co.uk
UK distributor: Grantham Book Services Ltd; tel. 01476 541080; fax 01476 541061; orders@gbs.tbs-ltd.co.uk
North American agent/distributor: National Book Network; tel. 301 459 3366; fax 301 429 5746; www.nbnbooks.com
Australian agent/distributor: Pan Macmillan Australia; tel. 1300 135 113; fax 1300 135 103; customer.service@macmillan.com.au
New Zealand agent/distributor: David Bateman Ltd; tel. (09) 415 7664; fax (09) 415 8892

Publisher: Joanna Lorenz
Project Editor: Felicity Forster
Consulting Editor: Anne Sheasby
Nutritional Analysis: Jill Scott
Recipes: Catherine Atkinson, Carla Capalbo, Kit Chan, Jacqueline Clarke, Maxine Clarke, Frances Cleary, Carol Clements, Roz Denny,
Matthew Drennan, Joanna Farrow, Christine France, Sarah Gates, Shirley Gill, Carole Handslip, Christine Ingram, Patricia Lousada, Norma
MacMillan, Sue Maggs, Elizabeth Martin, Sarah Maxwell, Janice Murfitt, Annie Nichols, Angela Nilsen, Maggie Pannell, Louise Pickford, Jennie
Shapter, Anne Sheasby, Hilaire Walden, Laura Washburn, Steven Wheeler, Kate Whiteman, Judy Williams, Elizabeth Wolf-Cohen, Jeni Wright
Photographers: Karl Adamson, Edward Allwright, David Armstrong, Steve Baxter, Nicki Dowey, James Duncan, Michelle Garrett, Amanda
Heywood, Tim Hill, David Jordan, Dave King, Don Last, Patrick McLeavey, Michael Michaels, Thomas Odulate, Peter Reilly, William Lingwood
Indexer: Helen Snaith
Editorial Reader: Marion Wilson

## ETHICAL TRADING POLICY

Because of our ongoing ecological investment programme, you, as our customer, can have the pleasure and reassurance of knowing that a
tree is being cultivated on your behalf to naturally replace the materials used to make the book you are holding. For further information
about this scheme, go to www.annesspublishing.com/trees

A CIP catalogue record for this book is available from the British Library.

## NOTES

For all recipes, quantities are given in both metric and imperial measures and, where appropriate, in standard cups and spoons.
Follow one set of measures, but not a mixture, because they are not interchangeable.

Standard spoon and cup measures are level. 1 tsp = 5ml, 1 tbsp = 15ml, 1 cup = 250ml/8fl oz.

Australian standard tablespoons are 20ml. Australian readers should use 3 tsp in place of 1 tbsp for measuring small quantities.

American pints are 16fl oz/2 cups. American readers should use 20fl oz/2.5 cups in place of 1 pint when measuring liquids.

Electric oven temperatures in this book are for conventional ovens. When using a fan oven, the temperature will probably need to be reduced
by about 10–20°C/20–40°F. Since ovens vary, you should check with your manufacturer's instruction book for guidance.

The nutritional analysis given for each recipe is calculated per portion (i.e. serving or item), unless otherwise stated. If the recipe
gives a range, such as Serves 4–6, then the nutritional analysis will be for the smaller portion size, i.e. 6 servings.
Medium (US large) eggs are used unless otherwise stated.

Main front cover image shows rigatoni with winter tomato sauce — for recipe, see page 193.

# CONTENTS

# INTRODUCTION

Italians are passionate about their food and always enjoy spending time preparing, cooking and eating food with family and friends. Food is one of their greatest pleasures, and Italians are fortunate to be able to enjoy many regional variations in the food and dishes they eat. Italian food is thought by many of us to be laden with calories and fat, but in fact the same appealing scope and variety of flavors from Italy can be enjoyed as part of a healthy, low-fat diet.

Many traditional Italian foods, such as the abundance of fresh Mediterranean sun-ripened vegetables, fresh herbs and many different types of pasta, are naturally low in fat, making them ideal to enjoy as part of a low-fat eating plan. Quality and freshness of foods are both of great importance to the Italians, and much of the fresh produce eaten in Italy is grown or produced locally. When it comes to cooking foods such as vegetables, they are often cooked in simple ways to bring out their delicious and natural flavors.

Olive oil is the primary fat used for cooking in Italy, and it is also commonly used for dressing foods such as salads. Olive oil is a "healthier" type of fat, which is high in monounsaturated fat and low in saturated fat, and as long as it is used in moderation, it can also be enjoyed as part of a low-fat diet.

Some other typical Italian ingredients, such as pancetta, salami, Parmesan and mozzarella, are high in fat but easily substituted with lower-fat foods such as turkey bacon and reduced-fat mozzarella, or, in many recipes, the amount of the high-fat food can often simply be reduced to lower the fat content of the dish.

*BELOW: Italian food is packed with flavor and color, and can be amazingly low in fat too.*

*ABOVE: Pasta, rice, olive oil, nuts, cheese, meat, olives, garlic, and fresh fruits and vegetables can all be enjoyed as part of a low-fat Italian diet.*

In Italy, pasta and rice dishes form a large part of the cuisine, and both are ideal for a low-fat diet, as they are naturally high in carbohydrates and low in fat, as long as the sauce served with the pasta and the other ingredients used in a rice dish are also low in fat!

Most of us eat fats in some form or another every day, and we all need a small amount of fat in our diet to maintain a healthy, balanced eating plan. However, most of us eat far too much fat, and we should all be looking to reduce our overall fat intake, especially saturated fats.

Weight for weight, dietary fats supply far more energy than all the other nutrients in our diet, and if you eat a diet that is high in fat but don't exercise enough to use up that energy, you will gain weight.

By cutting down on the amount of fat

you eat and making easy changes to your diet, such as choosing the right types of fat, using low-fat and fat-free products whenever possible and making simple changes to the way you prepare and cook food, you will soon be reducing your overall fat intake and enjoying a much healthier lifestyle—and you'll hardly notice the difference!

As you will see from this cookbook, it is certainly practical to eat and enjoy Italian food as part of a low-fat eating plan. We include lots of useful and informative advice, including an introduction to basic healthy eating guidelines; helpful hints and tips on low-fat and fat-free ingredients and low-fat or fat-free cooking techniques; practical tips on how to reduce fat and saturated fat in your diet; interesting insight into the traditional Italian kitchen and the types of ingredients and foods most commonly used in everyday Italian cooking; and, finally, an appealing selection of over 160 delicious and easy-to-follow low-fat Italian recipes for all the family to enjoy.

Each recipe includes a nutritional

breakdown, providing at-a-glance calorie and fat contents per serving. All the recipes in this cookbook are very low in fat—each contains five grams of fat or less per serving, some contain less than one gram of fat per serving.

You will be surprised and delighted by this tempting collection of recipes which ranges from soups, appetizers and salads to main-course pasta dishes, breads and desserts. All the recipes contain less fat than similar traditional Italian recipes and yet they are packed full of Italian flavor and appeal. This practical cookbook will give you valuable insight into low-fat and Italian cooking and will enable you to enjoy Italian food that is healthy, delicious and nutritious as well as being low in fat.

*BELOW: Fresh fruits are an ideal choice for fat-free cooking because they are naturally low in fat. They can be used in both sweet and savory Italian dishes.*

# HEALTHY EATING GUIDELINES

A healthy diet is one that provides us with all the nutrients we need. By eating the right types, balance and proportions of foods, we are more likely to feel healthy, have plenty of energy and a higher resistance to disease that will help prevent us from developing illnesses such as heart disease, cancers, bowel disorders and obesity.

By choosing a variety of foods every day, you will ensure that you are supplying your body with all the essential nutrients, including vitamins and minerals, it needs. To get the balance right, it is important to know just how much of each type of food you should be eating.

There are five main food groups, and it is recommended that we eat plenty of fruits and vegetables (at least five portions a day, not including potatoes) and foods such as cereals, pasta, rice and potatoes; moderate amounts of meat, fish, poultry and dairy products, and only small amounts of foods containing fat or sugar. By choosing a good balance of foods from these groups every day, and by choosing lower-fat or lower-sugar alternatives, we will be supplying our bodies with all the nutrients they need for optimum health.

## THE FIVE MAIN FOOD GROUPS

- Fruits and vegetables
- Rice, potatoes, bread, pasta and other cereals
- Meat, poultry, fish and alternative proteins, such as peas, beans and lentils
- Milk and other dairy foods
- Foods that contain fat and foods that contain sugar

### THE ROLE AND IMPORTANCE OF FAT IN OUR DIET

Fats shouldn't be cut out of our diets completely. We need a small amount of fat for general health and well-being—fat is a valuable source of energy, and also helps to make foods more palatable to eat. However, if you lower the fats, especially saturated fats, in your diet, it may help you to lose weight, as well as reducing your risk of developing some diseases, such as heart disease.

Aim to limit your daily intake of fats to no more than 30–35 percent of the total number of calories. Since each gram of fat provides nine calories, your total daily intake should be no more than around 70g fat. Your total intake of saturated fats should be no more than approximately ten percent of the total number of calories.

*ABOVE: By choosing a variety of foods from the five main food groups, you will ensure that you are supplying your body with all the nutrients it needs.*

### TYPES OF FAT

All fats in our foods are made up of building blocks of fatty acids and glycerol, and their properties vary according to each combination.

There are two main types of fat, which are referred to as saturated and unsaturated. The unsaturated group of fats is divided into further types—polyunsaturated and monounsaturated fats.

There is usually a combination of these types of fat (saturated, polyunsaturated and monounsaturated) in foods that contain fat, but the amount of each type varies from one kind of food to another.

### SATURATED FATS

These fats are usually hard at room temperature. They are not essential in the diet, and should be limited, as they are linked to increasing the level of cholesterol in the blood, which in turn can increase the likelihood that heart disease will develop.

The main sources of saturated fats are animal products, such as fatty meats, and spreading fats, such as butter and lard, that are solid at room temperature. However, there are also saturated fats of vegetable origin, notably coconut and

*BELOW: A selection of foods containing the three main types of fat: saturated, polyunsaturated and monounsaturated fats. Small amounts of poly- and monounsaturated fats can help to reduce the level of cholesterol in the blood.*

palm oils, and some margarines and oils, which, when processed, change the nature of the fat from unsaturated fatty acids to saturated ones. These fats are labeled "hydrogenated vegetable oil" and should be limited. Saturated fats are also found in many processed foods, such as chips and savory snacks, as well as cookies and cakes.

### POLYUNSATURATED FATS

There are two types of polyunsaturated fats: those of vegetable or plant origin (omega 6), such as sunflower oil, soft margarine and seeds, and those from oily fish (omega 3), such as salmon, herring, mackerel and sardines. Both fats are usually liquid at room temperature. Small amounts of polyunsaturated fats are essential for good health and are thought to help reduce the blood cholesterol level.

### MONOUNSATURATED FATS

Monounsaturated fats are also thought to have the beneficial effect of reducing the blood cholesterol level, and this could explain why in some Mediterranean countries there is such a low incidence of heart disease. Monounsaturated fats are found in foods such as olive oil, rapeseed oil, some nuts, such as almonds and hazelnuts, oily fish and avocados.

### CUTTING DOWN ON FATS AND SATURATED FATS IN THE DIET

About one-quarter of the fat we eat comes from meat and meat products, one-fifth from dairy products and margarine and the rest from cakes, cookies, pastries and other foods.

It is relatively easy to cut down on obvious sources of fat in the diet, such as butter, oils, margarine, cream, whole milk and full-fat cheese, but we also need to know about—and check our consumption of—"hidden" fats. Hidden fats can be found in foods such as cakes, chips, cookies and nuts.

By being aware of which foods are high in fats and particularly saturated fats, and by making simple changes to your diet, you can reduce the total fat content of your diet quite considerably.

Whenever possible, choose reduced-fat or low-fat alternatives to foods such as milk, cheese and salad dressings, and fill up on very low-fat foods, such as fruits and vegetables, and foods that are high in carbohydrates, such as pasta, rice, bread and potatoes.

Cutting down on fat doesn't mean sacrificing taste. It's easy to follow a healthy-eating plan without having to forgo all your favorite foods.

# EASY WAYS TO CUT DOWN ON FAT
# AND SATURATED FAT IN THE DAILY DIET

There are lots of simple no-fuss ways of reducing the fat in your diet. Just follow the simple "eat less—try instead" suggestions below to discover how easy it is.

• EAT LESS—Butter, margarine, other spreading fats and cooking oils.

• TRY INSTEAD—Low-fat spreads or fat-free spreads. If you must use butter or hard margarine, make sure they are softened at room temperature, and spread them very thinly, or try low-fat cream cheese for sandwiches and toast.

• EAT LESS—Fatty meats and high-fat products, such as meat pâtés, burgers, pies and sausages.

• TRY INSTEAD – Low-fat meats, such as chicken, turkey and venison. Use only the leanest cuts of meats such as lamb, beef and pork. Always cut and discard any visible fat and skin from meat before cooking. Choose reduced-fat sausages and meat products, and eat fish more often. Try using low-fat protein products such as peas, beans, lentils or tofu instead of meat in recipes.

• EAT LESS—Full-fat dairy products such as whole milk, cream, butter, hard margarine, crème fraîche, whole milk

*BELOW: Chicken and fish are low in fat; always use only the leanest cuts of meats.*

*ABOVE: Look for reduced-fat hard cheeses, low-fat yogurts and skim milk.*

yogurts and hard cheese.

• TRY INSTEAD —Low-fat or skim milk and milk products, low-fat yogurts, low-fat fromage frais and low-fat soft cheeses, reduced-fat hard cheeses such as Cheddar, and reduced-fat crème fraîche.

• EAT LESS—Hard cooking fats, such as lard or hard margarine.

• TRY INSTEAD—Polyunsaturated or monounsaturated oils, such as olive, sunflower or corn oil for cooking (but don't use too much).

• EAT LESS—Rich salad dressings, such as full-fat mayonnaise and salad dressings.

• TRY INSTEAD—Reduced-fat or fat-free mayonnaise or dressings. Make salad dressings at home with low-fat yogurt or fromage frais.

• EAT LESS—Fried foods.

• TRY INSTEAD—Fat-free cooking methods such as grilling, microwaving, steaming or baking whenever possible. Try cooking in a nonstick wok with only a very small amount of oil. Always roast or broil meat or poultry on a rack.

• EAT LESS—Deep-fried and sautéed potatoes.

• TRY INSTEAD—Low-fat starchy foods such as pasta, couscous and rice. Choose baked or boiled potatoes.

• EAT LESS—Added fat in cooking.

• TRY INSTEAD—To cook with little or no fat. Use heavy or good quality nonstick pans so that the food doesn't stick. Try using a small amount of spray oil in cooking to control exactly how much fat you are using. Use fat-free or low-fat ingredients for cooking, such as fruit juice, low-fat or fat-free stock, wine or even beer.

• EAT LESS—High-fat snacks, such as chips, fried snacks and pastries, chocolate cakes, muffins, doughnuts and cookies.

• TRY INSTEAD—Low-fat and fat-free fresh or dried fruits, breadsticks or vegetables. Make your own home-baked low-fat cakes. Buy low-fat and reduced-fat versions of cookies.

*BELOW: Rice is very low in fat, and there are many varieties to choose from.*

# FAT-FREE COOKING METHODS

It's extremely easy to cook without fat—whenever possible, grill, bake, microwave and steam foods without the addition of fat, or try stir-frying without fat—try using a little low-fat or fat-free stock, wine or fruit juice instead.

• By choosing good quality cookware, you'll find that the amount of fat needed for cooking foods can be kept to an absolute minimum. When making casseroles or meat sauces such as Bolognese, dry-fry the meat to brown it, and then drain off all the excess fat before adding the other ingredients. If you do need a little fat for cooking, choose an oil that is high in unsaturates, such as corn, sunflower, olive or canola oil, and always use as little as possible.

• When baking low-fat cakes and cookies, use good quality bakeware that doesn't need greasing before use, or use nonstick baking parchment and only lightly grease before lining.

• Look for nonstick coated fabric sheets. This re-usable nonstick material is amazingly versatile. It can be cut to size and used to line cake pans, baking sheets or frying pans. Heat-resistant up

*BELOW: Always cut and discard any visible fat and skin from meat before cooking.*

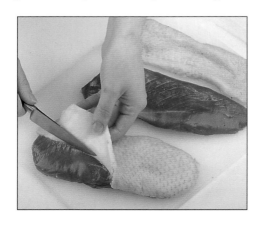

*ABOVE: Marinating helps to tenderize meat as well as adding flavor and color.*

to 550°F and microwave-safe, it will last for up to five years.

• When baking foods such as chicken or fish, rather than adding a pat of butter to the food, try baking it in a loosely sealed package of aluminum foil or parchment paper and adding some wine or fruit juice and herbs or spices before sealing the parcel.

• When broiling foods, the addition of fat is often unnecessary. If the food shows signs of drying, lightly brush with a small amount of unsaturated oil, such as sunflower or corn oil.

• Microwaved foods rarely need the addition of fat, so add herbs or spices for extra flavor and color.

• Steaming or boiling are easy, fat-free ways of cooking many foods, especially vegetables, fish and chicken.

• Try poaching foods, such as chicken, fish and fruits, in low-fat or fat-free stock or syrup—it is another easy, fat-free cooking method.

• Try braising vegetables in the oven in low-fat or fat-free stock, wine or simply water with the addition of some herbs.

• Sauté vegetables in low-fat or fat-free stock, wine or fruit juice instead of oil.

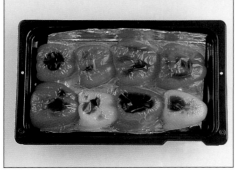

*ABOVE: Vegetables can be broiled without adding any fat at all.*

• Cook vegetables in a covered saucepan over low heat with a little water so they cook in their own juices.

• Marinate foods such as meat or poultry in mixtures of alcohol, herbs or spices, and vinegar or fruit juice. This will help to tenderize the meat and add flavor and color. In addition, the leftover marinade can be used to baste the food occasionally while it is cooking.

• When serving vegetables such as boiled potatoes, carrots or peas, resist the temptation to add a pat of butter or margarine. Instead, sprinkle with chopped fresh herbs or ground spices.

### LOW-FAT SPREADS IN COOKING

There is a huge variety of low-fat and reduced-fat spreads available at our supermarkets, along with some spreads that are very low in fat. Generally speaking, the very low-fat spreads with a fat content of around 20 percent or less have a high water content and so are unsuitable for cooking and only suitable for spreading.

# INGREDIENTS

## VEGETABLES

Vegetables play an important role in Italian cooking and, as many vegetables are also naturally low in fat, they are ideal for use in low-fat Italian cooking.

### EGGPLANT

Eggplant is a popular vegetable in Italian cooking. Many different types can be found at Italian markets, the deep purple, elongated variety being the most common. Choose firm eggplant with tight, glossy skins, that feel heavy for their size.

*RIGHT: Deep purple eggplant*

*BELOW: Clockwise from top left: beans, zucchini, potatoes, tomatoes, asparagus, carrots, bell peppers, broccoli and snowpeas.*

### ZUCCHINI

Zucchini is widely used in Italy, both as a vegetable and for its deep yellow flowers. They are available all year round but are at their best in spring and summer. The smaller and skinnier the zucchini are, the better they taste. Choose zucchini that are firm with glossy green skins and avoid those that are soft or have blemished skins. Zucchini are low in calories and fat and provide some vitamin C. They are used in many low-fat Italian dishes, and can be served raw in salads, cooked with other Mediterranean vegetables such as peppers and tomatoes, or simply stuffed and oven-baked.

*LEFT: Zucchini*

### FENNEL

Fennel has become a very popular vegetable and is used widely in low-fat Italian cooking. Bulb or Florence fennel resembles fat white celery root and has a delicate but distinctive flavor of aniseed and a crisp, refreshing texture. Fennel is available all year round. If possible, buy it with its topknot of feathery fronds, which you can chop and use as a herb or as a garnish. Choose fennel bulbs that feel firm with crisp white outer layers that are not wizened or yellowish. It should have a delicate, fresh scent of aniseed and the texture of green celery. Whole fennel bulbs will keep in the refrigerator for up to one week. Once cut, use them immediately or the cut surfaces will discolor and soften. Fennel is naturally low in calories and fat and is enjoyed in low-fat dishes throughout Italy. It is served raw in salads, lightly dressed with a vinaigrette, or sautéed, baked or braised in similar ways to celery. It is particularly good served with white fish.

*RIGHT: Fennel*

*LEFT: Porcini mushrooms*

### MUSHROOMS

During the spring and autumn months, throughout the Italian countryside avid fungi collectors are spotted searching for the flavorful edible wild mushrooms that are a popular delicacy of Italy. Cultivated mushrooms, such as button mushrooms, are rarely eaten in Italy, and Italians prefer to use dried or preserved wild fungi with their robust earthy taste. The most popular and highly prized mushroom used in Italian cooking is the porcini or cèpe which is also readily available dried. Other popular wild mushrooms used in Italy include field mushrooms and chanterelles.

Cultivated mushrooms and cèpes can be eaten raw (in salads or lightly dressed), but other edible wild mushrooms should be cooked before eating. In Italy, mushrooms may simply be lightly broiled or baked or added to many dishes, such as sauces, stocks, soups and risottos.

### ONIONS

Onions are an essential part of low-fat Italian cooking. Many varieties are grown, including white, mild yellow, baby and red onions.

*LEFT: Red onion*

Choose firm onions that show no signs of sprouting green leaves. Onions should have thin, almost papery skins that are unblemished. Onions are naturally low in calories and fat and are used in numerous low-fat Italian dishes. They can be served raw in salads, stuffed and baked or, in the case of baby onions, cooked in a sweet-and-sour sauce of sugar and wine vinegar and served cold or hot.

### BELL PEPPERS

Generically known as capsicums, bell peppers come in many colors including green (these are unripe red peppers), red, yellow, orange, white and purplish-black, all of which have the same sweetish flavor and crunchy texture and can be eaten raw or cooked.

*ABOVE: Mixed bell peppers*

Each region of Italy has its own low-fat specialities using peppers. These include raw or lightly cooked peppers added to salads, roasted and lightly dressed peppers, and stuffed and oven-baked peppers.

*RIGHT: Vine-ripened tomatoes*

### TOMATOES

It is impossible to imagine low-fat Italian cooking without tomatoes. Tomatoes are cultivated all over Italy and are incorporated into the cooking of every region. In Italy, many types of tomatoes are grown, from plum to cherry tomatoes, and they are at their best in summer. Choose bright, firm, ripe tomatoes, with tight, unwrinkled, unblemished skins and a good aroma. Ripe tomatoes will keep well for several days in the refrigerator, but always bring tomatoes to room temperature before serving to enjoy them at their best.

Tomatoes are naturally low in calories and fat and provide a good source of vitamin C. Tomatoes can be enjoyed raw or cooked, and they are often served with fresh basil leaves with which they have a great affinity. Tomatoes add flavor and color to almost any savory low-fat dish and can be enjoyed simply chopped and added to salads or made into a topping for bruschetta. They can be broiled, lightly fried, baked, stuffed or stewed and made into sauces and soups.

Canned or bottled peeled plum tomatoes, passata and tomato paste are also widely used in low-fat Italian cooking to add flavor, color and texture to many dishes.

# FRUITS AND NUTS

*LEFT:*
*Lemons*

The Italians prefer to enjoy fruits and nuts when they are in season and much of the fresh produce available in Italy is grown or produced locally. Most types of fruit are naturally low in fat and so play a significant part in low-fat Italian cooking to create some delicious dishes.

*ABOVE: Citrus fruits are an Italian favorite and can be used for both sweet and savory recipes, melons make an excellent accompaniment to prosciutto as an antipasto, and cherries—usually preserved in syrup—are used in desserts.*

cooked fish or lean meat to add flavor, or as an aromatic flavoring for low-fat cakes and baked goods.

## MELONS

Many different varieties of sweet aromatic melons are grown in Italy, the most common types being cantaloupe and watermelon. The best way to tell whether a melon is ripe is to smell it; it should have a mild, sweet scent. If it smells highly perfumed and musky, it will be overripe. The fruit should feel heavy for its size, and the skin should not be bruised or damaged. Gently press the rind with your thumbs at the stalk end; it should give a little. Melons are low in calories and fat and provide some vitamin C. Typically, Italians enjoy melon as a low-fat appetizer, simply served on its own or with wafer-thin slices of prosciutto, or as a tasty dessert served on its own or in a fresh fruit salad, sorbet or granita.

## FIGS

Figs are grown all over Italy, and there are two main types, green and purple. Both have thin, tender skins and very sweet, succulent red flesh. Choose fruits that are soft and yielding but not overripe. Fresh figs are low in calories and fat and provide some vitamin C. Fresh figs are delicious served on their own as a typical low-fat Italian dessert, but they can also be enjoyed raw or poached in both sweet and savory low-fat dishes.

## LEMONS

Lemons are grown all over Italy, and their aromatic flavor enhances many low-fat Italian dishes. Depending on the variety, lemons may have a thick indented skin, or be perfectly smooth. Their appearance does not affect the flavor, but they should feel heavy for their size. Buy unwaxed lemons if you intend to use the zest in recipes. Lemons will keep in the refrigerator for up to two weeks. They are low in calories and fat and a good source of vitamin C. Lemons are very versatile, and the juice and/or zest is added to many low-fat Italian dishes. Lemon is used in cold drinks, to add flavor to dressings and sauces, freshly squeezed over

*BELOW: Watermelon*

*LEFT: Purple figs*

*ABOVE: The Italian climate is perfect for growing oranges; they add a bright splash of color to salads and desserts.*

### ORANGES

Many varieties of oranges are grown in Sicily and southern Italy, the best-known Sicilian oranges being the small blood oranges with their bright ruby-red flesh. Other types include sweet navel and bitter oranges. Choose unwaxed oranges if you intend to use the zest in recipes. Oranges are naturally low in calories and fat and a good source of vitamin C. Oranges are served in both sweet and savory low-fat dishes across Italy, including in salads, desserts, sorbets or granitas.

### PEACHES AND NECTARINES

Peaches and nectarines with their sweet juicy flesh are summer fruits grown in Italy. Both fruits are available in either yellow or

*ABOVE: Peaches*

white fleshed varieties, all of which are succulent, juicy and full of flavor. They are naturally low in calories and fat and provide some vitamin C. Peaches and nectarines are interchangeable in recipes and are delicious served alone as a dessert but can also be macerated in fortified wine or spirits or poached in white wine or syrup to create a typical low-fat Italian dessert. They are also delicious served with raspberries or made into fruit drinks and low-fat ice creams and sorbets.

### ALMONDS AND OTHER NUTS

Two varieties of almonds are grown in Italy—sweet and bitter almonds. Sweet almonds are the most common and are eaten on their own or used in cooking and baking. Bitter almonds are not edible in their raw state and are used to flavor liqueurs such as amaretto. In Italy, sweet almonds are enjoyed raw as a dessert or dried and blanched, slivered or ground for use in cakes, baked goods and candy. Dried sweet almonds are the most common type used in many countries. Almonds are high in monounsaturated fat and low in saturated fat.

Other nuts, such as hazelnuts, walnuts and pistachios, are also grown and harvested in Italy and are used in many sweet and savory dishes, including desserts, candy, cakes and baked goods. Hazelnuts are usually dried before use, whereas walnuts can be enjoyed fresh or dried and pistachios are eaten raw or roasted. As with many nuts, they are all high in fat, although the type of fats they contain are the "healthier" types—either

*LEFT: Pine nuts (top) and almonds (below)*

monounsaturated or poly-unsaturated fats. They are all low in saturated fat but should be used sparingly in low-fat cooking.

### PINE NUTS

Pine nuts (or pine kernels) are very popular in Italy and are an essential ingredient in the classic Italian pesto sauce. They can be eaten either raw or toasted and are used in both sweet and savory dishes. Pine nuts are high in polyunsaturated fat and low in saturated fat and should be used in moderation.

*BELOW: Almonds are an extremely versatile ingredient, used raw or to flavor cakes and liqueurs. Red and white Italian grapes are particularly refreshing on a hot day; they have a wonderful Muscat flavor.*

# PASTA

Pasta is the one ingredient that probably sums up the essence of Italian cooking, and it is an essential part of many Italian meals. It is a wonderfully simple, nutritious and low-fat food, which is available in a whole wealth of shapes and sizes. There are two basic types of pasta, dried and fresh.

### FRESH PASTA

Homemade fresh pasta is usually made by hand using superfine white flour enriched with eggs. It is often wrapped around a low-fat stuffing of lean meat, fish, vegetables or low-fat cheese to make filled pasta such as ravioli or tortellini, or layered with lean meat or vegetable sauces to make a tasty low-fat lasagne. Commercially-made fresh pasta is made with durum wheat, water and eggs. The flavor and texture of all fresh pasta is very delicate, so it is best suited to slightly more creamy, low-fat sauces.

### DRIED PASTA

Dried pasta is produced from a dough made from hard durum wheat. It is then shaped into numerous different forms, from long, thin spaghetti to elaborate spirals and frilly bow shapes. Dried pasta can be made from basic pasta dough, which consists of durum wheat and water, or it can be made from a dough enriched with eggs or colored and flavored with ingredients

*LEFT: Dried rigatoni*

*ABOVE: Fresh pasta comes in a wide variety of interesting shapes, sizes and colors.*

*LEFT: Angel's hair pasta*

*RIGHT: Fettucine*

such as spinach, herbs, tomatoes or squid ink. Dried pasta has a nutty flavor and should always retain a firm texture when cooked. It is generally used in preference to fresh pasta for thinner-textured, more robust, low-fat sauces.

### BUYING AND STORING PASTA

Choose dried pasta that is made from Italian durum wheat, and store it in a cool, dry place. Once opened, dried pasta will keep for weeks in an airtight container. Homemade fresh pasta will only keep for a couple of days, but it also freezes very well. Commercially made fresh pasta (fresh pasta that is available in the refrigerated section of the supermarket) is

*RIGHT: Dried spaghetti*

pasteurized and vacuum-packed, so it will keep in the refrigerator for about two weeks or it can be frozen for up to six months. When buying colored and flavored pasta, make sure that it has been made with natural ingredients.

### COOKING PASTA

All pasta must be cooked in a large saucepan filled with plenty of fast-boiling, salted water. Cooking times vary according to the type, size and shape of the pasta but, as a general rule, filled pasta takes about 12 minutes, dried pasta needs 8–10 minutes and fresh pasta only 2–3 minutes. All pasta should be cooked until it is *al dente*, or still firm to the bite. Always test pasta for readiness just before you think it should be done, as it can easily overcook. To stop it from overcooking, take the pan off the heat and run a little cold water into it, then drain the pasta and serve.

### PASTA VARIETIES

Pasta shapes can be divided roughly into four categories: long strands or ribbons, flat, short and filled. When choosing the appropriate pasta for a sauce, there are no hard-and-fast rules; almost any pasta is suitable for a low-fat sauce.

*LEFT: Conchiglie*

*BELOW: Tomato and spinach orecchiette*

## SHORT PASTA

Short pasta covers a wide variety of shapes, the more common types being macaroni, rigati, rigatoni and tubetti. Pasta shapes vary, and the list is almost endless, with some wonderfully descriptive names. There are cappellacci (little hats), orecchiette (little ears) or maltagliati (badly cut) and penne (quills), conchiglie (little shells), farfalle (bows) and lumache (snails).

## LONG OR RIBBON PASTA

The best-known long variety is spaghetti, which also comes in a thinner version, spaghettini, and the flatter linguine, which means "little tongues." Bucatini are thicker and hollow—perfect for trapping low-fat sauces in the cavities. Ribbon pasta is wider than the strands, and fettucine, tagliatelle and trenette all fall into this category. Dried tagliatelle is sold folded into nests, which unravel during cooking. Pappardelle are the widest ribbon pasta; they are often served with a low-fat rabbit sauce. The thinnest pasta strands are vermicelli (little worms) and ultra-fine capelli d'angelo (angel hair).

## FLAT PASTA

In Italy, fresh flat pasta is often called maccheroni, not to be confused with the short tubes of macaroni with which we are familiar. Lasagne and cannelloni are larger flat rectangles of pasta, used for layering or rolling around a low-fat filling; dried cannelloni are already formed into wide tubes. Layered pasta dishes like this are baked.

*RIGHT: Lasagne*

*BELOW: Multi-colored tagliatelle*

*RIGHT: Tortelli*

## FILLED PASTA

Dried and fresh filled pastas are available in many varieties, and there are dozens of names for filled pasta, but the only difference lies in the shape and size. Ravioli are square, tortelli and agnolotti are usually round, and tortellini and anellini are ring-shaped. Fillings for fresh and dried pasta include lean meat, pumpkin, artichokes, ricotta and spinach, seafood, chicken and mushrooms.

## GNOCCHI

Gnocchi fall into a different category from other pasta, being similar to small dumplings. They can be made from semolina (milled durum wheat), flour, potatoes or ricotta and spinach and may be shaped like elongated shells, ovals, cylinders or flat discs, or roughly shredded into strozzapreti (priest stranglers). Gnocchi are extremely light and almost melt in your mouth and can be served like any pasta, as a low-fat first course, in clear soup or as an accompaniment to the main course.

*RIGHT: Gnocchi*

# BREAD, RICE, GRAINS AND PULSES

*ABOVE: Ciabatta*

Rice, grains and pulses form the basis of many delicious and nutritious low-fat Italian dishes, and fresh bread is always served in Italy as a tasty, low-fat accompaniment to every meal.

In Italy, no meal is ever served without bread. There are numerous different types of Italian breads with many regional variations. Several varieties, such as ciabatta and focaccia, are readily available at bakeries or supermarkets.

Rice and grains are staple foods in Italy and are almost as important as pasta in Italian cooking. Italy relied heavily on these low-fat, protein-rich foods when luxuries such as meat were in short supply, and a number of wholesome and delicious low-fat recipes were developed using these modest ingredients.

Many beans and pulses, both fresh and dried, are naturally low in fat and are used widely in low-fat Italian cooking, providing the basis for a variety of delicious dishes.

## CIABATTA

These flattish, slipper-shaped loaves with squared or rounded ends are made with olive oil and are often flavored with fresh or dried herbs, olives or sun-dried tomatoes. They have an airy texture inside and a pale, crisp crust. Ciabatta is delicious served warm and is excellent for low-fat sandwiches.

## FOCACCIA

Focaccia is a dimpled flat bread similar to pizza dough that is traditionally lightly oiled and baked in a wood oven. A whole traditional focaccia from an Italian bakery weighs several pounds and is sold by weight, cut into manageable pieces. A variety of low-fat ingredients can be worked into the dough or served as a topping—onions, rosemary or oregano, lean ham or olives.

*LEFT: Focaccia*

*RIGHT: Risotto rices like these arborio varieties are famous in Italy, and can be flavored with an almost endless array of ingredients.*

## RICE

Italy produces a great variety of rice, including the short-grain carnaroli and arborio rice, which make the best risottos. Italian rice is classified by size, ranging from the shortest, roundest ordinario (used for puddings), to semifino (for soups and salads), then fino and finally the longer grains of the finest risotto rice, superfino.

Rice is used in many low-fat Italian dishes. Baked rice dishes are also popular, and plain boiled rice may simply be served on its own.

The most famous of all Italian rice dishes, however, is risotto. A good risotto can be made only with superfine rice and is a delicious low-fat Italian dish. All risottos are basically prepared in the same way, although they can be flavored with an almost endless variety of exciting ingredients.

Buy only superfine risotto rice for use in Italian risottos. Shorter grain rice is best reserved for making soups and puddings. Store uncooked rice in an airtight container in a cool, dry place. The rice will keep for several months.

*ABOVE: Fine polenta*

### POLENTA

For centuries, polenta has been a staple low-fat food of northern Italy. Polenta is a grainy yellow flour that is a type of cornmeal. It is then cooked into a kind of porridge and used in a variety of ways. There are two main types of polenta—coarse and fine.

Polenta is very versatile and can be used to create many delicious low-fat dishes. It is most often served in Italy as a first

*LEFT: Dried cannellini beans*

*ABOVE: Canned borlotti beans*

*LEFT: Canned black-eyed peas*

course, but it can also be used as a vegetable dish or main course. Polenta can be served on its own and is a satisfying dish. It also goes well with lean meats and game, or it can be cooled and cut into squares before being broiled or baked and served with a low-fat sauce or topping.

Quick-cooking polenta, which can be prepared in only five minutes, and ready-prepared blocks of cooked polenta are also available, but traditional polenta only takes about 20 minutes to cook, so it is best to buy this for its superior texture and flavor. Once opened, polenta will keep in an airtight container for at least one month.

### HARICOT BEANS

Haricot beans are eaten all over Italy, the most popular varieties being borlotti beans, cannellini beans (a type of kidney bean) and black-eyed peas. All these are eaten in hearty low-fat stews, with pasta, in low-fat soups or salads or simply cooked and served as a side dish.

Both fresh and dried beans are available in Italy, and canned varieties make an acceptable substitute. Once opened, store dried beans in an airtight container in a cool, dry place for up to one year.

### FAVA BEANS

Fava beans are at their best when eaten fresh from the pod in late spring or in early summer when they are small and very tender, or cooked and skinned later in the season. They are popular in Italy and are excellent served with lean ham,

*LEFT: Canned fava beans*

in low-fat dishes such as risotto or simply served as a side dish. Dried fava beans, which need pre-cooking, are also used in Italian dishes such as low-fat soups and stews.

### CHICKPEAS

Chickpeas, which are round, golden pulses shaped much like hazelnuts, and which have a distinctive, nutty flavor, are also popular in low-fat Italian cooking. Chickpeas are cooked and used in the same way as haricot beans and they can also be served cold and lightly dressed to make a tasty salad.

### LENTILS

Lentils grow in pods, although they are always sold podded and dried. Italian lentils are the small brown variety, which do not break up during cooking and are often mixed with pasta or rice to create delicious and satisfying low-fat dishes. They are also delicious served cold, lightly dressed or in nutritious soups. Whole brown, green or puy lentils can also be used.

*ABOVE: Dried chickpeas*

*RIGHT: Dried brown lentils*

# MEAT, POULTRY AND FISH

Although meat and poultry did not feature largely in Italian cooking until recent years, a variety of lean cuts and a range of fish are used in many appetizing low-fat Italian dishes.

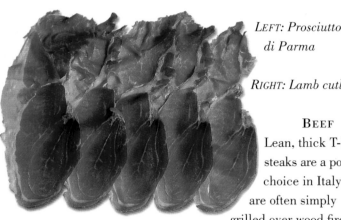

*LEFT: Prosciutto di Parma*

*RIGHT: Lamb cutlets*

## CURED MEATS

Italy is famous for its prosciutto crudo—salted and dried ham that requires no cooking. The most famous of these hams is prosciutto di Parma, or Parma ham, which has a medium-high fat content, but is served in wafer-thin slices, so it can be incorporated into low-fat Italian dishes.

Pancetta, bresaola, mortadella and salami are also popular Italian cured meats. Meats such as pancetta, mortadella and salami are high in fat and should be used sparingly in low-fat Italian recipes. Bresaola has a similar fat content to prosciutto.

## BEEF

Lean, thick T-bone steaks are a popular choice in Italy and are often simply grilled over wood fires. Leftover cooked lean beef can be sliced and made into a tasty salad. Less tender cuts of beef are usually braised, stewed or ground and used for a whole variety of tasty low-fat Italian dishes. Choose lean cuts of beef that are naturally low in fat or choose extra-lean ground beef.

*ABOVE: Ground beef*

## LAMB

Lambs in Italy are bred mainly in the southern region, and they are slaughtered at different ages, resulting in distinctive flavors. Young spring lambs are often spit-roasted whole or used for roasting or grilling. Older lamb has a stronger flavor and is suitable for roasting or stewing. Choose lean cuts of lamb for low-fat cooking to keep the fat content down.

## PORK

A lot of Italian pork is transformed into hams, sausages and salamis, but fresh pork is also enjoyed all over Italy. Lean

*BELOW: Chicken*

*BELOW: Bresaola*

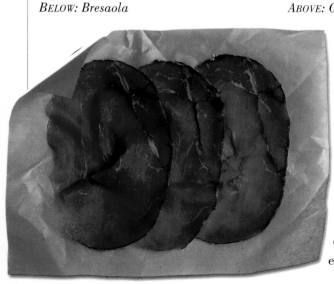

## CHICKEN AND TURKEY

Poultry is a popular food in Italy and is used to create a huge variety of simple and delicious low-fat Italian dishes. Factory farming does exist in Italy, but many flavorful free-range birds are also available. Chicken and turkey are usually filleted for quick cooking, and removing and discarding the skin before cooking ensures that the meat is very lean.

*ABOVE: Rabbit*

pork chops or cutlets can be grilled or braised with herbs or artichokes for a tasty, low-fat meal. Loin of pork can be braised in milk or roasted with rosemary or sage. Choose lean cuts of pork and remove and discard any visible fat before cooking to keep the fat content low.

### RABBIT

Rabbit often replaces chicken or veal in low-fat Italian cooking. The meat is very pale and is naturally lean and low in fat. Wild rabbit has a stronger flavor; farmed rabbit is very tender and has a much more delicate flavor. Farmed rabbit can replace chicken or turkey in almost any low-fat recipe. Wild rabbit can be stewed or braised either in white wine or Marsala, or with eggplant, lean bacon and tomatoes. It can also be roasted simply with root vegetables or fresh herbs.

### FISH

Italy's extensive coastal waters are host to a large variety of fish and shellfish of every description, many of which are unknown outside Italy. Italians like their seafood very fresh and tend to cook it simply. Large fish are usually grilled, barbecued or baked, smaller whole fish may be stuffed and grilled or baked, and small fish are often lightly pan-fried.

Popular fish in Italy include white fish such as monkfish, cod and sole, and oily fish such as salmon, swordfish, tuna, trout and sardines. Some fish are dried, salted or preserved in oil, the most popular being tuna, which is packed in olive oil. Salted dried cod is also a favorite and is often made into soups and stews.

White fish is very low in fat and is ideal for use in low-fat Italian cooking. Remove and discard the skin to keep the fat content low. Oily fish such as tuna and swordfish are also naturally low in fat, and although oily fish such as salmon are higher in fat, it is higher in the "healthier" types of fat—poly-unsaturated and monounsaturated fats—and low in saturated fat.

*RIGHT: Cod fillet*

*LEFT: Shrimp*

### SHELLFISH

The Italians enjoy a wide variety of shellfish and crustaceans from their coastal waters, and almost all seafood is considered edible, from mussels, clams and scallops to octopus, squid, razor-shells and sea snails. Shrimp come in all sizes and colors, from vibrant red to pale

*ABOVE: Fish and shellfish like sardines and mussels are often simply grilled or fried, or used as the basis of a soup or stew.*

gray, while crustaceans range from bright orange crawfish to blue-black lobsters.

Most shellfish and crustaceans are nutritious, naturally low in fat and ideal for creating many delicious low-fat Italian dishes. Squid and cuttlefish are served cut into rings either as part of a seafood salad or before being lightly fried with other types of fish. Octopus tend to be cooked slowly for long periods to tenderize them or, if very small ones are available, these can be cooked in the same way as squid.

Mussels make an attractive and tasty addition to many low-fat pasta and fish dishes, salads and pizza toppings. They are especially good served with a low-fat garlicky tomato sauce. Shrimp can be boiled and served with lemon juice and olive oil or in salads. They can also be grilled or barbecued and served with tomato sauce or rice.

# DAIRY PRODUCTS

Dairy products such as butter and cheeses play a part in low-fat Italian cooking, but due to their generally high fat content they should only be used in small amounts.

*LEFT: Butter*

*RIGHT: Mozzarella*

## BUTTER

Although olive oil is the primary fat used for cooking in Italy, butter is more common in northern Italian cooking. The amount of butter used in recipes in this book has been kept to a minimum, as butter is very high in fat, particularly saturated fat. Choose a polyunsaturated or mono-unsaturated margarine in place of butter if you prefer. Although the fat content of these margarines is similar to butter, the fats are "healthier" types. Very low-fat spreads are not suitable for cooking; only use these for spreading.

## CHEESES

Italy has a great variety of cheese, ranging from fresh, mild cheese such as mozzarella to aged hard cheeses such as Parmesan. All types of milk are used, including cow's, sheep's, goat's and buffalo's, and some cheeses are made from a mixture of milks. Other popular types of Italian cheese include Pecorino, Provolone, Bel Paese, Fontina, ricotta, Gorgonzola and mascarpone.

Many of the Italian cheeses are suitable for cooking and are used in a wide variety of dishes. However, many are also high in fat, especially saturated fat, but if used in moderation can be incorporated into low-fat Italian cuisine. Strong-flavored cheeses, such as Parmesan, can be used in smaller amounts and other cheeses, such as mozzarella, are available in reduced-fat versions.

*ABOVE: Parmesan*

## PARMESAN

Parmesan is the best-known and most important of the Italian hard cheeses. There are two basic types—Parmigiano Reggiano and Grana Padano—but the former is infinitely superior. A little finely grated Parmesan goes adds delicious flavor to many dishes, from pasta and polenta to risotto and minestrone.

*LEFT: Pecorino studded with peppercorns*

*RIGHT: Ricotta*

## MOZZARELLA

Italian cooking could hardly exist without mozzarella, the pure white egg-shaped fresh cheese, whose melting quality makes it perfect for so many dishes. The best mozzarella is made in the area around Naples, using water buffalo's milk. Reduced-fat mozzarella is also readily available and is ideal for use in low-fat Italian cooking. It is delicious in sandwiches or served with fresh red tomatoes and green basil (*insalata tricolore*, or three-color salad). When cooked, mozzarella becomes uniquely stringy and is ideal for topping pizzas.

## RICOTTA

Ricotta is a fresh, soft cheese made from cow's, sheep's or goat's milk. It is used widely in Italy in both sweet and savory dishes. Ricotta has a medium-high fat content, so should be used in moderation in low-fat Italian cooking. It has an excellent texture and a mild flavor, so it makes a perfect vehicle for seasonings such as black pepper, nutmeg or chopped fresh herbs. It is also puréed with cooked spinach to make a classic filling for ravioli, cannelloni or lasagne. It is often used in desserts and can be sweetened and then served with fresh fruit.

# OLIVE OIL AND FLAVORINGS

Olive oil and flavorings play an important role in Italian cooking. They are ideal for combining with staples such as rice and pasta to create speedy and nutritious low-fat meals.

### OLIVE OIL

Olive oil is perhaps the single most important ingredient in an Italian kitchen. The best olive oil is extra virgin, which must have an acidity level of less than one percent. It is ideal for using "raw" in salad dressings, uncooked sauces and for drizzling lightly on vegetables. Virgin olive oil has a higher acidity level and less refined flavor and is used as a condiment or for general cooking. Unclassified or pure olive oil is refined, then blended with virgin oil to add flavor and is ideal for cooking and baking.

Olive oil is high in monounsaturated fat and low in saturated fat and should be used in moderation when preparing low-fat Italian recipes.

*LEFT: Extra virgin olive oil*

*BELOW: Balsamic vinegar*

*ABOVE: A selection of Italian flavorings is essential for the authentic Italian pantry. Here we see a variety of oils, sun-dried tomatoes and tomato paste, passata, anchovies, capers and balsamic vinegar.*

*RIGHT: A mixture of black and green olives*

### BALSAMIC VINEGAR

Balsamic vinegar is the king of vinegars and is made in the area around Modena in Italy. It is the boiled and concentrated juice of local trebbiano grapes, which is aged over a very long period to give it a slightly syrupy texture and a rich, deep mahogany color. Balsamic vinegar is used as a dressing or to finish a delicate sauce for white fish, poultry or calf's liver.

### OLIVES

Black and green olives are used in low-fat Italian cooking, and both types are available whole or pitted, sold loose, in jars or vacuum-packed. Olives are added to many low-fat Italian dishes, such as salads and sauces. Olives are quite high in monounsaturated fat and low in saturated fat, but should be used in moderation.

### PESTO

Green pesto is traditionally made with fresh basil, pine nuts, Parmesan and olive oil, but a red version based on sweet red peppers is also available. It can be homemade or bought ready-made in jars or fresh in plastic containers. Pesto can be added to hot pasta or gnocchi, risottos, tomato sauces and tomato-based soups. However, pesto is high in fat and should be used sparingly.

### SUN-DRIED TOMATOES

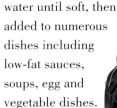

Wrinkled red sun-dried tomatoes are available dry in packages or preserved in oil in jars. Dry-packed tomatoes are lower in fat than the oil-packed ones and are used in many low-fat Italian dishes to add flavor and color. They can be eaten on their own as a snack, or soaked in hot water until soft, then added to numerous dishes including low-fat sauces, soups, egg and vegetable dishes.

*RIGHT: Sun-dried tomatoes*

# HERBS AND SPICES

Herbs and spices are vital to low-fat Italian cooking. Their aromatic flavor adds depth and interest to numerous dishes. Many wild herbs grow in the Italian countryside and are often incorporated into low-fat Italian recipes. Buy growing herbs in their pots if you can, as this ensures that the herbs are as fresh as possible. Better still, grow herbs in your own kitchen garden or on windowsills and enjoy the convenience of a continuous supply.

*ABOVE: Always use fresh herbs whenever you can. Their aromatic flavor adds depth and interest to all Italian cooking.*

*LEFT: Basil*

*RIGHT: Rosemary*

### BASIL

Basil, with its intense aroma and fresh, pungently sweet flavor, is associated with low-fat Italian cooking more than any other herb. There are many varieties of fresh basil, but sweet basil is the most common. It is an essential ingredient of pesto, but it is also used in low-fat soups, salads, fish and shellfish dishes and almost any dish based on tomatoes, with which it has a great affinity. It is best added at the end of cooking.

### MARJORAM AND OREGANO

These two highly aromatic herbs are closely related (oregano is the wild variety), but marjoram has a much milder flavor. Marjoram is more

*ABOVE: Marjoram*

*RIGHT: Parsley*

commonly used in northern Italy, to flavor meat, poultry, vegetables and low-fat soups, while oregano is widely used in the south to flavor low-fat tomato dishes, vegetables and pizza. Choose plants that have fresh-looking leaves of good color and even size.

### PARSLEY

Italian parsley is the flat-leaf variety that has a more robust flavor than curly parsley. It is used in low-fat savory dishes such as soups, sauces, stocks, stews and risottos. Chopped parsley or whole leaves may also be used as a garnish. If flat-leaf parsley is not available, curly parsley makes a good substitute. Choose parsley that has a good, fresh green color.

### ROSEMARY

Spiky evergreen rosemary bushes, with their attractive blue flowers, grow wild all over Italy. The herb has a delicious, highly aromatic flavor that can easily overpower a dish so should be used sparingly. Rosemary combines well with roast or grilled lean lamb, veal and chicken. It is also used to enhance low-fat dishes such as those based on baked fish and tomato. Some rosemary branches added to the charcoal on a grill impart a great flavor to whatever is being cooked.

### SAGE

Wild sage grows in profusion in the Italian countryside. There are several varieties, all of which have a slightly bitter, aromatic flavor, which contrasts well with lean meat such as pork, veal and chicken. Sage should be used sparingly and combines well with almost all low-fat meat and vegetable dishes, including minestrone, calf's liver and white haricot beans. Choose leaves that look fresh and bright in color. Fresh sage should be stored in a plastic bag in the refrigerator for up to one week.

*RIGHT: Sage*

*BELOW: Black peppercorns*

## BLACK PEPPERCORNS

Black peppercorns are the green berries of a vine that are dried on mats in the sun until they are all wrinkled and black. They are used for seasoning many low-fat Italian dishes and are best used freshly ground in a mill or crushed to enjoy their delicious flavor and aroma. Store peppercorns in an airtight container in a cool, dry place.

## CHILES

Chopped fresh chiles or hot flakes of dried chiles are added to many low-fat Italian dishes. Fresh chiles vary in taste, from mild to fiery hot, and they are unusual in that their "hotness" is usually in inverse proportion to their size, so larger, round fleshly varieties are generally milder than the smaller, thin-skinned pointed ones. For a milder, but still spicy flavor, remove and discard the seeds and veins from fresh chiles before use. A small pinch of dried chile flakes spices up low-fat stews and sauces, particularly those made with tomatoes. For a really hot low-fat pizza,

*RIGHT: Fresh red chiles*

crumble a few dried chile flakes on top. Dried chiles are extremely fiery and should be used sparingly.

Be careful when preparing fresh chiles, and always wear rubber or plastic gloves, or wash your hands and utensils thoroughly after use, as chiles contain volatile oils, which can irritate and burn if they touch sensitive areas, especially the eyes.

## SAFFRON

Saffron is the world's most expensive spice and consists of the hand-picked dried stigmas of the saffron crocus. Saffron has a highly aromatic flavor and will impart a rich golden color to many dishes. In Italy, saffron is mainly used to flavor and color risottos, and it is excellent in low-fat sauces for fish and poultry. It can also be used to flavor cookies and cakes. Saffron threads are sold in small boxes or jars containing only a few grams, and powdered saffron is also available in jars.

## SALT

Salt is the universal seasoning ingredient used to bring out the flavor of both sweet and savory dishes. It is odorless and without it our food would be insipid and bland. Several types of salt are widely available, including rock salt, sea salt and refined table salt. Due to its intensity,

*ABOVE: Saffron threads*

salt should be used sparingly in cooking and for seasoning food. Always store salt in an airtight container in a cool, dry place.

*LEFT: Fine and coarse sea salt*

*BELOW: Italian chiles are generally milder than their South American counterparts, but should still be used with caution—it can often be quite difficult to gauge their heat.*

# THE FAT AND CALORIE CONTENTS OF FOOD

The following figures show the weight of fat (g) and the energy content per 100 grams of each food.

| VEGETABLES | FAT (G) | ENERGY |
|---|---|---|
| Artichokes, raw | 0.2 | 18cals |
| Bell Peppers, red, raw | 0.4 | 32cals |
| Broccoli, raw | 0.9 | 33cals |
| Carrots, raw | 0.3 | 35cals |
| Cauliflowers, raw | 0.9 | 34cals |
| Chard, Swiss, raw | 0.2 | 19cals |
| Cucumbers, raw | 0.1 | 10cals |
| Eggplant, raw | 0.4 | 15cals |
| Eggplant, fried in corn oil | 31.9 | 302cals |
| Endive, raw | 0.6 | 11cals |
| Fennel, Florence, raw | 0.2 | 12cals |
| Mushrooms, raw | 0.4 | 13cals |
| Olives, in brine | 11.0 | 103cals |
| Onions, raw | 0.2 | 36cals |
| Peas, raw | 1.5 | 83cals |
| Potatoes, raw | 0.2 | 75cals |
| Radicchio, raw | 0.2 | 14cals |
| Spinach, raw | 0.8 | 25cals |
| Squash, butternut | 0.1 | 36cals |
| Tomatoes, raw | 0.3 | 17cals |
| Zucchini, raw | 0.4 | 18cals |

| FRUITS AND NUTS | FAT (G) | ENERGY |
|---|---|---|
| Apples, raw | 0.1 | 47cals |
| Apricots, raw | 0.1 | 31cals |
| Avocados | 19.5 | 190cals |
| Bananas | 0.3 | 95cals |
| Dried mixed fruits | 0.4 | 268cals |
| Figs, raw | 0.3 | 43cals |
| Figs, dried | 1.5 | 209cals |
| Grapefruits, raw | 0.1 | 30cals |
| Grapes | 0.1 | 60cals |
| Melons | 0.1 | 24cals |
| Nectarines | 0.1 | 40cals |
| Oranges | 0.1 | 37cals |
| Peaches | 0.1 | 33cals |
| Pears | 0.1 | 40cals |
| Almonds | 55.8 | 612cals |
| Brazil nuts | 68.2 | 682cals |
| Cashews, plain | 48.2 | 573cals |
| Chestnuts | 2.7 | 170cals |
| Hazelnuts | 63.5 | 650cals |
| Pine nuts | 68.6 | 688cals |
| Pistachios | 55.4 | 601cals |
| Walnuts | 68.5 | 688cals |

| CEREALS AND BAKING | FAT (G) | ENERGY |
|---|---|---|
| Brown rice, uncooked | 2.8 | 357cals |
| White rice, uncooked | 3.6 | 383cals |
| Pasta, white, uncooked | 1.8 | 342cals |
| Pasta, whole-wheat, uncooked | 2.5 | 324cals |
| Brown bread | 2.0 | 218cals |
| White bread | 1.9 | 235cals |
| Whole-wheat bread | 2.5 | 215cals |
| Sugar, white | 0 | 394cals |
| Chocolate, milk | 30.7 | 520cals |
| Chocolate, semi-sweet | 28.0 | 510cals |
| Honey | 0 | 288cals |
| Fruit jam | 0 | 261cals |

| BEANS AND PULSES | FAT (G) | ENERGY |
|---|---|---|
| Black-eyed peas, cooked | 0.7 | 116cals |
| Chickpeas, canned | 2.9 | 115cals |
| Fava beans, raw | 1.0 | 59cals |
| Green and brown lentils, cooked | 0.7 | 105cals |
| Lima beans, canned | 0.5 | 77cals |
| Red kidney beans, canned | 0.6 | 100cals |

| MEAT AND MEAT PRODUCTS | FAT (G) | ENERGY |
|---|---|---|
| Bacon | 23.6 | 276cals |
| Beef, ground, raw | 16.2 | 225cals |
| Beef, ground, extra lean, raw | 9.6 | 174cals |
| Beef, average, lean, raw | 5.1 | 136cals |
| Lamb, average, lean, raw | 8.3 | 156cals |
| Pork, average, lean, raw | 4.0 | 123cals |
| Chicken breast, no skin, raw | 1.1 | 106cals |
| Chicken, roasted, meat and skin | 12.5 | 218cals |
| Duck, meat only, raw | 6.5 | 137cals |
| Duck, roasted, meat, fat, skin | 38.1 | 423cals |
| Turkey, meat only, raw | 1.6 | 105cals |
| Liver, lamb, raw | 6.2 | 137cals |
| Salami | 39.2 | 438cals |
| Prosciutto | 12.7 | 223cals |
| Liver, calf, raw | 3.4 | 104cals |

| FISH AND SHELLFISH | FAT (G) | ENERGY |
|---|---|---|
| Anchovies, canned in oil | 19.9 | 280cals |
| Clams, canned in brine | 0.6 | 77cals |
| Cod fillets, raw | 0.7 | 80cals |
| Crab, canned | 0.5 | 77cals |
| Flounder, raw | 1.4 | 79cals |
| Haddock, raw | 0.6 | 81cals |
| Monkfish, raw | 0.4 | 66cals |
| Mussels, raw | 1.8 | 74cals |
| Red snapper, raw | 3.8 | 109cals |
| Sardines, raw | 9.2 | 165cals |
| Sea bass, raw | 2.5 | 100cals |
| Shrimp, boiled | 0.9 | 99cals |
| Squid, raw | 1.7 | 81cals |
| Tuna, canned in water | 0.6 | 99cals |
| Tuna, canned in oil | 9.0 | 189cals |
| Tuna, fresh | 4.6 | 136cals |

| DAIRY, FATS AND OILS | FAT (G) | ENERGY |
|---|---|---|
| Cream, heavy | 48.0 | 449cals |
| Cream, light | 19.1 | 198cals |
| Crème fraîche | 40.0 | 379cals |
| Reduced-fat crème fraîche | 15.0 | 165cals |
| Milk, skim | 0.1 | 33cals |
| Milk, whole | 3.9 | 66cals |
| Cheddar cheese | 34.4 | 412cals |
| Cheddar-type, reduced-fat | 15.0 | 261cals |
| Cream cheese | 47.4 | 439cals |
| Fromage frais, plain | 7.1 | 113cals |
| Fromage frais, very low-fat | 0.2 | 58cals |
| Mozzarella cheese | 21.0 | 289cals |
| Ricotta cheese | 11.0 | 144cals |
| Skim milk soft cheese | Trace | 74cals |
| Feta cheese | 20.2 | 250cals |
| Parmesan cheese | 32.7 | 452cals |
| Low-fat yogurt, plain | 0.8 | 56cals |
| Butter | 81.7 | 737cals |
| Margarine | 81.6 | 739cals |
| Corn oil | 99.9 | 899cals |
| Olive oil | 99.9 | 899cals |
| Safflower oil | 99.9 | 899cals |
| Eggs, whole, raw | 10.8 | 147cals |
| Egg yolk, raw | 30.5 | 339cals |
| Egg white, raw | Trace | 36cals |
| Dressing, fat-free | 1.2 | 67cals |
| Dressing, French | 49.4 | 462cals |
| Mayonnaise | 75.6 | 691cals |
| Mayonnaise, reduced-calorie | 28.1 | 288cals |

# EQUIPMENT

Many of the utensils in the Italian kitchen are everyday items found in most kitchens, but some specialized ones are particularly useful.

For pasta you need to have a large saucepan for cooking the pasta and a colander for draining, while for making sauces you need only a sharp knife and a cutting board for chopping ingredients and a saucepan for cooking. You will also need a large bowl plus spoons and forks for tossing and serving.

You can make pasta by hand, but a pasta machine will make it much lighter work. Pasta machines come in electric or hand-cranked varieties.

*BELOW: If you make pasta frequently, a pasta machine is an excellent buy because it is inexpensive, easy and fun to use, and makes excellent pasta in a very short time.*

A special spoon with "teeth" or a perforated ladle are ideal for lifting spaghetti out of the saucepan. If you are making pizza, a cutting wheel will cut it into clean slices.

To keep fat to an absolute minimum, choose heavy, good quality cookware that doesn't need greasing before use, or use nonstick baking parchment and only lightly grease the pan before lining it. Also look for nonstick coated fabric sheets, which are reusable.

### BAKING SPATULA
Useful whenever you need to spread and smooth ingredients.

### COLANDER
A colander is and indispensable item of equipment for quickly draining hot pasta and cooked vegetables.

### COOKIE CUTTER
Usually used for cutting cookie dough into fancy shapes but equally good for cutting fresh pasta shapes.

### EARTHENWARE POT
Excellent for slow-cooking stews, soups or sauces. It can be used either in the oven or on top of the stove over low heat with a metal heat diffuser under it to prevent cracking. Many shapes and sizes are available. To season a terra-cotta pot before using it for the first time, immerse it in cold water overnight. Remove from the water and rub the unglazed bottom with a garlic clove. Fill with water and bring slowly to a boil. Discard the water. Repeat, changing the water, until the "earth" taste disappears.

### FLUTED COOKIE CUTTER
Good for cutting out fresh pasta shapes or for cutting freshly rolled pastry.

### HAND FOOD MILL
Excellent for soups, sauces and tomato "passata": the pulp passes through the holes of the mill, leaving the seeds and skin behind.

### ICE CREAM SCOOP
Suited to scooping firm and well-frozen ice creams, sorbets and frozen yogurt.

### ITALIAN ICE CREAM SCOOP
Good for soft ices or sorbets that are not too solid.

### MEAT POUNDER
Good for pounding cutlets. As well as pounding meat, it can be used to crush nuts and whole spices.

*ABOVE: 1 Earthenware pot, 2 olive pitter, 3 whisk, 4 fluted cookie cutter, 5 cookie cutters, 6 pasta rolling pin, 7 mortar and pestle, 8 hand food mill, 9 colander, 10 Parmesan cheese knife, 11 pizza cutting wheel, 12 baking spatula, 13 spaghetti spoon, 14 meat pounder, 15 pasta machine, 16 wide vegetable peeler, 17 Italian ice cream scoop, 18 ice cream scoop.*

### MORTAR AND PESTLE
For hand-grinding spices, rock salt, whole peppercorns, fresh herbs and bread crumbs.

### OLIVE PITTER
Useful for pitting olives or fresh cherries.

### PARMESAN CHEESE KNIFE
Break Parmesan off the large cheese wheels using this wedge-shaped tool.

### PASTA MACHINE
Many models are available, including sophisticated electric and industrial models. Most have an adjustable roller width and both thin and wide noodle cutters.

### PASTA ROLLING PIN
Ideal for rolling out homemade pasta dough. A length of dowelling 2 inches in diameter can also be used. Smooth the surface with fine sandpaper before using for the first time.

### PIZZA CUTTING WHEEL
Useful for cutting slices of pizza, although a sharp knife may also be used.

### SPAGHETTI SPOON
The wooden "teeth" catch the spaghetti strands and make cooked spaghetti easier to serve.

### WHISK
Excellent for smoothing sauces and beating egg whites.

### WIDE VEGETABLE PEELER
Very effective and easy to use for peeling all sizes of vegetable. Can also be used for peeling fruit.

# TECHNIQUES

## CHICKEN STOCK

This classic, flavorful low-fat stock forms the base for many Italian soups and sauces.

### INGREDIENTS
*2¼ pounds chicken wings or thighs*
*1 onion*
*2 whole cloves*
*1 bay leaf*
*1 sprig of fresh thyme*
*3–4 sprigs of fresh parsley*
*10 black peppercorns*

#### MAKES 6¼ CUPS

**1** Cut the chicken into pieces and put into a saucepan. Peel the onion and stud it with cloves. Tie the bay leaf, thyme, parsley and peppercorns in a piece of muslin and add to the saucepan with the onion.

**2** Pour in 7½ cups cold water. Slowly bring to the simmering point, skimming off and discarding any scum that rises to the surface with a slotted spoon. Continue to simmer very gently, uncovered, for 1½ hours.

**3** Strain the stock through a sieve into a large bowl and let sit until it is cold. Discard the contents of the sieve. Remove and discard any chicken fat from the surface of the stock with a spoon. Keep the stock chilled and covered in the refrigerator until needed, or freeze in usable amounts for up to six months.

## VEGETABLE STOCK

### INGREDIENTS
*2 carrots*
*2 celery stalks*
*2 onions*
*2 tomatoes*
*10 mushroom stalks*
*2 bay leaves*
*1 sprig of fresh thyme*
*3–4 sprigs of fresh parsley*
*10 black peppercorns*

#### MAKES 6¼ CUPS

### COOK'S TIP
To make fish stock, follow the recipe for chicken stock, substituting fish bones or trimmings for the chicken, and let it simmer for 20–30 minutes.

**1** Roughly chop the carrots, celery, onions, tomatoes and mushroom stalks. Place them in a large heavy saucepan. Tie the bay leaves, thyme, parsley and peppercorns in a piece of muslin and add to the saucepan.

**2** Pour in 7½ cups of cold water. Slowly bring to the simmering point. Continue to simmer very gently, uncovered, for 1½ hours.

**3** Strain the stock through a sieve into a large bowl and let sit until it is cold. Discard the contents of the sieve. Keep the stock chilled and covered in the refrigerator until needed, or freeze in usable amounts for up to one month.

## PEELING AND SEEDING TOMATOES

The best tomatoes for cooking are plum tomatoes, which hold their shape well and should have a fine flavor.
Try to buy "vine-ripened" varieties, as they will be properly ripened. The following method is an efficient way of
preparing tomatoes and can be done in advance of making a recipe.

**1** Use a sharp knife to cut a small cross on the bottom of the tomato. Turn the tomato over and carefully cut out the core. Immerse the tomato in boiling water for 30 seconds, then transfer to a bowl of cold water using a slotted spoon.

**2** Lift out the tomato and peel (the skin should be easy to remove). Cut the peeled tomato in half crosswise and squeeze out the seeds.

**3** Use a large knife to cut the peeled tomato into strips, then chop across the strips to make dice. Use as required.

## CHOPPING ONIONS

Cutting onion into uniform-size dice makes cooking easy. This method can't be beaten.

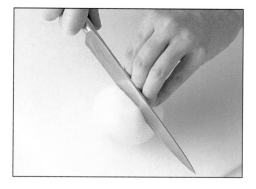

**1** Peel the onion. Cut it in half with a large knife and set it cut-side down on a board. Make lengthwise vertical cuts along the onion, cutting almost but not quite through to the root.

**2** Make two horizontal cuts from the stalk end and toward the root, but not through it.

**3** Cut the onion crosswise to form small, even dice. Use as required.

> ### COOK'S TIP
> This technique also works for shallots, but because they are smaller, you may not need to make the horizontal cuts.

## MAKING BASIC PASTA DOUGH ON A WORK SURFACE

The best place to make, knead and roll out pasta dough is on a wooden kitchen table—the larger the better. The surface should be warm, so marble is not suitable.

### INGREDIENTS
*1¾ cups all-purpose flour*
*pinch of salt*
*2 eggs*
*2 teaspoons cold water*

### SERVES 3–4

#### VARIATIONS
TOMATO: add 4 teaspoons concentrated tomato paste to the eggs before mixing.
SPINACH: add 4 ounces frozen spinach, thawed and with the moisture squeezed out. Liquidize with the eggs, before adding to the flour.
HERBS: add 3 tablespoons finely chopped fresh herbs to the eggs before mixing the dough.

**1** Sift the flour and salt onto a clean work surface, and make a well in the center with your hand.

**2** Put the eggs and water into the well. Using a fork, beat the eggs gently together, then gradually draw in the flour from the sides to make a thick paste.

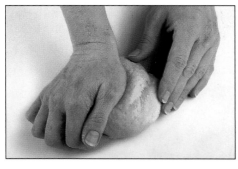

**3** When the mixture becomes too stiff to use a fork, use your hands to mix into a firm dough. Knead the dough for about 5 minutes, until smooth. (This can be done in an electric food mixer with a dough hook.) Wrap in plastic wrap to prevent it from drying out and let rest for 20–30 minutes.

## MAKING BASIC PASTA DOUGH IN A BOWL

**1** Sift the flour and salt into a glass bowl and make a well in the center. Add the eggs and water.

**2** Using a fork, beat the eggs gently together, then gradually draw in the flour from the sides, to make a thick paste.

**3** When the mixture becomes too stiff to use a fork, use your hands to mix into a firm dough. Knead the dough for 5 minutes until smooth. (This can be done in an electric food mixer with a dough hook.) Wrap in plastic wrap to prevent it from drying out and let sit for 20–30 minutes.

## ROLLING OUT PASTA DOUGH BY HAND

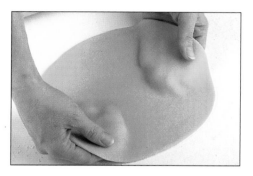

**1** Cut the basic dough in quarters. Use one quarter at a time and re-wrap the rest in plastic wrap so it does not dry out. Flatten the dough and dust liberally with flour. Start rolling out the dough, making sure you roll it evenly.

**2** As the dough becomes thinner, keep rotating it on the work surface by gently lifting the edges with your fingers and supporting it over the rolling pin. Make sure you don't tear the dough.

**3** Continue rolling out the dough until it has reached the desired thickness, about 1/8 inch thick.

## ROLLING OUT DOUGH USING A PASTA MACHINE

**1** Cut the basic dough into quarters. Use one quarter at a time and re-wrap the rest in plastic wrap so it does not dry out. Flatten the dough and dust liberally with flour. Start with the machine set to roll at the thickest setting. Pass the dough through the rollers several times, dusting the dough occasionally with flour until it is smooth.

**2** Fold the strip of dough into thirds, press the folds down and pass through the machine again. Repeat the folding and rolling several times on each setting.

**3** Guide the dough through the machine, but do not pull or stretch it, or the dough will tear. As the dough is worked through all the settings, it will become thinner and longer. Guide the dough over your hand, as the dough is rolled out to a thin sheet. Pasta used for stuffing, such as ravioli or tortellini, should be used immediately. Otherwise, lay the rolled sheets on a clean dish towel, lightly dusted with sifted flour, and let dry for 10 minutes before cutting. This makes it easier to cut and prevents the strands of pasta from sticking together.

## CUTTING PASTA SHAPES

Until you are confident handling and shaping pasta dough, it is easier to work with small amounts.
Always keep the dough well wrapped in plastic wrap to prevent it from drying out, before
you are ready to work with it.

 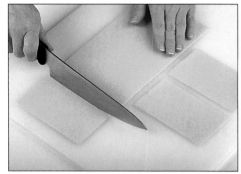 

### CUTTING OUT TAGLIATELLE
To cut tagliatelle, fit the appropriate attachment to the machine or move the handle to the appropriate slot. Cut the pasta sheets into 10-inch lengths and pass these through the machine as for spaghetti.

### CUTTING OUT LASAGNE
Take a sheet of pasta dough and cut out neat rectangles about 7 × 3 inches to make sheets of lasagne. Lay on a clean dish towel to dry.

### CUTTING OUT SPAGHETTI
To cut spaghetti, put the appropriate attachment on the machine or move the handle to the appropriate slot. Cut the pasta sheets into 10-inch lengths and pass these through the machine. Guide the strands over the back of your hand as they appear out of the machine.

## SHAPING RAVIOLI

Ravioli made in this way are not perfectly square, but they look charmingly homemade.

  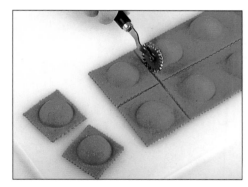

**1** To make ravioli, place spoonfuls of filling on a sheet of dough at intervals of 2–3 inches, leaving a 1-inch border. Brush the dough between the spoonfuls of filling with lightly beaten egg white.

**2** Lay a second sheet of pasta carefully on top. Press around each mound of filling, excluding any air pockets.

**3** Using a fluted pastry wheel or a sharp knife, cut between the stuffing to make square-shaped parcels.

## MAKING FARFALLE (PASTA BOWS)

**1** Roll the pasta dough through a pasta machine until the sheets are very thin. Then cut into long strips 1½ inches wide.

**2** Cut the strips into small rectangles. Run a pastry wheel along the two shorter edges of the little rectangles—this will give the bows a decorative edge.

**3** Moisten the center of the strips and, using a finger and thumb, gently pinch each rectangle together in the middle to make little pasta bows.

## MAKING TAGLIATELLE

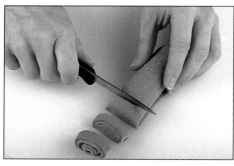

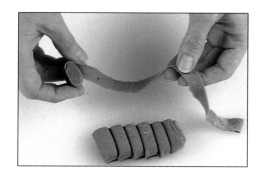

**1** Lightly flour some spinach-flavored pasta dough, cut into a rectangle 12 × 4 inches and roll it up.

**2** Using a sharp knife, cut across the pasta roll.

**3** Carefully unravel each little roll as you cut it to make ribbons of fresh tagliatelle.

### COOKING PASTA

**1** Before starting to cook either sauce or pasta, read through the recipe carefully. It is important to know which needs to be cooked for the longest time—sometimes it is the pasta and sometimes the sauce, so don't always assume one or the other. The sauce can often be made ahead of time and reheated, but pasta is almost like a hot soufflé—it waits for no one.

**2** There needs to be plenty of room for the pasta to move around in the large amount of water it needs, so a big pan is essential. The best type of pan is a tall, lightweight, straight-sided, stainless steel pasta cooking pot with its own in-built draining pan. Both outer and inner pans have two handles each, which ensures easy and safe lifting and draining. It is well worth investing in one of these pans.

**3** Use a large amount of water. If there is not enough water, the pasta shapes will stick together as they swell, and the pan will become overcrowded. This will result in gummy-textured pasta. Before adding the pasta, the water should be at a fast rolling boil. The quickest way to do this is to boil water in a kettle, then pour it into the pasta pot, which should be set over high heat.

# SOUPS

DELICIOUS *soups can be made in no time at all and they provide a* TEMPTING *start to a meal or make a complete* LIGHT *meal on their own when served with a hunk of fresh crusty* ITALIAN *bread. We include a selection of homemade* FAT-FREE *and low-fat Italian soups for you to make and enjoy, such as Roasted Bell* PEPPER *Soup, Italian Vegetable Soup, Chicken and Pasta Soup and Roasted* TOMATO *and Pasta Soup.*

# ITALIAN VEGETABLE SOUP

Fresh vegetables, cooked beans and pasta combine well with vegetable stock to create this tasty, virtually fat-free Italian soup.

### INGREDIENTS

*1 small carrot*
*1 baby leek*
*1 celery stalk*
*2 ounces green cabbage*
*3¾ cups vegetable stock*
*1 bay leaf*
*1 cup cooked cannellini or white beans*
*¼ cup dried soup pasta, such as tiny shells, bows, stars or elbows*
*salt and freshly ground black pepper*
*snipped fresh chives, to garnish*

### SERVES 4

**2** Add the cabbage, beans and pasta shapes. Stir, then simmer, uncovered, for another 4–5 minutes or until the vegetables and pasta are tender or *al dente*, stirring occasionally.

**3** Remove the bay leaf and season with salt and pepper to taste. Ladle into soup bowls and garnish with snipped chives. Serve immediately.

**1** Cut the carrot, leek and celery into 2-inch long julienne strips. Slice the cabbage very finely. Set aside. Put the stock and bay leaf into a large saucepan and bring to a boil. Add the carrot, leek and celery, cover and simmer for 6 minutes, stirring occasionally.

### NUTRITIONAL NOTES
*Per portion:*

| | |
|---|---|
| Energy | 63cals |
| Total fat | 0.48g |
| Saturated fat | 0.07g |
| Cholesterol | 0mg |
| Fiber | 1.48g |

# VEGETABLE MINESTRONE

**This vegetable and pasta soup makes a tasty appetizer or snack and is very low in fat.**

### INGREDIENTS

*large pinch of saffron threads*
*1 onion, chopped*
*1 leek, sliced*
*1 celery stalk, sliced*
*2 carrots, diced*
*2–3 garlic cloves, crushed*
*2¹/2 cups chicken stock*
*2 14-ounce cans chopped tomatoes*
*¹/2 cup frozen peas*
*¹/2 cup dried soup pasta,*
*such as anellini*
*1 teaspoon sugar*
*1 tablespoon chopped fresh parsley*
*1 tablespoon chopped fresh basil*
*salt and freshly ground black pepper*

*SERVES 4*

**1** Soak the saffron threads in 1 tablespoon boiling water in a small bowl. Let stand for 10 minutes.

**2** Meanwhile, put the onion, leek, celery, carrots and garlic into a large saucepan. Add the chicken stock, bring to a boil, cover and simmer for about 10 minutes.

**3** Add the tomatoes, the saffron with its liquid and the frozen peas. Bring back to a boil and add the soup pasta. Simmer for 10 minutes, until tender or *al dente*, stirring occasionally.

**4** Season with sugar, salt and pepper to taste. Stir in the chopped herbs just before serving. Ladle into soup bowls and serve.

### NUTRITIONAL NOTES
*Per portion:*

| | |
|---|---|
| Energy | 77cals |
| Total fat | 0.6g |
| Saturated fat | 0.1g |
| Cholesterol | 0mg |
| Fiber | 2.9g |

# LITTLE STUFFED HATS IN BROTH

—

This soup is served in northern Italy on Santo Stefano (St. Stephen's Day)
and on New Year's Day. It makes a light change from all the rich foods of the day before.

### INGREDIENTS
*5 cups chicken stock*
*1 cup fresh or dried cappelletti*
*2 tablespoons dry white wine (optional)*
*about 1 tablespoon finely chopped fresh*
*flat-leaf parsley (optional)*
*salt and freshly ground black pepper*
*shredded flat-leaf parsley, to garnish*
*1 tablespoon grated fresh Parmesan*
*cheese, to serve*

### SERVES 4

**1** Pour the chicken stock into a large
saucepan and bring to a boil. Add a little
salt and pepper to taste.

**2** Drop in the pasta, stir well and bring
back to a boil. Reduce the heat to a
simmer and cook, according to the
package instructions, until the pasta
is tender or *al dente*. Stir the pasta
frequently during cooking to ensure that
it cooks evenly.

**3** Swirl in the wine and parsley, if using,
then adjust the seasoning. Ladle into
warmed soup bowls, then sprinkle with
shredded flat-leaf parsley and grated
Parmesan. Serve immediately.

### NUTRITIONAL NOTES
*Per portion:*

| | |
|---|---|
| Energy | 103cals |
| Total fat | 1.7g |
| Saturated fat | 0.8g |
| Cholesterol | 3.7mg |
| Fiber | 0.8g |

# TINY PASTA IN BROTH

—

In Italy this tasty pasta soup is often served with bread for a light evening supper or for a quick
midday snack. You can use any other dried tiny soup pastas in place of the funghetti.

### INGREDIENTS
*5 cups beef stock*
*3/4 cup dried tiny soup pasta,*
*such as funghetti*
*2 pieces bottled roasted red bell pepper,*
*about 2 ounces*
*salt and freshly ground black pepper*
*1 ounce coarsely shaved fresh Parmesan*
*cheese, to serve*

### SERVES 4

**1** Bring the beef stock to a boil in a large
saucepan. Add salt and pepper to taste,
then drop in the dried soup pasta. Stir
well and bring the stock back to a boil.

**2** Reduce the heat to a simmer and cook
for 7–8 minutes or according to the
package instructions, until the pasta is
tender or *al dente*. Stir frequently during
cooking to prevent the pasta shapes from
sticking together.

### NUTRITIONAL NOTES
*Per portion:*

| | |
|---|---|
| Energy | 108cals |
| Total fat | 3.7g |
| Saturated fat | 1.5g |
| Cholesterol | 6.2mg |
| Fiber | 0.8g |

**3** Drain the pieces of roasted pepper and
dice them finely. Place them in the
bottom of four soup bowls. Taste the soup
and adjust the seasoning. Ladle into the
soup bowls and serve immediately, with
shavings of Parmesan passed separately.

# FRESH TOMATO SOUP

—

**Intensely flavored sun-ripened tomatoes need little embellishment in this fresh-tasting
low-fat soup. For the best flavor, choose the ripest looking tomatoes you can find.**

## INGREDIENTS

*3–3¹/₂ pounds ripe tomatoes*
*1²/₃ cups chicken or vegetable stock*
*3 tablespoons sun-dried tomato paste*
*2–3 tablespoons balsamic vinegar*
*2–3 teaspoons sugar*
*small handful fresh basil leaves*
*salt and freshly ground black pepper*
*fresh basil leaves, to garnish*
*6 small toasted cheese croûtes, and*
*2 tablespoons low-fat sour cream, to serve*

*SERVES 6*

---

### COOK'S TIP

Add the vinegar and sugar a little at a
time, tasting the soup as you go, to ensure
you use just the right amount of each.

**1** Plunge the tomatoes into a bowl of
boiling water for 30 seconds, then refresh
in cold water. Drain. Peel and discard the
skins and quarter the tomatoes. Put them
in a large saucepan and pour in the
chicken or vegetable stock. Bring to a
boil, reduce the heat, cover and simmer
gently for 10 minutes, until the tomatoes
are pulpy.

**2** Stir in the tomato paste, vinegar, sugar
and basil. Season with salt and pepper,
then cook gently, stirring, for 2 minutes.
Purée the soup in a blender or food
processor, then return to the rinsed-out
saucepan and reheat gently until piping
hot. Serve in soup bowls topped with one
or two toasted cheese croûtes and a
teaspoonful of sour cream. Garnish with
basil leaves.

### NUTRITIONAL NOTES
*Per portion:*

| | |
|---|---|
| Energy | 108cals |
| Total fat | 3.5g |
| Saturated fat | 1.8g |
| Cholesterol | 2.6mg |
| Fiber | 2.7g |

# CHICKEN AND PASTA SOUP

Skinless cooked chicken, mushrooms and pasta combine well with a flavorful stock, to create this tasty, low-fat soup, ideal for an appetizer or snack.

**3** Remove and discard the skin from the chicken and slice the meat thinly using a sharp knife. Add to the soup and season to taste. Heat the soup through for 2–3 minutes.

**4** Stir in the pasta, bring to a boil, cover and simmer for 7–8 minutes, until tender or *al dente*. Just before serving, remove and discard the bay leaf. Stir in the white wine and chopped parsley, heat through for 2–3 minutes, then adjust the seasoning and serve in soup bowls.

### INGREDIENTS

*3³⁄₄ cups chicken stock*
*1 bay leaf*
*4 scallions, sliced*
*3 cups button*
*mushrooms, sliced*
*4 ounces cooked chicken breast*
*¹⁄₂ cup dried soup pasta,*
*such as stellette*
*²⁄₃ cup dry white wine*
*1 tablespoon chopped fresh parsley*
*salt and freshly ground black pepper*

**SERVES 4–6**

**1** Put the stock and bay leaf into a saucepan and bring to a boil.

**2** Add the scallions and mushrooms and stir to mix.

### NUTRITIONAL NOTES
*Per portion:*

| | |
|---|---|
| Energy | 74cals |
| Total fat | 1g |
| Saturated fat | 0.3g |
| Cholesterol | 8.24mg |
| Fiber | 0.75g |

# TOMATO AND FRESH BASIL SOUP

A soup for late summer, when fresh plum tomatoes are at their most flavorful, this fresh tomato soup flavored with basil is a tasty supper dish.

**2** Stir in the chopped tomatoes and garlic, then add the stock, white wine and tomato paste, with salt and pepper to taste. Bring to a boil, then reduce the heat, half-cover the pan and simmer gently for 20 minutes, stirring the mixture occasionally to stop the tomatoes from sticking to the bottom of the pan.

### INGREDIENTS
*1 tablespoon olive oil*
*1 onion, finely chopped*
*2 pounds ripe Italian plum tomatoes, roughly chopped*
*1 garlic clove, roughly chopped*
*about 3 cups chicken or vegetable stock*
*1/2 cup dry white wine*
*2 tablespoons sun-dried tomato paste*
*2 tablespoons shredded fresh basil, plus a few whole leaves to garnish*
*2 tablespoons light cream*
*salt and freshly ground black pepper*

**SERVES 4**

**1** Heat the olive oil in a large saucepan over medium heat. Add the chopped onion and cook gently for about 5 minutes, stirring frequently, until it is softened but not brown.

### NUTRITIONAL NOTES
*Per portion:*

| | |
|---|---|
| Energy | 77cals |
| Total fat | 3.9g |
| Saturated fat | 1.1g |
| Cholesterol | 2.74mg |
| Fiber | 1.75g |

**3** Purée the soup with the shredded basil in a blender or food processor until smooth, then press through a sieve into a clean pan. Discard the remaining contents of the sieve.

**4** Add the cream to the soup in the pan and heat through, stirring. Do not let the soup boil. Check the consistency of the soup and add more hot stock if necessary, then adjust the seasoning. Pour into soup bowls and garnish with whole basil leaves. Serve immediately.

# FARMHOUSE SOUP
—

**Root vegetables form the basis of this low-fat, chunky, minestrone-style soup. For a more substantial meal, serve with fresh crusty bread.**

### INGREDIENTS

*1 tablespoon olive oil*
*1 onion, roughly chopped*
*3 carrots, cut into large chunks*
*6–7 ounces turnips, cut into large chunks*
*6 ounces rutabaga, cut into large chunks*
*14-ounce can chopped Italian tomatoes*
*1 tablespoon tomato paste*
*1 teaspoon dried mixed herbs*
*1 teaspoon dried oregano*
*1/2 cup dried peppers, washed and thinly sliced (optional)*
*6 1/4 cups vegetable stock or water*
*1/2 cup dried small macaroni or conchiglie*
*14-ounce can red kidney beans, rinsed and drained*
*2 tablespoons chopped fresh flat-leaf parsley*
*salt and freshly ground black pepper*
*1 tablespoon grated fresh Parmesan cheese, to serve*

### SERVES 6

**1** Heat the oil in a large saucepan, add the onion and cook over low heat for about 5 minutes, until softened. Add the prepared fresh vegetables, canned tomatoes, tomato paste, dried herbs and dried peppers, if using. Stir in salt and pepper to taste. Pour in the stock or water and bring to a boil. Stir well, cover, reduce the heat and simmer for 30 minutes, stirring occasionally.

**2** Add the pasta and bring to a boil, stirring, then simmer, uncovered, for about 5 minutes or according to the package instructions, until the pasta is just tender or *al dente*. Stir frequently.

**3** Stir in the beans. Heat through for 2–3 minutes, then remove from heat and stir in the parsley. Adjust the seasoning. Serve hot in soup bowls, sprinkled with a little grated Parmesan.

### COOK'S TIP
Dried Italian peppers are piquant and firm with a "meaty" bite, which makes them ideal for adding substance to vegetarian soups.

### NUTRITIONAL NOTES
*Per portion:*

| | |
|---|---|
| Energy | 159cals |
| Total fat | 4g |
| Saturated fat | 0.9g |
| Cholesterol | 2.36mg |
| Fiber | 6.6g |

# ROASTED BELL PEPPER SOUP

Broiling intensifies the flavor of red and yellow bell peppers and helps this soup keep its stunning color. No added fat is used for this recipe, creating a delicious and virtually fat-free soup.

### INGREDIENTS
*3 red bell peppers*
*1 yellow bell pepper*
*1 onion, chopped*
*1 garlic clove, crushed*
*3 cups vegetable stock*
*1 tablespoon all-purpose flour*
*salt and freshly ground black pepper*
*red and yellow bell peppers, diced,*
*to garnish*
### SERVES 4

**1** Preheat the broiler. Halve the red and yellow peppers and cut out and discard their tops and white pith. Scrape out and discard the seeds.

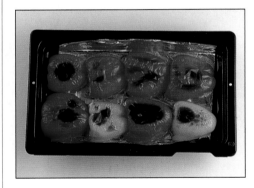

**2** Line a broiler pan with aluminum foil and arrange the halved peppers, skin-side up, in a single layer. Broil until the skins have blackened and blistered.

**3** Transfer the peppers to a plastic bag and let sit for a few minutes. Once cool, gently peel away and discard their skins. Roughly chop the pepper flesh. Set aside.

**4** Put the onion, garlic clove and ²/₃ cup stock into a large saucepan. Bring to a boil and boil for about 5 minutes, until most of the stock has reduced in volume. Reduce the heat and stir until the onion and garlic are softened and just beginning to color.

### NUTRITIONAL NOTES
*Per portion:*

| | |
|---|---|
| Energy | 28cals |
| Total fat | 0.2g |
| Saturated fat | 0.04g |
| Cholesterol | 0mg |
| Fiber | 0.8g |

**5** Sprinkle the flour on the onions, then gradually stir in the remaining stock. Add the chopped peppers and bring to a boil, stirring. Cover and let simmer for 5 minutes.

**6** Let cool slightly, then purée in a blender or food processor until smooth. Season to taste. Return to the rinsed-out saucepan and reheat until piping hot. Ladle into soup bowls and garnish each portion with a sprinkling of diced peppers. Serve.

### COOK'S TIP
Sautéeing onions and garlic in stock, as described in Step 4, is a very useful technique in low-fat cooking. The trick is to let the stock reduce almost entirely, from which point the onions and garlic will start to brown, rather than simply being boiled.

# PASTA AND CHICKPEA SOUP

A simple, country-style Italian soup, ideal for a flavorful, low-fat appetizer. You can use other pasta shapes, but conchiglie are ideal because they scoop up the chickpeas and beans.

### INGREDIENTS
*1 onion*
*2 carrots*
*2 celery sticks*
*1 tablespoon olive oil*
*14-ounce can chickpeas, rinsed and drained*
*7-ounce can cannellini beans, rinsed and drained*
*2/3 cup passata*
*1/2 cup water*
*6 1/4 cups vegetable or chicken stock*
*1 fresh or dried rosemary sprig*
*scant 2 cups dried conchiglie*
*salt and freshly ground black pepper*
*fresh rosemary leaves, to garnish*
*1 tablespoon grated fresh Parmesan cheese, to serve*

### SERVES 6

**1** Chop the onion, carrots and celery finely, either in a food processor or by hand.

**2** Heat the olive oil in a large saucepan, add the chopped vegetables and cook over low heat, stirring frequently, for 5–7 minutes.

**3** Add the chickpeas and cannellini beans, stir well to mix, then cook for 5 minutes. Stir in the passata and water. Cook, stirring, for 2–3 minutes.

**4** Add 2 cups of the stock, the rosemary sprig and salt and pepper to taste. Bring to a boil, cover, then simmer gently, stirring occasionally, for 1 hour.

### NUTRITIONAL NOTES
*Per portion:*

| | |
|---|---|
| Energy | 201cals |
| Total fat | 4.5g |
| Saturated fat | 0.9g |
| Cholesterol | 1.84mg |
| Fiber | 3.4g |

**5** Pour in the remaining stock, add the pasta and bring to a boil, stirring. Reduce the heat and simmer, stirring frequently for 7–8 minutes or according to the package instructions, until the pasta is tender or *al dente*. Adjust the seasoning. Remove and discard the rosemary sprig and serve the hot soup in soup bowls, topped with a few rosemary leaves and a little grated Parmesan.

# LENTIL AND PASTA SOUP

**This rustic Italian vegetarian soup makes a warming winter meal. It goes well with crusty Italian bread to create a healthy, low-fat supper.**

### INGREDIENTS
*3/4 cup brown lentils*
*3 garlic cloves*
*4 cups water*
*1 tablespoon olive oil*
*1 onion, finely chopped*
*2 celery stalks, finely chopped*
*2 tablespoons sun-dried tomato paste*
*7 1/2 cups vegetable stock*
*a few fresh marjoram leaves*
*a few fresh basil leaves*
*leaves from 1 fresh thyme sprig*
*1/2 cup dried small pasta shapes,*
*such as tubetti*
*salt and freshly ground black pepper*
*tiny fresh herb leaves, to garnish*

### SERVES 6

1 Put the lentils in a large saucepan. Smash 1 garlic clove (there's no need to peel it first) and add it to the lentils. Pour in the water and bring to a boil. Reduce the heat to a gentle simmer and cook, stirring occasionally, for about 20 minutes or until the lentils are just tender. Put the lentils into a sieve, remove the garlic and set it aside. Rinse the lentils under the cold tap, then let them drain.

2 Heat the oil in a large saucepan. Add the onion and celery and cook over low heat, stirring frequently, for 5–7 minutes, until softened.

3 Crush the remaining garlic, then peel and mash the reserved garlic. Add to the vegetables with the tomato paste and the lentils. Stir, then add the stock, the fresh herbs and salt and pepper to taste. Bring to a boil, then simmer for 30 minutes, stirring occasionally.

4 Add the pasta and bring back to a boil, stirring. Simmer, stirring frequently for 7–8 minutes or according to the package instructions, until the pasta is tender or *al dente*. Adjust the seasoning. Serve hot, sprinkled with the herb leaves.

### COOK'S TIP
Use green lentils instead of brown if you want to, but don't use the orange or red ones, as they get mushy.

### NUTRITIONAL NOTES
*Per portion:*

| | |
|---|---|
| Energy | 145cals |
| Total fat | 3.2g |
| Saturated fat | 0.4g |
| Cholesterol | 0mg |
| Fiber | 3.2g |

# PUGLIA-STYLE MINESTRONE

—

**This is a tasty low-fat soup for a supper early in the week because it can be made with the leftover carcass of Sunday's roast chicken.**

### INGREDIENTS

*1 roast chicken carcass*
*1 onion, quartered lengthwise*
*1 carrot, roughly chopped*
*1 celery stalk, roughly chopped*
*a few black peppercorns*
*1 small handful mixed fresh herbs, such as parsley and thyme*
*1 chicken bouillon cube*
*1/2 cup dried tubetti*
*salt and freshly ground black pepper*
*1 ounce ricotta salata or feta cheese, coarsely grated or crumbled, and*
*2 tablespoons fresh mint leaves, to serve*

SERVES 4

**1** Break the chicken carcass into pieces and place these in a large saucepan. Add the onion, carrot, celery, peppercorns and fresh herbs, then crumble in the bouillon cube and add a good pinch of salt. Cover the chicken generously with cold water (you will need about 6¼ cups) and bring to a boil over high heat.

**2** Reduce the heat, half cover the pan and simmer gently for about 1 hour. Remove the pan from heat and let the mixture cool, then strain the liquid through a colander or sieve into a clean, large saucepan.

**3** Remove any meat from the chicken bones, cut it into bite-size pieces and set aside. Discard the carcass and all the flavoring ingredients.

**4** Bring the stock in the pan to a boil, add the pasta and simmer, stirring frequently for 5–6 minutes or according to the package instructions, until only just tender or *al dente*.

**5** Add the chicken and heat through for a few minutes, by which time the pasta will be ready. Adjust the seasoning. Serve hot in soup bowls, sprinkled with the ricotta salata or feta cheese and mint leaves.

### NUTRITIONAL NOTES
*Per portion:*

| | |
|---|---|
| Energy | 59cals |
| Total fat | 1.5g |
| Saturated fat | 0.9g |
| Cholesterol | 4.38mg |
| Fiber | 0.4g |

# PASTA, BEAN AND VEGETABLE SOUP

**This tasty soup is a specialty from the Calabrian region of Italy. The combination of pulses, pasta and vegetables creates a filling, low-fat soup.**

### INGREDIENTS

*scant 1/2 cup brown lentils*
*1/2 cup dried mushrooms*
*1 tablespoon olive oil*
*1 carrot, diced*
*1 celery stalk, diced*
*1 onion, finely chopped*
*1 garlic clove, finely chopped*
*a little chopped fresh flat-leaf parsley*
*a good pinch of crushed*
*red chiles (optional)*
*6 1/4 cups vegetable stock*
*scant 1 cup each canned red kidney beans,*
*cannellini beans and chickpeas, rinsed*
*and drained*
*1 cup dried small pasta shapes, such as*
*rigatoni, penne or penne rigate*
*salt and freshly ground black pepper*
*chopped flat-leaf parsley, to garnish*
*2 tablespoons grated fresh Pecorino*
*cheese, to serve*

### SERVES 6

**1** Put the lentils in a medium saucepan, add 2 cups water and bring to a boil over high heat. Reduce the heat to a gentle simmer and cook, stirring occasionally, for 15–20 minutes or until just tender. Meanwhile, soak the dried mushrooms in 3/4 cup warm water for 15–20 minutes.

**2** Put the lentils in a sieve to drain, then rinse under the cold tap. Drain the soaked mushrooms and reserve the soaking liquid. Finely chop the mushrooms and set aside.

**3** Heat the oil in a large saucepan and add the carrot, celery, onion, garlic, parsley and chiles, if using. Cook over low heat for 5–7 minutes, stirring occasionally. Add the stock, then the mushrooms and their soaking liquid.

**4** Bring to a boil, then add the beans, chickpeas and lentils. Season to taste. Cover, and simmer gently for 20 minutes.

**5** Add the pasta and bring the soup back to a boil, stirring. Simmer, stirring frequently for 7–8 minutes or according to the package instructions, until the pasta is tender or *al dente*. Check the seasoning, and serve hot, sprinkled with parsley and Pecorino.

### NUTRITIONAL NOTES
*Per portion:*

| | |
|---|---|
| Energy | 202cals |
| Total fat | 5g |
| Saturated fat | 1.1g |
| Cholesterol | 3.02mg |
| Fiber | 4.9g |

# ROASTED TOMATO AND PASTA SOUP

When the only tomatoes you can buy are not particularly flavorful, make this soup.
The oven-roasting compensates for any lack of flavor in the tomatoes.

### INGREDIENTS

*1 pound ripe Italian plum tomatoes,*
*halved lengthwise*
*1 large red bell pepper, quartered*
*lengthwise and deseeded*
*1 large red onion, quartered lengthwise*
*2 garlic cloves, unpeeled*
*1 tablespoon olive oil*
*5 cups vegetable stock or water*
*good pinch of sugar*
*scant 1 cup dried small pasta shapes, such*
*as tubetti or small macaroni*
*salt and freshly ground black pepper*
*fresh basil leaves, to garnish*

### SERVES 4

**1** Preheat the oven to 375°F. Spread out the tomatoes, red pepper, onion and garlic in a roasting pan and drizzle with the olive oil. Roast for 30–40 minutes, until the vegetables are soft and charred, stirring and turning them halfway through the cooking time.

**2** Put the vegetables in a blender or food processor, add about 1 cup of the stock or water and blend until puréed. Scrape into a sieve placed over a large saucepan, and press the purée through the sieve into the pan. Discard the contents of the sieve.

**4** Add the pasta and simmer, stirring frequently, for 7–8 minutes or according to the package instructions, until the pasta is tender or *al dente*. Adjust the seasoning. Serve hot in soup bowls, garnished with fresh basil leaves.

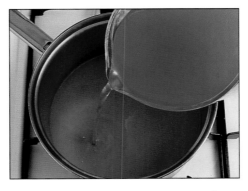

**3** Add the remaining stock or water, the sugar and salt and pepper to taste. Bring to a boil, stirring.

### COOK'S TIP

The soup can be frozen without the pasta. Thaw and bring to a boil before adding the pasta.

### NUTRITIONAL NOTES
*Per portion:*

| | |
|---|---|
| Energy | 145cals |
| Total fat | 4.6g |
| Saturated fat | 0.7g |
| Cholesterol | 0mg |
| Fiber | 2.4g |

# WILD MUSHROOM SOUP

Dried porcini mushrooms have an intense flavor, so only a small amount is needed for this delicious soup. The beef stock helps to strengthen the earthy flavor of the mushrooms.

### INGREDIENTS

*1/2 cup dried porcini mushrooms*
*1 tablespoon olive oil*
*2 leeks, thinly sliced*
*2 shallots, roughly chopped*
*1 garlic clove, roughly chopped*
*3 cups fresh wild mushrooms*
*about 5 cups beef stock*
*1/2 teaspoon dried thyme*
*2 tablespoons light cream*
*salt and freshly ground black pepper*
*fresh thyme sprigs, to garnish*

### SERVES 4

**1** Put the dried porcini in a bowl, add 1 cup warm water and let soak for 20–30 minutes. Lift out of the liquid and squeeze over the bowl to remove as much of the soaking liquid as possible. Strain all the liquid and reserve to use later. Finely chop the porcini and set aside.

**2** Heat the olive oil in a large saucepan. Add the leeks, shallots and garlic and cook gently for about 5 minutes, stirring the mixture frequently, until softened but not colored.

**3** Chop or slice the fresh mushrooms and add to the pan. Stir over medium heat for a few minutes, until they begin to soften. Pour in the beef stock and bring to a boil. Add the chopped porcini, reserved soaking liquid, dried thyme and salt and pepper. Reduce the heat, half-cover the pan and simmer gently for 30 minutes, stirring occasionally.

**4** Pour about three-quarters of the soup into a blender or food processor and blend until smooth. Return to the soup remaining in the pan, stir in the cream and heat through gently. Check the consistency and add more stock if the soup is too thick. Adjust the seasoning. Serve hot in soup bowls, garnished with fresh thyme sprigs.

### NUTRITIONAL NOTES

*Per portion:*

| | |
|---|---|
| Energy | 66cals |
| Total fat | 4.7g |
| Saturated fat | 1.2g |
| Cholesterol | 3.32mg |
| Fiber | 1.2g |

# FRESH TOMATO AND ONION SOUP

—

This delicious wholesome soup is full of flavor and is low in fat too. Serve with slices of whole-grain bread for a more substantial snack.

### INGREDIENTS

*2 teaspoons sunflower oil*
*1 large onion, chopped*
*2 celery stalks, chopped*
*¾ cup split red lentils*
*2 large tomatoes, skinned and*
*roughly chopped*
*3¾ cups vegetable stock*
*2 teaspoons mixed dried Italian herbs,*
*such as oregano and thyme*
*salt and freshly ground black pepper*
*chopped fresh parsley, to garnish*

### SERVES 4

**1** Heat the oil in a large saucepan. Add the chopped onion and celery and cook for 5 minutes, stirring occasionally. Add the lentils and cook for 1 minute.

**2** Stir in the tomatoes, stock, herbs and seasoning. Cover, bring to a boil and simmer for about 20 minutes, stirring occasionally, until the lentils and vegetables are cooked and tender. Remove the pan from heat and set the soup aside to cool slightly.

**3** Purée the soup in a blender or food processor until smooth. Adjust the seasoning, return to the rinsed-out saucepan and reheat gently until piping hot. Serve garnished with chopped parsley.

### NUTRITIONAL NOTES
*Per portion:*

| | |
|---|---|
| Energy | 117cals |
| Total fat | 2.0g |
| Saturated fat | 0.3g |
| Cholesterol | 1mg |
| Fiber | 1.9g |

# MIXED VEGETABLE SOUP WITH CONCHIGLIETTE

Lean bacon adds delicious flavor to this Italian-style low-fat
vegetable and pasta soup.

**3** Add the milk and season with salt and pepper. Purée half of the soup in a blender or food processor until smooth, then return to the pan with the pasta shells. Bring to a boil and simmer for 10 minutes, stirring occasionally.

**4** Meanwhile, fry the bacon quickly in a nonstick frying pan for 2–3 minutes, until the meat is cooked, stirring frequently. Stir into the soup and ladle into soup bowls to serve. Serve with breadsticks, if desired.

### INGREDIENTS

*1 small green bell pepper*
*1 pound potatoes, peeled and diced*
*2 cups canned or frozen corn*
*1 onion, chopped*
*1 celery stalk, chopped*
*1 bouquet garni (bay leaf, parsley stems*
*and thyme)*
*2<sup>1</sup>/2 cups chicken stock*
*1<sup>1</sup>/4 cups skim milk*
*2 ounces small dried pasta*
*shells (conchigliette)*
*4 ounces lean bacon, diced*
*breadsticks, to serve (optional)*
*salt and freshly ground black pepper*

### SERVES 6

**1** Halve the green pepper and remove and discard the top and seeds. Cut the flesh into small dice. Place in a bowl, cover with boiling water and let stand for 2 minutes. Rinse and drain.

**2** Put the green pepper into a saucepan with the diced potatoes, corn, onion, celery, bouquet garni and chicken stock. Bring to a boil, cover and simmer for 20 minutes, until the vegetables are tender, stirring occasionally.

### NUTRITIONAL NOTES
*Per portion:*

| | |
|---|---|
| Energy | 177cals |
| Total fat | 3.6g |
| Saturated fat | 1.2g |
| Cholesterol | 10.82mg |
| Fiber | 1.8g |

# LENTIL SOUP WITH TOMATOES

—

**This classic rustic Italian soup is low in fat and flavored with rosemary, and is delicious served with crusty bread or low-fat garlic bread.**

### INGREDIENTS

*1 cup dried green or brown lentils*
*2 teaspoons extra virgin olive oil*
*2 strips lean bacon, cut into small dice*
*1 onion, finely chopped*
*2 celery stalks, finely chopped*
*2 carrots, finely diced*
*2 fresh rosemary sprigs, finely chopped*
*2 bay leaves*
*14-ounce can chopped plum tomatoes*
*7 1/2 cups vegetable stock*
*salt and freshly ground black pepper*
*fresh bay leaves and rosemary sprigs,*
*to garnish*

*SERVES 4*

**1** Place the lentils in a bowl and cover with cold water. Let soak for 2 hours. Rinse and drain well.

**2** Heat the oil in a large saucepan. Add the bacon and cook for about 3 minutes, then stir in the chopped onion and cook for 5 minutes, until softened, stirring occasionally. Stir in the celery, carrots, chopped rosemary, bay leaves and lentils.

**3** Add the tomatoes and stock and bring to a boil. Reduce the heat, half-cover the pan, and simmer for about 1 hour or until the lentils are perfectly tender, stirring occasionally.

**4** Remove and discard the bay leaves, add salt and pepper to taste and serve garnished with bay leaves and rosemary.

### NUTRITIONAL NOTES
*Per portion:*

| | |
|---|---|
| Energy | 235cals |
| Total fat | 4.9g |
| Saturated fat | 0.9g |
| Cholesterol | 3.48mg |
| Fiber | 6.9g |

# SPINACH AND RICE SOUP

—

**Use very fresh, young spinach leaves to prepare this light and fresh-tasting low-fat Italian soup.**

### INGREDIENTS

*1 1/2 pound fresh spinach, washed*
*1 tablespoon extra virgin olive oil*
*1 small onion, finely chopped*
*2 garlic cloves, finely chopped*
*1 small fresh red chile, deseeded and*
*finely chopped*
*generous 1/2 cup risotto rice*
*5 cups vegetable stock*
*salt and freshly ground black pepper*
*4 teaspoons grated fresh Pecorino cheese,*
*to serve*

*SERVES 4*

**1** Place the spinach in a large saucepan with just the water clinging to the leaves. Add a large pinch of salt and heat gently until wilted. Remove from heat and drain, reserving any liquid.

**2** Either chop the spinach finely or place in a food processor and blend into a purée.

**3** Heat the oil in a saucepan and cook the onion, garlic and chile for 4–5 minutes, stirring occasionally. Stir in the rice, then the stock and spinach liquid. Boil, then simmer for 10 minutes. Add the spinach and seasoning and cook for 5–7 minutes. Serve with the Pecorino cheese.

### NUTRITIONAL NOTES
*Per portion:*

| | |
|---|---|
| Energy | 235cals |
| Total fat | 4.9g |
| Saturated fat | 0.9g |
| Cholesterol | 3.48mg |
| Fiber | 6.9g |

# RIBOLLITA

Ribollita is a lot like minestrone, but includes beans instead of pasta. In Italy it is traditionally
served ladled over bread and a rich green vegetable, making it a delicious and wholesome soup.

## INGREDIENTS

*1 tablespoon olive oil*
*2 onions, chopped*
*2 carrots, sliced*
*4 garlic cloves, crushed*
*2 celery stalks, thinly sliced*
*1 fennel bulb, trimmed and chopped*
*2 large zucchini, thinly sliced*
*14-ounce can chopped tomatoes*
*1 tablespoon homemade or bought pesto*
*3¾ cups vegetable stock*
*14-ounce can white or borlotti
beans, drained*
*salt and freshly ground black pepper*

## TO FINISH

*1 pound young spinach or other dark
greens, such as chard or cabbage*
*2 teaspoons extra virgin olive oil*
*8 small slices white bread*
*1 tablespoon shaved fresh Parmesan
cheese (optional)*

### SERVES 8

**1** Heat the oil in a large saucepan. Add
the onions, carrots, garlic, celery and
fennel and cook gently for 10 minutes,
stirring occasionally. Add the zucchini
and cook for another 2 minutes.

**2** Add the chopped tomatoes, pesto, stock
and beans and bring to a boil. Reduce the
heat, cover and simmer gently for
25–30 minutes, until the vegetables are
completely tender, stirring occasionally.
Season with salt and pepper to taste.

**3** To serve, cook the spinach or greens in
the oil for 2 minutes or until wilted.
Spoon onto the bread in soup bowls, then
ladle in the soup and serve. Serve with
Parmesan cheese shavings sprinkled on
top, if desired.

## NUTRITIONAL NOTES
*Per portion:*

| | |
|---|---|
| Energy | 181cals |
| Total fat | 4.85g |
| Saturated fat | 0.75g |
| Cholesterol | 0mg |
| Fiber | 6.1g |

# CLAM AND PASTA SOUP

—

This recipe uses staple ingredients to create a delicious and filling low-fat soup. Serve it with hot focaccia or ciabatta for an informal supper with friends.

### INGREDIENTS

*1 tablespoon olive oil*
*1 large onion, finely chopped*
*2 garlic cloves, crushed*
*14-ounce can chopped tomatoes*
*1 tablespoon sun-dried tomato paste*
*1 teaspoon sugar*
*1 teaspoon dried mixed Italian herbs*
*about 3 cups fish or vegetable stock*
*2/3 cup red wine*
*1/2 cup small dried pasta shapes*
*5-ounce jar or can clams in natural juice*
*2 tablespoons finely chopped fresh flat-leaf*
*parsley, plus a few whole leaves, to garnish*
*salt and freshly ground black pepper*

### SERVES 4

**1** Heat the oil in a large saucepan. Cook the onion gently for 5 minutes, stirring frequently, until softened.

### NUTRITIONAL NOTES
*Per portion:*

| | |
|---|---|
| Energy | 165cals |
| Total fat | 3.4g |
| Saturated fat | 0.4g |
| Cholesterol | 0mg |
| Fiber | 1.5g |

**2** Add the garlic, tomatoes, tomato paste, sugar, herbs, stock and wine, and salt and pepper to taste. Bring the mixture to a boil. Reduce the heat, half cover the pan and simmer for 10 minutes, stirring the mixture occasionally.

**3** Add the pasta and continue simmering, uncovered, for 10 minutes or until the pasta is tender or *al dente*. Stir occasionally.

**4** Add the clams and their juice to the soup and heat through for 3–4 minutes, adding more stock if needed. Do not let it boil or the clams will be tough. Remove from heat, stir in the chopped parsley and adjust the seasoning. Serve hot, ladled into soup bowls and sprinkled with coarsely ground black pepper and parsley leaves, to garnish.

# CONSOMMÉ WITH AGNOLOTTI

—

**A flavorful Italian pasta soup, ideal for a tasty appetizer or snack.**

### INGREDIENTS

*3 ounces cooked, peeled shrimp*
*3 ounces canned crabmeat, drained*
*1 teaspoon fresh ginger root, peeled and*
*finely grated*
*1 tablespoon fresh white bread crumbs*
*1 teaspoon light soy sauce*
*1 scallion, finely chopped*
*1 garlic clove, crushed*
*1 batch of basic pasta dough (see*
*Techniques section)*
*egg white, beaten*
*14-ounce can chicken or fish consommé*
*2 tablespoons sherry or vermouth*
*salt and freshly ground black pepper*
*2 ounces cooked, peeled shrimp and*
*cilantro leaves, to garnish*

**SERVES 6**

**1** Put the shrimp, crabmeat, ginger, bread crumbs, soy sauce, onion, garlic and seasoning into a blender or food processor and blend until smooth. Set aside.

**2** Roll the pasta into thin sheets. Stamp out 32 rounds 2 inches in diameter, with a fluted cookie cutter.

**3** Place a small teaspoon of the puréed filling in the center of half the pasta rounds. Brush the edges of each round with egg white and sandwich together by placing a second pasta round on top. Pinch the edges together firmly to stop the filling from seeping out.

**4** Cook the pasta in a large saucepan of boiling, salted water for 5 minutes (cook in batches to keep them from sticking together). Remove from the pan and drop into a bowl of cold water for 5 seconds before removing and placing on a tray.

**5** Heat the chicken or fish consommé in a saucepan with the sherry or vermouth. When piping hot, add the cooked pasta shapes and simmer for 1–2 minutes.

**6** Serve the cooked pasta in shallow soup bowls with hot consommé. Garnish with shrimp and cilantro.

### NUTRITIONAL NOTES
*Per portion:*

| | |
|---|---|
| Energy | 177cals |
| Total fat | 2.7g |
| Saturated fat | 0.7g |
| Cholesterol | 89.66mg |
| Fiber | 1g |

### COOK'S TIP
You can make these pasta shapes a day in advance. Cover with plastic wrap and store in the refrigerator.

# APPETIZERS, SALADS AND SNACKS

*This* APPETIZING *array of fat-free and low-fat Italian recipes provides tempting dishes to launch a meal,* HEALTHY *and* REFRESHING *salads and tasty low-fat snacks to enjoy at any time of the day. Choose from* ITALIAN *dishes such as Eggplant, Garlic and Bell* PEPPER *Pâté,* ARUGULA, *Pear and Parmesan Salad, Tomato Pesto Toasts and* PROSCIUTTO *and Bell Pepper Pizzas.*

# EGGPLANT SUNFLOWER PÂTÉ

—

This delicious eggplant pâté, flavored with sunflower seeds and fresh herbs, makes a tempting
low-fat appetizer or snack.

### INGREDIENTS
*1 large eggplant*
*1 garlic clove, crushed*
*1 tablespoon lemon juice*
*2 tablespoons sunflower seeds*
*3 tablespoons low-fat plain yogurt*
*handful of cilantro or parsley,*
*plus extra to garnish*
*ground black pepper*
*vegetable sticks, to serve*

### SERVES 4

**1** Cut the eggplant in half and place, cut-side down, on a baking sheet. Place under a hot broiler for 15–20 minutes, until the skin is blackened and the flesh is soft.

**2** Let sit for a few minutes to cool slightly, then scoop the flesh into a blender or food processor. Discard the skin. Add the garlic, lemon juice, sunflower seeds and yogurt to the processor. Blend together until smooth.

**3** Roughly chop the cilantro or parsley and mix into the eggplant mixture. Season with black pepper, then spoon into a serving dish. Garnish with cilantro or parsley and serve with vegetable sticks.

| NUTRITIONAL NOTES | |
|---|---|
| *Per portion:* | |
| Energy | 59cals |
| Total fat | 4g |
| Saturated fat | 0.5g |
| Cholesterol | 0.44mg |
| Fiber | 1.5g |

# BELL PEPPER DIPS WITH CRUDITÉS

—

Make one or both of these colorful Italian vegetable dips—if you have time to make both they
look spectacular together and are both low-fat too!

### INGREDIENTS
*2 red bell peppers, halved and deseeded*
*2 bell yellow peppers, halved and deseeded*
*2 garlic cloves*
*2 tablespoons lemon juice*
*4 teaspoons olive oil*
*1 cup fresh white bread crumbs*
*salt and freshly ground black pepper*
*prepared fresh vegetables,*
*for dipping*

### SERVES 6

**1** Place the peppers in two separate saucepans with a peeled clove of garlic. Add just enough water to cover.

**2** Bring to a boil, then cover and simmer for 15 minutes, until tender. Drain, cool, then purée the peppers separately in a blender or food processor, adding half the lemon juice and olive oil to each purée.

**3** Stir half the bread crumbs into each purée and season to taste with salt and pepper. Spoon the dips into serving dishes, garnish with a grinding of black pepper and serve with a selection of fresh vegetables for dipping.

| NUTRITIONAL NOTES | |
|---|---|
| *Per portion:* | |
| Energy | 60cals |
| Total fat | 3g |
| Saturated fat | 0.5g |
| Cholesterol | 0mg |
| Fiber | 1.1g |

# EGGPLANT, GARLIC AND BELL PEPPER PÂTÉ

Serve this Italian-style chunky, garlicky pâté of smoky baked eggplant and red bell peppers on a bed of salad, accompanied by crisp toasts.

### INGREDIENTS

3 eggplant
2 red bell peppers
5 garlic cloves
1½ teaspoons pink peppercorns in brine, drained and crushed
2 tablespoons chopped cilantro

### SERVES 4

### NUTRITIONAL NOTES

*Per portion:*

| | |
|---|---|
| Energy | 15cals |
| Total fat | 0.4g |
| Saturated fat | 0.1g |
| Cholesterol | 0mg |
| Fiber | 1.8g |

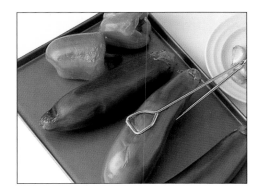

**1** Preheat the oven to 400°F. Arrange the whole eggplant, peppers and garlic cloves on a baking sheet and place in the oven. After 10 minutes remove the garlic cloves. Turn over the eggplant and peppers and return to the oven.

**2** Carefully peel the garlic cloves and place them in the bowl of a blender or food processor.

**3** After another 20 minutes remove the blistered and charred peppers from the oven and place in a plastic bag. Let cool.

**4** After another 10 minutes remove the eggplant from the oven. Split in half and scoop the flesh into a sieve placed over a bowl. Discard the skin. Press the flesh with a spoon to remove the bitter juices. Discard the juices.

**5** Add the eggplant flesh to the garlic in the blender or food processor and blend until smooth. Place in a large bowl.

**6** Peel and chop the red peppers and stir into the eggplant mixture. Mix in the peppercorns and cilantro, spoon into a serving dish and serve immediately.

# CANNELLINI BEAN PURÉE WITH GRILLED ENDIVE

The slightly bitter flavors of the endive and radicchio make a wonderful marriage with the
creamy bean purée to create this low-fat appetizer or snack.

**3** Cut each radicchio head into eight
wedges. Preheat the broiler.

**4** Lay the endive and radicchio on a
baking sheet and brush lightly with the
walnut oil. Broil for 2–3 minutes. Serve
with the bean purée and sprinkle on the
orange shreds to garnish, if using.

### INGREDIENTS

*14-ounce can cannellini beans*
*3 tablespoons low-fat sour cream*
*finely grated zest and juice of*
*1 large orange*
*1 tablespoon finely chopped fresh rosemary*
*4 heads of endive*
*2 heads of radicchio*
*2 teaspoons walnut oil*
*longer shreds of orange zest,*
*to garnish (optional)*

### SERVES 4

### COOK'S TIP
Other good pulses to use are white,
mung or fava beans.

**1** Drain the beans, rinse, and drain them
again. Purée the beans in a blender or
food processor with the sour cream,
orange zest and juice and rosemary.
Set aside.

**2** Cut the heads of endive in half along
the length.

### NUTRITIONAL NOTES
*Per portion:*

| | |
|---|---|
| Energy | 142cals |
| Total fat | 3.4g |
| Saturated fat | 0.5g |
| Cholesterol | 0.11mg |
| Fiber | 1.1g |

# ROASTED PLUM TOMATOES WITH GARLIC

A very typical Italian dish, these roast tomatoes flavored with garlic are so simple to prepare, yet
taste absolutely wonderful. A shallow earthenware dish will let the tomatoes char.

### INGREDIENTS
*8 plum tomatoes*
*12 garlic cloves*
*4 teaspoons extra virgin olive oil*
*3 bay leaves*
*salt and freshly ground black pepper*
*3 tablespoons fresh oregano leaves,*
*to garnish*

### SERVES 4

**1** Preheat the oven to 450°F. Cut the plum tomatoes in half, leaving a small part of the green stem intact for the final decoration.

**2** Select an ovenproof dish that will hold all the tomatoes snugly together in a single layer. Place them in the dish with the cut-side facing upward, and push each of the whole, unpeeled garlic cloves among them.

**3** Lightly brush the tomatoes with the oil, add the bay leaves and sprinkle black pepper on top.

**4** Bake for 35–45 minutes, until the tomatoes have softened and are sizzling in the dish. They should be charred around the edges. Season with salt and a little more black pepper, if needed. Garnish with the fresh oregano leaves and serve immediately.

### COOK'S TIP
Select ripe, juicy tomatoes without any blemishes to get the best flavor.

### VARIATION
For a sweet alternative, use halved and seeded red or yellow bell peppers instead of the tomatoes.

### NUTRITIONAL NOTES
*Per portion:*

| | |
|---|---|
| Energy | 57cals |
| Total fat | 4.0g |
| Saturated fat | 0.6g |
| Cholesterol | 0mg |
| Fiber | 1.1g |

# ARTICHOKE SALAD WITH SALSA AGRODOLCE

Agrodolce is an Italian sweet-and-sour sauce that makes an ideal accompaniment for this
artichoke and bean salad.

### INGREDIENTS
*6 small artichokes*
*juice of 1 lemon*
*1 tablespoon olive oil*
*2 onions, roughly chopped*
*1 cup fresh or frozen fava beans*
*(shelled weight)*
*1¹/2 cups fresh or frozen peas*
*(shelled weight)*
*salt and freshly ground black pepper*
*fresh mint leaves, to garnish*

### FOR THE SALSA AGRODOLCE
*¹/2 cup white wine vinegar*
*1 tablespoon sugar*
*handful of fresh mint leaves, roughly torn*

### SERVES 4–6

**1** Peel and discard the outer leaves from
the artichokes and cut into quarters.
Place the artichokes in a bowl of water
with the lemon juice.

**2** Heat the oil in a large saucepan and
add the onions. Cook until the onions are
golden, stirring occasionally. Add the fava
beans and stir, then drain the artichokes
and add to the pan. Pour in about
1¹/4 cups of water, bring to a boil, then
cook, covered, for 10–15 minutes.

**3** Add the peas, season with salt and
pepper and cook for another 5 minutes,
stirring occasionally, until the vegetables
are tender. Strain through a sieve, discard
the liquid, then place all the vegetables
in a bowl, let cool, cover and chill.

**4** To make the salsa agrodolce, mix all
the ingredients in a saucepan. Heat gently
for 2–3 minutes, until the sugar has
dissolved. Simmer for 5 minutes, stirring
occasionally. Remove from heat and let
cool. To serve, drizzle the salsa on the
vegetables and garnish with mint leaves.

### NUTRITIONAL NOTES
*Per portion:*

| | |
|---|---|
| Energy | 182cals |
| Total fat | 4g |
| Saturated fat | 0.6g |
| Cholesterol | 0mg |
| Fiber | 5.5g |

# GARLIC BAKED TOMATOES

For the best results, use Italian plum tomatoes, which have a warm, slightly sweet flavor.
Serve this tasty dish with fresh Italian bread or crisp toasts.

## INGREDIENTS

*2 tablespoons unsalted butter*
*1 large garlic clove, crushed*
*1 teaspoon finely grated orange zest*
*4 firm plum tomatoes, or 2 large
beefsteak tomatoes*
*salt and freshly ground black pepper*
*fresh basil leaves, to garnish*

### SERVES 4

**1** Soften the butter in a small bowl and blend with the crushed garlic, orange zest, and seasoning. Chill for a few minutes.

**2** Preheat the oven to 400°F. Halve the tomatoes crosswise and trim the bottoms so they stand upright.

**3** Place the tomatoes in an ovenproof dish and spread the butter equally on each.

**4** Bake the tomatoes for 15–25 minutes, depending on the size of the tomato halves, until just tender. Serve sprinkled with the fresh basil leaves.

### NUTRITIONAL NOTES
*Per portion:*

| | |
|---|---|
| Energy | 49cals |
| Total fat | 5g |
| Saturated fat | 3.3g |
| Cholesterol | 13.88mg |
| Fiber | 0.3g |

# LEMON CARROT SALAD

This tangy, colorful and refreshing salad is an ideal low-fat snack or accompaniment.

## INGREDIENTS

*1 pound small, young carrots*
*finely grated zest and juice of 1/2 lemon*
*1 tablespoon light brown sugar*
*2 tablespoons sunflower oil*
*1 teaspoon hazelnut or sesame oil*
*1 teaspoon chopped fresh oregano*
*salt and freshly ground black pepper*

### SERVES 6

### NUTRITIONAL NOTES
*Per portion:*

| | |
|---|---|
| Energy | 76cals |
| Total fat | 4.7g |
| Saturated fat | 0.6g |
| Cholesterol | 0mg |
| Fiber | 1.8g |

**1** Finely grate the carrots and place them in a large bowl. Stir in the lemon zest and 1–2 tablespoons of the lemon juice.

### VARIATION
Experiment with different herbs.
Tarragon goes well with carrots.

**2** Add the sugar, sunflower and hazelnut or sesame oils, and mix well. Add more lemon juice and seasoning to taste, then sprinkle on the oregano and toss lightly to mix. Let the salad sit for 1 hour before serving, garnished with a sprig of oregano.

# ARUGULA, PEAR AND PARMESAN SALAD

**For a sophisticated start to a meal with friends, try this simple Italian salad of fresh, ripe pears, tasty Parmesan and aromatic leaves of arugula. Serve with fresh Italian bread or crisp toasts.**

### INGREDIENTS

*3 ripe pears, such as Williams
or Packhams
2 teaspoons lemon juice
1 tablespoon hazelnut or walnut oil
4 ounces of arugula
1 ounce fresh Parmesan cheese
ground black pepper*

### SERVES 4

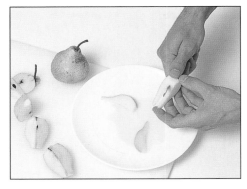

**1** Peel and core the pears and slice thickly. Place in a bowl and moisten with lemon juice to keep the flesh white.

**2** Combine the nut oil with the pears. Add the arugula leaves and toss to mix.

**3** Divide the salad among four small plates and top each portion with shavings of Parmesan cheese. Season with ground black pepper and serve.

---

### COOK'S TIP

You can grow your own arugula from early spring to late summer. You can also use watercress instead.

---

### NUTRITIONAL NOTES

*Per portion:*

| | |
|---|---|
| Energy | 102cals |
| Total fat | 5g |
| Saturated fat | 1.6g |
| Cholesterol | 6.24mg |
| Fiber | 2.6g |

# MELON, PROSCIUTTO AND STRAWBERRY SALAD

Sections of cool fragrant melon wrapped with thin slices of air-dried Italian ham make this delicious Italian appetizer or snack.

### INGREDIENTS

*1 large melon, cantaloupe, Galia or charentais*
*4 ounces prosciutto or Serrano ham, thinly sliced*

#### FOR THE SALSA

*8 ounces strawberries*
*1 teaspoon sugar*
*4 teaspoons peanut or sunflower oil*
*1 tablespoon unsweetened orange juice*
*1/2 teaspoon finely grated orange zest*
*1/2 teaspoon finely grated fresh ginger root*
*salt and freshly ground black pepper*

#### SERVES 4

**1** Halve the melon and remove the seeds with a spoon. Cut off the rind with a paring knife. Discard the seeds and rind, then slice the melon flesh thickly. Chill until ready to serve.

### NUTRITIONAL NOTES
*Per portion:*

| | |
|---|---|
| Energy | 89cals |
| Total fat | 4.9g |
| Saturated fat | 0.8g |
| Cholesterol | 13.66mg |
| Fiber | 0.8g |

**2** To make the salsa, hull the strawberries and cut them into large dice. Place in a small mixing bowl with the sugar and crush lightly to release the juices. Add the oil, orange juice, orange zest and ginger. Season with salt and a generous twist of black pepper.

**3** Arrange the melon on a serving plate, lay the prosciutto on top and serve with the bowl of salsa alongside.

### COOK'S TIP
Melon has a very subtle flavor. To enjoy it at its best, do not over-chill it.

# THREE-COLOR SALAD

—

This classic Italian dish, *insalata tricolore*, is a delicious and colorful appetizer
or snack. Use plum or vine-ripened tomatoes for the best flavor.

### INGREDIENTS

*1 small red onion, thinly
sliced
6 large full-flavored tomatoes
1 small bunch arugula or watercress,
roughly chopped
4 ounces reduced-fat mozzarella cheese,
thinly sliced or grated
4 teaspoons extra virgin
olive oil
2 tablespoons pine nuts
(optional)
salt and freshly ground black pepper*

### SERVES 6

**1** Soak the onion slices in a bowl of
cold water for 30 minutes, then drain
and pat dry.

**2** Prepare the tomatoes for skinning by
slashing them with a sharp knife and
dipping briefly in boiling water.

**3** Peel off the skins and then slice each
tomato using a sharp knife.

**4** Arrange half the tomato slices on a
large platter, or divide them among
six small plates if you prefer.

**5** Layer with half the chopped arugula
or watercress and half the onion slices,
seasoning well. Add half the cheese,
sprinkling on a little more seasoning.

**6** Repeat with the remaining tomato and
onion slices, salad leaves and cheese.

**7** Season well to finish, and sprinkle the
oil on the salad. Sprinkle the pine nuts
on top, if using. Cover the salad and chill
for at least 2 hours before serving.

### NUTRITIONAL NOTES

*Per portion:*

| | |
|---|---|
| Energy | 75cals |
| Total fat | 5g |
| Saturated fat | 2g |
| Cholesterol | 7.36mg |
| Fiber | 0.6g |

### VARIATIONS

Instead of the fresh arugula or
watercress, use chopped fresh basil,
which goes particularly well with the
flavor of ripe tomatoes. To reduce
the fat content even more, omit the
oil and sprinkle the salad with
a fat-free vinaigrette dressing.

# ROASTED BELL PEPPER AND TOMATO SALAD

**This recipe brings together perfectly the colors, flavors and textures of southern Italian food.
Serve this low-fat dish at room temperature with a green salad.**

### INGREDIENTS
*3 red bell peppers*
*6 large plum tomatoes*
*1/2 teaspoon dried red chile flakes*
*1 red onion, thinly sliced*
*3 garlic cloves, finely chopped*
*finely grated zest and juice of 1 lemon*
*3 tablespoons chopped fresh flat-leaf parsley*
*4 teaspoons extra virgin olive oil*
*salt and freshly ground black pepper*
*1 ounce black and green olives and extra*
*chopped fresh flat-leaf parsley, to garnish*

### SERVES 4

**1** Preheat the oven to 425°F. Place the peppers on a baking sheet and roast, turning occasionally, for 10 minutes or until the skins are almost blackened. Add the tomatoes to the baking sheet and bake for another 5 minutes.

**2** Place the peppers in a plastic bag, close the top loosely, trapping in the steam, and then set them aside with the tomatoes until they are cool enough to handle.

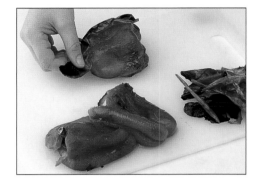

**3** Carefully pull off and discard the skin from the peppers. Remove and discard the seeds, then chop the peppers and tomatoes roughly and place them together in a mixing bowl.

**4** Add the chile flakes, onion, garlic, lemon zest and juice. Sprinkle on the parsley. Mix well, then transfer to a serving dish. Sprinkle with a little salt and pepper, drizzle on the olive oil and sprinkle the olives and extra parsley on top to garnish. Serve the salad at room temperature.

### NUTRITIONAL NOTES
*Per portion:*

| | |
|---|---|
| Energy | 78cals |
| Total fat | 4.9g |
| Saturated fat | 0.8g |
| Cholesterol | 0mg |
| Fiber | 2.1g |

# MARINATED ZUCCHINI

**This is a simple vegetable dish that is prepared all over Italy using the best of the season's
zucchini. It can be eaten hot or cold and is a delicious accompaniment to a main course.**

### INGREDIENTS
*4 zucchini*
*8 teaspoons extra virgin olive oil*
*2 tablespoons chopped fresh mint, plus*
*whole leaves, to garnish*
*2 tablespoons white wine vinegar*
*salt and freshly ground black pepper*

### SERVES 6

**1** Cut the zucchini into thin slices. Heat 4 teaspoons of the oil in a wide heavy saucepan.

**2** Fry the zucchini in batches, for 4–6 minutes, until tender and brown around the edges. Transfer the zucchini to a bowl. Season well.

### NUTRITIONAL NOTES
*Per portion:*

| | |
|---|---|
| Energy | 50cals |
| Total fat | 5.0g |
| Saturated fat | 0.7g |
| Cholesterol | 0mg |
| Fiber | 0.3g |

**3** Heat the remaining oil, then add the mint and vinegar and let bubble for a few seconds. Stir into the zucchini. Marinate for 1 hour, then serve with mint leaves.

# DUCK BREAST SALAD

Succulent duck breasts are broiled, then sliced and tossed with pasta and fruit in a delicious
virtually fat-free dressing to create this tempting salad.

### INGREDIENTS

*2 duck breasts, boned*
*1 teaspoon coriander seeds, crushed*
*12 ounces dried rigatoni*
*2/3 cup fresh orange juice*
*1 tablespoon lemon juice*
*2 teaspoons honey*
*1 shallot, finely chopped*
*1 garlic clove, crushed*
*1 celery stalk, chopped*
*3 ounces dried cherries*
*3 tablespoons port or red wine*
*1 tablespoon chopped fresh mint, plus*
*extra to garnish*
*2 tablespoons chopped cilantro, plus extra*
*to garnish*
*1 apple, cored and diced*
*2 oranges, segmented*
*salt and freshly ground black pepper*

### SERVES 6

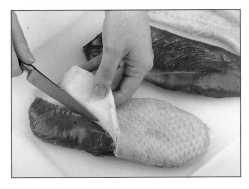

**1** Remove and discard the skin and fat from
the duck breasts and season with salt and
pepper. Rub the duck breasts all over with
crushed coriander seeds. Preheat the broiler,
then broil the duck for 7–10 minutes
depending on size. Wrap in aluminum foil
and set aside for about 20 minutes.

**2** Meanwhile, cook the pasta in a large
saucepan of boiling, salted water until
tender or *al dente*. Drain thoroughly and
rinse under cold running water, then
drain again. Let cool.

**3** In the meantime, make the dressing.
Put the orange juice, lemon juice, honey,
shallot, garlic, celery, cherries, port or red
wine, chopped mint and cilantro in a
bowl, whisk together then set aside for
20–30 minutes.

### NUTRITIONAL NOTES
*Per portion:*

| | |
|---|---|
| Energy | 298cals |
| Total fat | 2.3g |
| Saturated fat | 0.5g |
| Cholesterol | 27.5mg |
| Fiber | 3g |

**4** Slice the duck very thinly. (It should be
pink in the center.)

**5** Put the pasta in a bowl, add the duck,
dressing, diced apple and segments of
orange. Toss well to mix. Transfer the
salad to a serving plate and garnish with
the extra mint and cilantro. Serve.

### COOK'S TIP
To skin the duck breasts, slide your
fingers between the skin and breast
and gently pull to separate. Use a sharp
knife to loosen any stubborn parts.

### VARIATION
Other shapes of pasta may be
substituted for the rigatoni. Penne work
well, although long varieties, such as
tagliatelle, are also good.

# WARM CHICKEN SALAD

Succulent cooked chicken pieces are combined with vegetables and rice in a light chili dressing to create this appetizing lunch or supper salad.

### INGREDIENTS

*2 ounces mixed greens*
*2 ounces baby spinach leaves*
*2 ounces watercress*
*2 tablespoons chili sauce*
*2 tablespoons dry sherry*
*1 tablespoon light soy sauce*
*1 tablespoon ketchup*
*2 teaspoons olive oil*
*8 shallots, finely chopped*
*1 garlic clove, crushed*
*12 ounces skinless, boneless chicken breasts, cut into thin strips*
*1 red bell pepper, deseeded and sliced*
*6 ounces snowpeas, trimmed*
*14-ounce can baby corn, drained and halved lengthwise*
*10 ounces cooked brown rice*
*salt and freshly ground black pepper*
*fresh parsley sprig,*
*to garnish*

### SERVES 6

**1** Arrange the mixed greens and the spinach leaves on a serving dish, tearing up any large ones. Add the watercress and toss to mix. Set aside.

**2** In a small bowl, combine the chili sauce, sherry, soy sauce and ketchup and set aside.

### NUTRITIONAL NOTES
*Per portion:*

| | |
|---|---|
| Energy | 191cals |
| Total fat | 4g |
| Saturated fat | 1g |
| Cholesterol | 25mg |
| Fiber | 2.6g |

**3** Heat the oil in a large nonstick frying pan or wok. Add the shallots and garlic and stir-fry for 1 minute over medium heat. Add the chicken and stir-fry for 3–4 minutes.

**4** Add the pepper, snowpeas, corn and rice and stir-fry for 2–3 minutes.

**5** Pour in the chili sauce mixture and stir-fry for 2–3 minutes, until hot and bubbling. Season to taste with salt and pepper. Spoon the chicken mixture onto the greens, toss to mix and serve immediately, garnished with a fresh parsley sprig.

# CRAB PASTA SALAD WITH SPICY DRESSING

White crabmeat and fusilli pasta are tossed together in a spicy dressing to create this flavorful
Italian-style salad that is very low in fat.

### INGREDIENTS

*12 ounces dried fusilli*
*1 small red bell pepper, deseeded and*
*finely chopped*
*2 6-ounce cans white crabmeat*
*4 ounces cherry tomatoes, halved*
*1/4 cucumber, halved, deseeded and sliced*
*into crescents*
*1 tablespoon lemon juice*
*1 1/4 cups low-fat plain yogurt*
*2 celery stalks, finely chopped*
*2 teaspoons horseradish sauce*
*1/2 teaspoon ground paprika*
*1/2 teaspoon Dijon mustard*
*2 tablespoons sweet tomato pickle*
*or chutney*
*salt and freshly ground black pepper*
*fresh basil, to garnish*

### SERVES 6

**1** Cook the pasta in a large saucepan of
boiling salted water, according to the
package instructions, until tender or
*al dente*. Drain and rinse the pasta
thoroughly under cold water. Drain
again and set aside.

**2** Put the red pepper in a bowl and cover
with boiling water. Let stand for 1 minute.
Drain and rinse under cold water. Pat dry
on paper towels and set aside.

**3** Drain the crabmeat and pick over
carefully. Discard any pieces of shell. Put
the crabmeat into a bowl with the
tomatoes and cucumber. Season with salt
and pepper and sprinkle with lemon
juice. Set aside.

**4** To make the dressing, put the yogurt in
a bowl and add the red pepper, celery,
horseradish, paprika, mustard and sweet
tomato pickle or chutney. Mix the pasta
with the crab mixture and dressing and
transfer to a serving dish. Garnish with
fresh basil and serve.

### NUTRITIONAL NOTES
*Per portion:*

| | |
|---|---|
| Energy | 293cals |
| Total fat | 2.3g |
| Saturated fat | 0.5g |
| Cholesterol | 45mg |
| Fiber | 2.4g |

# SPICY CHICKEN SALAD

—

This tasty Italian-style low-fat chicken and pasta salad creates an ideal lunch or
supper dish for family or friends.

### INGREDIENTS

*1 teaspoon ground cumin seeds*
*1 teaspoon ground paprika*
*1 teaspoon ground turmeric*
*1–2 garlic cloves, crushed*
*3–4 tablespoons fresh lime juice*
*4 small chicken breasts, boned
and skinned*
*8 ounces dried rigatoni*
*1 red bell pepper, deseeded and chopped*
*2 celery stalks, thinly sliced*
*1 shallot or small onion, finely chopped*
*1/2 ounce stuffed green olives, halved*
*2 tablespoons honey*
*2 teaspoons whole-grain mustard*
*salt and freshly ground black pepper*
*mixed greens, to serve*

### SERVES 6

**1** Mix the cumin, paprika, turmeric,
garlic, seasoning and 2 tablespoons lime
juice in a bowl. Lay the chicken in a
shallow nonmetallic dish and rub the
mixture over the chicken breasts. Cover
with plastic wrap and set in a cool place
for about 3 hours or overnight.

**2** Preheat the oven to 400°F. Put the
chicken on a broiler rack in a single layer
and bake for 20 minutes until cooked.
(Alternatively, broil for 8–10 minutes on
each side.)

**3** Meanwhile, cook the rigatoni in a large
saucepan of boiling, salted water until
tender or *al dente*. Drain and rinse under
cold water. Let drain thoroughly.

**4** Put the red pepper, celery, shallot or
onion and olives into a large bowl with
the pasta and toss to mix.

**5** Combine the honey, mustard and
remaining lime juice in a bowl and pour
over the pasta. Toss to mix well.

**6** Cut the chicken into bite-size pieces.
Arrange the mixed greens on a serving
dish, spoon the pasta mixture in the
center of the leaves and top with the
spicy chicken pieces.

### NUTRITIONAL NOTES
*Per portion:*

| | |
|---|---|
| Energy | 234cals |
| Total fat | 4g |
| Saturated fat | 1.1g |
| Cholesterol | 37.88mg |
| Fiber | 1.6g |

# FARFALLE SALAD WITH PIQUANT BELL PEPPERS

Bell peppers, pasta and cilantro add delicious flavor to this quick and easy
Italian appetizer or supper dish.

### INGREDIENTS

*1 red, 1 yellow and 1 orange bell pepper*
*1 garlic clove, crushed*
*2 tablespoons capers*
*2 tablespoons raisins*
*1 teaspoon whole-grain mustard*
*finely grated zest and juice of 1 lime*
*1 teaspoon honey*
*2 tablespoons chopped cilantro*
*8 ounces dried farfalle*
*salt and freshly ground black pepper*
*shaved fresh Parmesan cheese,*
*to serve (optional)*

### SERVES 8

**1** Quarter the peppers and remove and discard the tops and seeds. Put into a saucepan of boiling water and cook for 10–15 minutes, until tender. Drain and rinse under cold water. Drain again. Peel off and discard the skin and cut the flesh into strips lengthwise. Set aside.

### NUTRITIONAL NOTES

*Per portion:*

| | |
|---|---|
| Energy | 160cals |
| Total fat | 1g |
| Saturated fat | 0.2g |
| Cholesterol | 0mg |
| Fiber | 1.9g |

**2** Put the garlic, capers, raisins, mustard, lime zest and juice, honey, cilantro and seasoning into a bowl and whisk together. Set aside.

### VARIATION

If you prefer, make this salad with only one color of pepper. The green ones are too bitter, however, and are not suitable.

**3** Cook the pasta in a large saucepan of boiling, salted water for 10–12 minutes, until tender or *al dente*. Drain.

**4** Return the pasta to the pan, add the reserved peppers and dressing. Heat gently and toss to mix. Transfer to a warm serving bowl and serve. Serve sprinkled with a few shavings of Parmesan cheese, if using.

# LEMON AND HERB RISOTTO CAKE

This unusual Italian rice dish can be served as a low-fat main course with salad, or as a satisfying side dish. It is also good served cold, and packs well for picnics.

### INGREDIENTS

*1 small leek, thinly sliced*
*2¹/2 cups chicken stock*
*1 cup short-grain rice*
*finely grated zest of 1 lemon*
*2 tablespoons chopped fresh chives*
*2 tablespoons chopped fresh parsley*
*³/4 cup grated reduced-fat*
*mozzarella cheese*
*salt and freshly ground black pepper*
*fresh parsley sprigs and lemon wedges,*
*to garnish*

### SERVES 6

**1** Preheat the oven to 400°F. Lightly oil an 8¹/2-inch round, springform cake pan. Set aside.

**2** Cook the leek in a large saucepan with 3 tablespoons stock, stirring over medium heat, to soften.

**3** Add the rice and the remaining stock. Bring to a boil. Cover and simmer, stirring occasionally, for about 20 minutes or until all the liquid is absorbed.

### NUTRITIONAL NOTES
*Per portion:*

| | |
|---|---|
| Energy | 165cals |
| Total fat | 3g |
| Saturated fat | 1.4g |
| Cholesterol | 4.94mg |
| Fiber | 0.4g |

### VARIATION

The best type of rice to choose for this recipe is the Italian round-grain arborio rice, but if it is not available, use pudding rice instead.

**4** Remove the pan from heat, stir in the lemon zest, chopped herbs, cheese and seasoning and mix well. Spoon the mixture into the prepared pan, level the surface and cover with aluminum foil.

**5** Bake for 30–35 minutes or until lightly browned. Turn out onto a serving plate and serve hot or cold in slices, garnished with parsley sprigs and lemon wedges.

# TOMATO PESTO TOASTS

Ready-made pesto is high in fat but, as its flavor is so powerful, it can be used in very small
amounts with good effect, as in these tasty low-fat toasts.

**3** Cut the tomato and onion, crosswise, into thin slices using a large sharp knife.

**4** Arrange the tomato and onion slices, overlapping, on top of the toast and season. Cook under a hot broiler until heated through, then serve, garnished with a sprig of thyme.

### COOK'S TIP
Almost any type of crusty bread can be used, but Italian ciabatta and French bread give the best flavor.

### NUTRITIONAL NOTES
*Per portion:*

| | |
|---|---|
| Energy | 149cals |
| Total fat | 4g |
| Saturated fat | 1g |
| Cholesterol | 2.57mg |
| Fiber | 1.2g |

### INGREDIENTS
*2 thick slices of crusty bread*
*3 tablespoons low-fat cream cheese or
low-fat sour cream*
*2 teaspoons red or green pesto*
*1 beefsteak tomato*
*1 red onion*
*salt and freshly ground black pepper*

### SERVES 2

**1** Toast the bread slices under a hot broiler until golden brown on both sides, turning once. Let cool.

**2** Combine the cream cheese or sour cream and pesto in a small bowl until well blended, then spread thickly on the toasted bread.

# PROSCIUTTO AND BELL PEPPER PIZZAS

The delicious flavors of these quick and easy Italian pizzas are hard to beat.
Serve with mixed salad greens and sliced plum tomatoes.

### INGREDIENTS

*1/2 loaf of ciabatta bread*
*1 red bell pepper, roasted, peeled*
*and deseeded*
*1 yellow bell pepper, roasted, peeled*
*and deseeded*
*4 thin slices prosciutto, cut into thick strips*
*2 ounces reduced-fat mozzarella cheese*
*ground black pepper*
*tiny fresh basil leaves,*
*to garnish*

*MAKES 4*

**3** Thinly slice the mozzarella and arrange on top, then grind on plenty of black pepper. Broil for 2–3 minutes, until the cheese is bubbling.

### NUTRITIONAL NOTES
*Per portion:*

| | |
|---|---|
| Energy | 213cals |
| Total fat | 3.9g |
| Saturated fat | 1.67g |
| Cholesterol | 8.76mg |
| Fiber | 1.5 |

**4** Sprinkle the basil leaves on top to garnish and serve immediately.

**1** Cut the bread into four thick slices and toast until golden.

**2** Cut the roasted peppers into thick strips and arrange on the toasted bread with the strips of prosciutto. Preheat the broiler.

# MEAT, POULTRY
### AND
# FISH DISHES

WHITE FISH *is naturally low in fat,*
*and by choosing* LEAN CUTS *of meat*
*and poultry these foods can also be* ENJOYED
*as part of a* HEALTHY *low-fat diet.*
*Choose from this nourishing collection of*
*fat-free and low-fat Italian meat, poultry and*
*fish dishes including* PANCETTA *and Fava*
*Bean* RISOTTO, *Tuscan Chicken and Roast*
*Monkfish with* GARLIC *and Fennel.*

# FILLET OF BEEF WITH HERBED TAGLIATELLE

This Italian-style fillet of beef served with herbed pasta is a delicious
low-fat main course or supper dish.

## INGREDIENTS

*1 pound lean beef fillet*
*1 pound fresh tagliatelle made with*
*sun-dried tomatoes and herbs*
*4 ounces cherry tomatoes*
*1/2 cucumber*

## FOR THE MARINADE

*1 tablespoon soy sauce*
*1 tablespoon sherry*
*1 teaspoon fresh ginger root, peeled*
*and grated*
*1 garlic clove, crushed*

## FOR THE HERB DRESSING

*2/3 cup low-fat plain yogurt*
*1 garlic clove, crushed*
*2–3 tablespoons chopped fresh herbs*
*(chives, parsley, thyme)*
*salt and freshly ground black pepper*

### SERVES 6

**1** Combine all the marinade ingredients
in a shallow nonmetallic dish, put the
beef in and turn it over to coat it.
Cover with plastic wrap and let sit for
30 minutes to let the flavors penetrate
the meat.

**2** Preheat the broiler. Lift the fillet out of
the marinade and pat it dry with paper
towels. Broil on a broiler pan for 8 minutes
on each side, basting with the marinade.

**3** Transfer to a plate, cover with aluminum
foil and let stand for 20 minutes.

**4** Mix the dressing ingredients thoroughly.
Cook the pasta in a large saucepan of
lightly salted boiling water, according to
the package instructions, until tender or
*al dente*. Drain thoroughly, rinse under
cold water and drain again.

**5** Cut the cherry tomatoes in half. Cut the
cucumber in half lengthwise, scoop out
and discard the seeds with a teaspoon
and slice the flesh thinly into crescents.

**6** Put the pasta, cherry tomatoes,
cucumber and dressing in a bowl and toss
to mix well. Slice the beef thinly and
arrange on serving plates with the pasta
salad served alongside.

### NUTRITIONAL NOTES
*Per portion:*

| | |
|---|---|
| Energy | 201cals |
| Total fat | 4.3g |
| Saturated fat | 1.7g |
| Cholesterol | 45.25mg |
| Fiber | 1.2g |

# BEEF STEW WITH TOMATOES, WINE AND PEAS

—

This is a traditional Italian recipe known as spezzatino, which is perfect for a winter lunch or dinner. Serve it with boiled or mashed potatoes to soak up the delicious sauce.

### INGREDIENTS
*2 tablespoons all-purpose flour*
*2 teaspoons chopped fresh thyme or*
*1 teaspoon dried thyme*
*1 pound lean braising or stewing beef,*
*cut into cubes*
*2 teaspoons olive oil*
*2 onions, roughly chopped*
*1 pound jar passata*
*1 cup beef stock*
*1 cup red wine*
*2 garlic cloves, crushed*
*2 tablespoons tomato paste*
*2 1/2 cups shelled fresh peas*
*1 teaspoon sugar*
*salt and freshly ground black pepper*
*fresh thyme sprigs, to garnish*

### SERVES 6

**1** Preheat the oven to 325°F. Put the flour in a shallow dish and season with the chopped thyme and salt and pepper. Add the beef cubes and turn to coat evenly with the flour.

### VARIATION
Use thawed frozen peas instead of fresh. Add them 10 minutes before the end of cooking.

**2** Heat the oil in a large flameproof casserole, add the beef and seal on all sides over medium heat. Remove with a slotted spoon and place on a plate.

**3** Add the onion to the pan, scraping the bottom of the pan to mix in any sediment. Cook gently for 3 minutes, stirring frequently, then stir in the passata, stock, wine, garlic and tomato paste. Bring to a boil, stirring. Return the beef to the pan and stir well to coat with the sauce. Cover and cook for 1 1/2 hours.

**4** Stir in the peas and sugar. Cover, return the casserole to the oven and cook for another 30 minutes or until the beef is tender. Adjust the seasoning to taste. Garnish with fresh thyme sprigs and serve immediately.

### NUTRITIONAL NOTES
*Per portion:*

| | |
|---|---|
| Energy | 183cals |
| Total fat | 4.9g |
| Saturated fat | 1.5g |
| Cholesterol | 38.3mg |
| Fiber | 2.8g |

# CALF'S LIVER WITH BALSAMIC VINEGAR

This delicious sweet-and-sour liver dish is a specialty of Venice. Serve it very simply, with green
beans sprinkled with toasted fresh bread crumbs, for an appetizing supper dish.

**2** Heat the oil in a wide, heavy saucepan
or frying pan. Add the onion rings and
cook gently, stirring frequently, for about
5 minutes, until softened but not colored.
Remove with a spatula, place on a plate
and set aside.

**3** Add the coated liver to the juices in the
pan and cook over medium heat for
2–3 minutes on each side. Transfer to
warmed serving plates and keep hot.

**4** Add the wine and vinegar to the pan
and stir to mix with the pan juices and
any sediment. Add the onions and sugar
and heat through until hot and bubbling,
stirring. Spoon the sauce onto the liver,
garnish with fresh sage sprigs and
serve immediately.

### INGREDIENTS
*1 tablespoon all-purpose flour*
*1/2 teaspoon finely chopped fresh sage*
*4 thin slices calf's liver, cut into
serving pieces*
*1 tablespoon olive oil*
*2 small red onions, sliced and separated
into rings*
*2/3 cup dry white wine*
*3 tablespoons balsamic vinegar*
*pinch of sugar*
*salt and freshly ground black pepper*
*fresh sage sprigs, to garnish*

**SERVES 4**

**1** Spread out the flour in a shallow bowl.
Season it with the chopped sage and
plenty of salt and pepper. Add the liver
and turn it in the flour until well coated.

### NUTRITIONAL NOTES
*Per portion:*

| | |
|---|---|
| Energy | 110cals |
| Total fat | 4.9g |
| Saturated fat | 1g |
| Cholesterol | 102.85mg |
| Fiber | 0.3g |

# VEAL WITH TOMATOES AND WHITE WINE

—

**This famous Milanese dish is delicious and hearty and is an ideal main course
for special occasions. It goes very well with a green salad.**

### INGREDIENTS
*2 tablespoons all-purpose flour*
*4 pieces of lean veal shank*
*2 small onions*
*2 teaspoons olive oil*
*1 large celery stalk,
finely chopped*
*1 carrot, finely chopped*
*2 garlic cloves, finely chopped*
*14-ounce can chopped tomatoes*
*1¼ cups dry
white wine*
*1¼ cups chicken or veal stock*
*1 strip of thinly pared lemon zest*
*2 bay leaves, plus extra for garnishing*
*salt and freshly ground black pepper*

### FOR THE GREMOLATA
*2 tablespoons finely chopped fresh
flat-leaf parsley*
*finely grated zest of 1 lemon*
*1 garlic clove, finely chopped*

### SERVES 4

**1** Preheat the oven to 325°F. Season the flour with salt and pepper and spread it out in a shallow bowl. Add the pieces of veal and turn them in the flour until they are evenly coated. Shake off any excess flour.

**2** Slice one of the onions into rings. Heat the olive oil in a large flameproof casserole, then add the veal pieces, with the onion rings, and brown the veal on both sides over medium heat. Remove the veal with tongs, place on a plate and set aside to drain.

**3** Chop the remaining onion and add to the pan with the celery, carrot and garlic. Stir the bottom of the pan to mix in the juices and sediment. Cook gently, stirring frequently, for about 5 minutes, until the vegetables soften slightly.

**4** Add the tomatoes, wine, stock, lemon zest and bay leaves, then season to taste with salt and pepper. Bring the mixture to a boil, stirring.

**5** Return the veal pieces to the pan and stir to coat thoroughly with the sauce. Cover and cook for 2 hours or until the veal feels tender when pierced with a fork.

**6** Meanwhile, make the gremolata. Combine the parsley, lemon zest and garlic in a small bowl. Remove the casserole from the oven and discard the lemon zest and bay leaves. Adjust the seasoning. Serve hot, sprinkled with the gremolata and garnished with bay leaves.

### NUTRITIONAL NOTES
*Per portion:*

| | |
|---|---|
| Energy | 219cals |
| Total fat | 4.8g |
| Saturated fat | 1.2g |
| Cholesterol | 84.8mg |
| Fiber | 1.3g |

# PANCETTA AND FAVA BEAN RISOTTO

This delicious Italian risotto makes a healthy and filling low-fat meal, served with cooked fresh seasonal vegetables or a mixed green salad.

### INGREDIENTS

*2 teaspoons olive oil*
*1 onion, chopped*
*2 garlic cloves, finely chopped*
*4 ounces smoked pancetta or smoked lean bacon, diced*
*1³/4 cups risotto rice*
*6¹/4 cups simmering chicken stock*
*1¹/3 cups frozen baby fava beans*
*2 tablespoons chopped fresh mixed herbs, such as parsley, thyme and oregano*
*salt and freshly ground black pepper*
*shaved fresh Parmesan cheese, to serve (optional)*

SERVES 6

**1** Heat the oil in a large saucepan. Add the onion, garlic and pancetta or bacon and cook gently for about 5 minutes, stirring occasionally. Do not let the onion and garlic brown.

**2** Add the rice and cook for 1 minute, stirring. Add a ladleful of stock and cook, stirring, until absorbed.

**3** Add more ladlefuls of stock until the rice is tender and almost all the liquid absorbed. This will take 30–35 minutes. Meanwhile, cook the fava beans in salted, boiling water for about 3 minutes. Drain and stir into the risotto, with the herbs. Season to taste. Sprinkle with shavings of Parmesan cheese, if using.

### NUTRITIONAL NOTES
*Per portion:*

| | |
|---|---|
| Energy | 294cals |
| Total fat | 5g |
| Saturated fat | 1.6g |
| Cholesterol | 8.5mg |
| Fiber | 2.7g |

# HUNTER'S CHICKEN

This traditional Italian dish combines chicken in a flavorful tomato, mushroom and herb sauce
to create a tempting main course, ideal served with mashed potatoes or cooked polenta.

**3** Add the onion and chopped porcini mushrooms to the pan. Cook gently, stirring frequently, for about 3 minutes, until the onion has softened but not browned. Stir in the chopped tomatoes, wine and reserved mushroom soaking liquid, then add the crushed garlic and chopped rosemary, with salt and pepper to taste. Bring to a boil, stirring constantly.

**4** Return the chicken to the pan and turn to coat it with the sauce. Cover and simmer gently for 30 minutes.

**5** Add the fresh mushrooms and stir into the sauce. Continue simmering gently for 10 minutes or until the chicken is tender. Adjust the seasoning to taste. Serve hot, garnished with fresh rosemary sprigs.

### INGREDIENTS

*1/4 cup dried porcini mushrooms*
*2 teaspoons olive oil*
*4 small chicken portions, on the bone, skinned*
*1 large onion, thinly sliced*
*14-ounce can chopped tomatoes*
*2/3 cup red wine*
*1 garlic clove, crushed*
*leaves of 1 sprig of fresh rosemary, finely chopped*
*1 3/4 cups fresh field mushrooms, thinly sliced*
*salt and freshly ground black pepper*
*fresh rosemary sprigs, to garnish*

### SERVES 4

**1** Put the porcini in a bowl, add 1 cup warm water and let soak for 20–30 minutes. Remove from the liquid and squeeze over the bowl. Strain the liquid and reserve. Finely chop the porcini.

**2** Heat the oil in a large flameproof casserole. Add the chicken. Sauté over medium heat for 5 minutes or until golden. Remove and drain on absorbent paper towels.

### NUTRITIONAL NOTES
*Per portion:*

| | |
|---|---|
| Energy | 190cals |
| Total fat | 5g |
| Saturated fat | 1.3g |
| Cholesterol | 44.12mg |
| Fiber | 1.2g |

# TUSCAN CHICKEN

This simple Italian peasant casserole has all the flavors of traditional Tuscan ingredients and is a delicious, low-fat supper dish.

**3** Lower the heat and simmer gently, stirring occasionally, for 30–35 minutes or until the chicken is tender and the juices run clear, not pink, when pierced with the point of a knife.

**4** Stir in the cannellini beans and simmer for another 5 minutes, until heated through. Sprinkle with the bread crumbs and cook under a hot broiler until golden brown. Serve immediately, garnished with fresh oregano sprigs.

### INGREDIENTS
*8 chicken thighs, skinned*
*1 teaspoon olive oil*
*1 onion, thinly sliced*
*2 red bell peppers, deseeded and sliced*
*1 garlic clove, crushed*
*1¹/4 cups passata*
*2/3 cup dry white wine*
*a large sprig of fresh oregano, chopped, or*
*1 teaspoon dried oregano*
*14-ounce can cannellini beans, drained*
*3 tablespoons fresh bread crumbs*
*salt and freshly ground black pepper*
*fresh oregano sprigs, to garnish*

### SERVES 6

**1** Fry the chicken in the oil in a nonstick or heavy pan until golden brown all over. Remove from the pan, place on a plate and keep hot. Add the onion and peppers to the pan and gently sauté until softened, but not brown. Add the garlic.

**2** Add the chicken, passata, wine and oregano and stir. Season well and bring to a boil, stirring, then cover the pan tightly.

### NUTRITIONAL NOTES
*Per portion:*

| | |
|---|---|
| Energy | 256cals |
| Total fat | 4.8g |
| Saturated fat | 1.3g |
| Cholesterol | 49.3mg |
| Fiber | 1.1g |

# CHICKEN IN A SALT CRUST

Cooking food in a casing of salt gives a deliciously moist, tender flavor that, surprisingly,
is not too salty. Serve with a selection of cooked fresh seasonal vegetables.

## INGREDIENTS
*4–4¹/₂-pound chicken*
*5¹/₄ pounds coarse sea salt*

### SERVES 6

**1** Preheat the oven to 425°F. Choose a deep ovenproof dish into which the whole chicken will fit snugly. Line the dish with a double thickness of heavy aluminum foil, letting plenty of foil overhang.

**2** Truss the chicken tightly so that the salt cannot fall into the cavity. Place the chicken on a thin layer of salt in the dish.

### COOK'S TIP
This recipe makes a stunning and unusual main course. Garnish the salt-encrusted chicken with fresh mixed herbs and take to the table. Scrape off the salt and transfer to a clean plate to carve.

**3** Pour the remaining salt all around and on top of the chicken until it is completely encased. Sprinkle the top with a little water.

**4** Cover tightly with the foil and bake the chicken on the lower shelf in the oven for 1³/₄ hours, until the chicken is cooked and tender.

**5** To serve the chicken, open out the foil and ease it out of the dish. Place on a large serving platter. Crack open the salt crust on the chicken and brush off the salt. Remove and discard the skin from the chicken and carve the meat into slices. Serve.

### NUTRITIONAL NOTES
*Per portion:*

| | |
|---|---|
| Energy | 156cals |
| Total fat | 4.4g |
| Saturated fat | 1.3g |
| Cholesterol | 61.6mg |
| Fiber | 0g |

# SHRIMP IN FRESH TOMATO SAUCE

**Fresh shrimp are cooked and served in a fresh tomato sauce to create this appetizing Italian-style low-fat dish.**

## INGREDIENTS

*4 teaspoons olive oil*
*1 onion, finely chopped*
*1 celery stalk, finely chopped*
*1 small red bell pepper, deseeded and chopped*
*¹/2 cup red wine*
*1 tablespoon wine vinegar*
*14-ounce can plum tomatoes, chopped, with their juice*
*2¹/4 pounds uncooked shrimp, in their shells*
*2–3 garlic cloves, finely chopped*
*3 tablespoons finely chopped fresh parsley*
*1 dried chile, crumbled or chopped (optional)*
*salt and freshly ground black pepper*

### SERVES 6

**1** Heat half the oil in a heavy saucepan. Add the onion and cook over low heat until soft, stirring occasionally. Stir in the chopped celery and pepper and cook for 5 minutes. Increase the heat and add the wine, vinegar and tomatoes. Bring the mixture to a boil and cook for 5 minutes, stirring occasionally. Reduce the heat, cover the pan and simmer for about 30 minutes, until the vegetables are soft, stirring occasionally.

### NUTRITIONAL NOTES
*Per portion:*

| | |
|---|---|
| Energy | 114cals |
| Total fat | 3.2g |
| Saturated fat | 0.6g |
| Cholesterol | 49.2mg |
| Fiber | 0.8g |

**2** Remove the pan from heat and let the vegetable mixture cool a little, then purée through a food mill to make a tomato sauce. Set aside.

**3** Shell the shrimp. Make a shallow incision with a small, sharp knife along the back of each shrimp and remove the long, black vein. Set the shrimp aside.

**4** Heat the remaining oil in a clean, heavy saucepan. Stir in the garlic and parsley, plus the chile, if using. Cook over medium heat, stirring, until the garlic is golden. Stir in the prepared tomato sauce and bring to a boil.

**5** Stir in the prepared shrimp. Bring the sauce back to a boil. Reduce the heat slightly and simmer, stirring occasionally, until the shrimp are pink and stiff: this will take 6–8 minutes, depending on their size. Season to taste and serve.

# MEDITERRANEAN FISH CUTLETS

These low-fat fish cutlets are ideal served with boiled potatoes, broccoli and carrots for
a delicious Italian supper.

**2** Meanwhile, place the fish in a frying pan, pour in the stock and/or wine and add the bay leaf, peppercorns and lemon zest. Cover and simmer for 10 minutes or until the fish is cooked and the flesh flakes easily.

**3** Using a slotted spoon, transfer the fish to a heated serving dish. Strain the fish stock into the tomato sauce and boil to reduce slightly. Season the sauce, pour it over the fish and serve immediately, sprinkled with the chopped fresh parsley to garnish.

### INGREDIENTS

*4 white fish cutlets, about 5 ounces each*
*about ⅔ cup fish stock or dry white wine*
*(or a mixture of the two), for poaching*
*1 bay leaf, a few black peppercorns and a*
*strip of pared lemon zest, for flavoring*
*chopped fresh parsley, to garnish*

### FOR THE TOMATO SAUCE

*14-ounce can chopped tomatoes*
*1 garlic clove, crushed*
*1 tablespoon pastis or other aniseed-*
*flavored liqueur*
*1 tablespoon drained capers*
*12–16 pitted black olives*
*salt and freshly ground black pepper*

**SERVES 4**

**1** To make the tomato sauce, place the chopped tomatoes, garlic, pastis or other liqueur, capers and olives in a saucepan. Season to taste with salt and pepper and cook over low heat for about 15 minutes, stirring occasionally.

### COOK'S TIP

Remove the skin from the fish cutlets and use fewer olives to reduce calories and fat even more. Use 1 pound fresh tomatoes, skinned and chopped, instead of canned.

### NUTRITIONAL NOTES
*Per portion:*

| | |
|---|---|
| Energy | 165cals |
| Total fat | 3.55g |
| Saturated fat | 0.5g |
| Cholesterol | 69mg |
| Fiber | 0.8g |

# ITALIAN FISH PARCELS

—

**Fresh sea bass fillets are topped with mixed Italian vegetables, then grilled or oven-baked to create this tasty dish, ideal for eating *al fresco*.**

### INGREDIENTS

*4 pieces skinless sea bass fillet or 4 whole
small sea bass
2 teaspoons olive oil for brushing
2 shallots, thinly sliced
1 garlic clove, chopped
1 tablespoon capers
6 sun-dried tomatoes, finely chopped
4 black olives, pitted and thinly sliced
finely grated zest and juice of 1 lemon
1 teaspoon paprika
salt and freshly ground black pepper*

### SERVES 4

**1** If you are using whole fish, gut them, taking care not to insert the knife too far. Use a teaspoon or your fingers to scrape out the contents. Leave the scales on, as they will hold the fragile fish together during cooking.

**2** Wash the cavity and the outside of the fish thoroughly with cold water.

### COOK'S TIPS

• When choosing fish, look for bright, slightly bulging eyes and shiny, faintly slimy skin. Open up the gills to check that they are clear red or dark pink and prod the fish lightly to check that the flesh is springy. All fish should have only a faint, pleasant smell; you can tell a stale fish a mile off by its disagreeable odor.
• Sea bass are prized for their delicate white flesh, and these slim, elegant fish are almost always sold whole. They don't have any irritating small bones, and as a result are never cheap.

**3** Cut four large squares of double-thickness aluminum foil, large enough to enclose the fish. Brush each square with a little olive oil.

**4** Place a piece of fish in the center of each piece of aluminum foil and season well with salt and pepper.

### NUTRITIONAL NOTES
*Per portion:*

| | |
|---|---|
| Energy | 117cals |
| Total fat | 4.5g |
| Saturated fat | 0.6g |
| Cholesterol | 50.2mg |
| Fiber | 0.1g |

**5** Sprinkle on the shallots, garlic, capers, sun-dried tomatoes, olives and grated lemon zest. Sprinkle with the lemon juice and paprika.

**6** Fold the foil over to enclose the fish loosely, sealing the edges firmly so none of the juices can escape.

**7** Place on a medium hot grill and cook for 8–10 minutes. Then open up the tops of the parcels and serve.

### VARIATIONS

• These parcels can also be baked: place them on a baking sheet and cook at 400°F for 15–20 minutes.
• Sea bass is good for this recipe, but you could also use small whole trout, or white fish such as cod or haddock.

# ROAST MONKFISH WITH GARLIC AND FENNEL

—

**Fresh monkfish quickly roasted with garlic and fennel is delicious served with boiled new potatoes for a summertime Italian meal.**

### INGREDIENTS

*2¹/2 pounds monkfish tail*
*8 garlic cloves*
*1 tablespoon olive oil*
*2 fennel bulbs, sliced*
*juice and zest of 1 lemon*
*1 bay leaf, plus extra*
*to garnish*
*salt and freshly ground black pepper*

**SERVES 6**

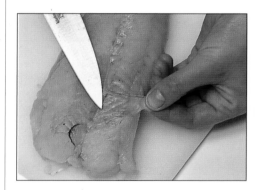

**1** Preheat the oven to 425°F. With a sharp filleting knife, carefully cut off the thin membrane covering the outside of the monkfish; keep the knife flat against the fish to avoid cutting off too much of the flesh. When finished, discard the membrane.

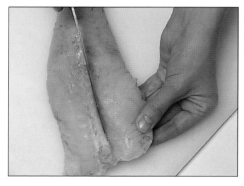

**2** Cut along one side of the central bone to remove the fillet. Repeat on the other side. Discard the bone.

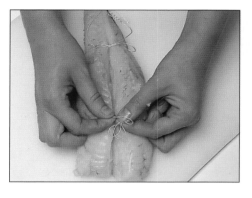

**3** Tie the separated fillets together with string to reshape as a tailpiece.

**4** Peel and slice the garlic cloves and cut incisions into the fish flesh. Place the garlic slices in the incisions.

**5** Heat the oil in a large, heavy saucepan and cook the fish until sealed on all sides.

**6** Place the fish in a roasting dish together with the fennel slices, lemon juice, bay leaf and seasoning.

**7** Roast for about 20 minutes, until tender and cooked through. Serve immediately, garnished with bay leaves and lemon zest.

---

### COOK'S TIPS

• Monkfish is usually available year round, but if it is not, then you could substitute another firm white fish, such as huss.
• The aniseed-like flavor of fennel goes particularly well with fish. The leaves can be used as a garnish if desired.

---

### NUTRITIONAL NOTES
*Per portion:*

| | |
|---|---|
| Energy | 234cals |
| Total fat | 4.7g |
| Saturated fat | 0.6g |
| Cholesterol | 123.5mg |
| Fiber | 1.2g |

# MONKFISH WITH PEPPERED CITRUS MARINADE

A fresh citrus fruit marinade adds delicious flavor to monkfish fillets and creates a low-fat, appetizing dish ideal for cooking and eating *al fresco*.

### INGREDIENTS

*2 monkfish tails, about 12 ounces each*
*1 lime*
*1 lemon*
*2 oranges*
*a handful of fresh thyme sprigs*
*4 teaspoons olive oil*
*1 tablespoon mixed peppercorns,*
*roughly crushed*
*salt and freshly ground black pepper*

### SERVES 4

**1** Remove and discard any skin from the monkfish tails.

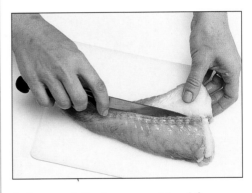

**2** Cut carefully down one side of the backbone, sliding the knife between the bone and flesh, to remove the fillet on one side. (You can ask your fishmonger to do this for you.)

### NUTRITIONAL NOTES
*Per portion:*

| | |
|---|---|
| Energy | 176cals |
| Total fat | 5g |
| Saturated fat | 0.7g |
| Cholesterol | 80.6mg |
| Fiber | 0g |

**3** Turn the fish and repeat on the other side. Repeat on the second tail. Discard the bones. Lay the fillets out flat.

**4** Cut two slices from each of the citrus fruits and arrange over two fillets. Add a few sprigs of thyme and season. Finely grate the w from the remaining fruit and sprinkle on the fish.

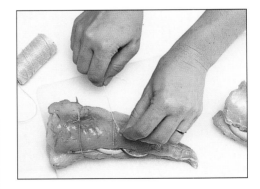

**5** Lay the other two fillets on top and tie them firmly at intervals, with fine cotton string, to hold them in shape. Place in a wide, shallow, nonmetallic dish.

**6** Squeeze the juice from the citrus fruits and mix it with the oil and more salt and black pepper.

**7** Spoon the juice mixture onto the fish. Cover and let marinate for about an hour, turning occasionally and spooning the marinade on it.

**8** Drain the monkfish, reserving the marinade, and sprinkle with the crushed peppercorns. Cook over a medium hot grill for 15–20 minutes, basting the fish with the marinade and turning it occasionally, until it is evenly cooked. Serve immediately.

### VARIATION
You can also use this marinade for monkfish kebabs.

# BAKED FLOUNDER WITH ITALIAN VEGETABLE SAUCE

**Fresh flounder fillets are oven-baked in an Italian mixed vegetable sauce to create a very low-fat meal for family or friends.**

### INGREDIENTS
*4 large flounder fillets*
*2 small red onions*
*1/2 cup vegetable stock*
*1/4 cup dry red wine*
*1 garlic clove, crushed*
*2 zucchini, sliced*
*1 yellow bell pepper, deseeded and sliced*
*14-ounce can chopped tomatoes*
*1 tablespoon chopped fresh thyme*
*salt and freshly ground black pepper*
*fresh thyme sprigs, to garnish*
*potato gratin, to serve*

### SERVES 4

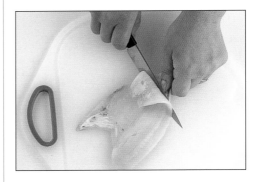

**1** Preheat the oven to 350°F. Lay the fillets skin-side down and, holding the tail end, push a sharp knife between the skin and flesh in a sawing movement. Hold the knife at a slight angle with the blade toward the skin. Discard the skin and set the fish aside.

### NUTRITIONAL NOTES
*Per portion:*

| | |
|---|---|
| Energy | 144cals |
| Total fat | 2.7g |
| Saturated fat | 0.4g |
| Cholesterol | 46.2mg |
| Fiber | 1.5g |

**2** Cut each onion into eight wedges. Put into a heavy saucepan with the vegetable stock. Cover, bring to a boil and simmer for 5 minutes. Uncover and continue to cook, stirring occasionally, until the stock has reduced entirely. Add the red wine and crushed garlic to the pan and continue to cook until the onions are soft, stirring occasionally.

**3** Stir in the zucchini, yellow pepper, tomatoes and chopped thyme and season to taste. Simmer for 3 minutes. Spoon the sauce into a large casserole.

**4** Fold each flounder fillet in half and put on top of the vegetable sauce. Cover and cook for 15–20 minutes, until the fish is opaque and flakes easily. Garnish with fresh thyme sprigs and serve with a potato gratin.

### COOK'S TIP
Skinless white fish fillets such as flounder are low in fat and make an ideal tasty and nutritious basis for many low-fat recipes such as this one.

# BAKED COD WITH TOMATOES

For the very best flavor, use firm sun-ripened tomatoes for this Italian tomato sauce and make
sure it is fairly thick before spooning it onto the cod. Serve with boiled new potatoes and a salad.

**2** Bring the sauce just to a boil, then
reduce the heat slightly and cook,
uncovered, for 15–20 minutes, until thick,
stirring occasionally. Stir in the parsley.

**3** Lightly grease an ovenproof dish, put
in the cod and spoon an equal quantity of
the tomato sauce on each. Sprinkle the
bread crumbs on top.

**4** Bake for 20–30 minutes, basting
occasionally with the sauce, until the fish
is cooked through, and the bread crumbs
are golden. Serve hot with new potatoes
and a mixed green salad.

### INGREDIENTS

*2 teaspoons olive oil*
*1 onion, chopped*
*2 garlic cloves, finely chopped*
*1 pound tomatoes, peeled, deseeded*
*and chopped*
*1 teaspoon tomato paste*
*¼ cup dry white wine*
*¼ cup chopped fresh flat-leaf parsley*
*4 cod fillets*
*2 tablespoons dried bread crumbs*
*salt and freshly ground black pepper*
*boiled new potatoes and mixed green*
*salad, to serve*

**SERVES 4**

**1** Preheat the oven to 375°F. Heat the oil
in a frying pan and sauté the onion for
about 5 minutes, stirring occasionally.
Add the garlic, tomatoes, tomato paste,
wine and seasoning and stir to mix.

### COOK'S TIP

For extra speed, use a 14-ounce can
of chopped tomatoes instead of the
fresh tomatoes and 1–2 teaspoons
ready-minced garlic in place of the
garlic cloves.

### NUTRITIONAL NOTES

*Per portion:*

| | |
|---|---|
| Energy | 151cals |
| Total fat | 1.5g |
| Saturated fat | 0.2g |
| Cholesterol | 55.2mg |
| Fiber | 2.42g |

# ITALIAN FISH STEW

**The different regions of Italy have their own variations on this low-fat dish. Buy some of the fish
whole so you can simmer them, then remove the cooked flesh and strain the juices for the stock.**

### INGREDIENTS

*2 pounds mixture of fish fillets or steaks,
such as monkfish, cod, haddock, halibut
or hake
2 pounds mixture of conger eel, red
snapper or small white fish
1 onion, halved
1 celery stalk, roughly chopped
8 ounces squid
8 ounces fresh mussels
1 1/2 pounds ripe tomatoes
1 tablespoon olive oil
1 large onion, thinly sliced
3 garlic cloves, crushed
1 teaspoon saffron threads
2/3 cup dry white wine
6 tablespoons chopped fresh parsley
salt and freshly ground black pepper
croutons, to serve (optional)*

### SERVES 6

**1** Remove and discard any skin and
bones from the fish fillets or steaks, cut
the fish into large pieces and reserve.
Place the bones in a saucepan with all
the remaining fish.

**2** Add the onion and celery and cover with
water. Bring almost to a boil, then reduce
the heat and simmer for about 30 minutes.
Lift out the fish and remove the flesh from
the bones. Reserve the flesh and discard
the bones. Strain and reserve the stock
and discard the contents of the sieve.

**3** To prepare the squid, twist the head
and tentacles off of the body. Cut the head
from the tentacles. Discard the body
contents and peel the skin. Wash the
tentacles and bodies and dry on paper
towels. Scrub the mussels, discarding any
that are damaged, or open ones that do
not close when tapped.

**4** Plunge the tomatoes into a bowl of
boiling water for 30 seconds, then refresh
in cold water. Peel off and discard the
skins and chop the tomatoes roughly.

**5** Heat the oil in a large saucepan or
sauté pan. Add the onion and garlic and
sauté gently for 3 minutes. Add the squid
and the reserved uncooked white fish, and
fry quickly on all sides, stirring frequently.
Remove from the pan, and drain.

**6** Add 2 cups reserved fish stock, the
tomatoes and the saffron to the pan. Pour
in the wine. Bring to a boil, then reduce
the heat and simmer for about 5 minutes.
Add the mussels, cover, and cook for
3–4 minutes, until the mussels have
opened. Discard any that remain closed.
Season the sauce and add all the fish.
Cook gently for 5 minutes until hot,
stirring occasionally. Sprinkle on with the
parsley and serve with croutons, if using.

### NUTRITIONAL NOTES
*Per portion:*

| | |
|---|---|
| Energy | 321cals |
| Total fat | 5g |
| Saturated fat | 0.7g |
| Cholesterol | 136.8mg |
| Fiber | 1g |

# MONKFISH WITH TOMATO AND OLIVE SAUCE

This low-fat Italian dish comes from the coast of Calabria in southern Italy. Serve with garlic-flavored mashed potatoes for an ideal family meal.

### INGREDIENTS

*1 pound fresh mussels in their shells, scrubbed*
*a few fresh basil sprigs*
*2 garlic cloves, roughly chopped*
*1¼ cups dry white wine*
*1 tablespoon olive oil*
*2 pounds monkfish fillets, skinned and cut into large chunks*
*1 onion, finely chopped*
*1¼-pound jar or carton passata*
*1 tablespoon sun-dried tomato paste*
*½ cup pitted black olives*
*salt and freshly ground black pepper*
*extra fresh basil leaves, to garnish*

### SERVES 4

**1** Put the mussels in a flameproof casserole with some of the basil leaves, the garlic and wine. Cover and bring to a boil. Lower the heat and simmer for 5 minutes, shaking the pan frequently. Remove the mussels, discarding any that fail to open. Strain and reserve the cooking liquid.

**2** Heat the oil in a flameproof casserole, add the monkfish pieces and sauté over medium heat until they just change color. Remove the fish from the pan, place on a plate and set aside.

**3** Add the onion to the juices in the casserole and cook gently for about 5 minutes, stirring frequently, until softened. Add the passata, the reserved cooking liquid from the mussels and the tomato paste. Season to taste with salt and pepper. Bring to a boil, stirring, then reduce the heat, cover and let simmer for 20 minutes, stirring occasionally.

### NUTRITIONAL NOTES

*Per portion:*

| | |
|---|---|
| Energy | 221cals |
| Total fat | 4.6g |
| Saturated fat | 0.7g |
| Cholesterol | 81.9mg |
| Fiber | 1.1g |

**4** Pull off and discard the top shells from the cooked mussels and set them aside. Add the monkfish pieces to the tomato sauce and cook gently for 5 minutes. Gently stir in the olives and remaining basil, then adjust the seasoning to taste. Place the mussels in their half shells on top of the sauce, cover the pan and heat the mussels through for 1–2 minutes. Serve immediately, garnished with basil leaves.

# TROUT AND PROSCIUTTO RISOTTO ROLLS

—

This makes a delicious and elegant low-fat meal. The risotto—made with porcini or chanterelle mushrooms and shrimp—is an ideal accompaniment for the flavorful trout rolls.

### INGREDIENTS
*4 trout fillets, skinned*
*4 thin slices of prosciutto*
*capers, to garnish*

### FOR THE RISOTTO
*2 teaspoons olive oil*
*8 large raw shrimp, peeled and deveined*
*1 onion, chopped*
*generous 1 cup risotto rice*
*about 7 tablespoons white wine*
*about 3 cups simmering fish or*
*chicken stock*
*2 tablespoons dried porcini or chanterelle*
*mushrooms, soaked for 10 minutes in*
*warm water to cover*
*salt and freshly ground black pepper*

### SERVES 4

**2** Add the onion to the oil in the pan. Sauté over low heat for 3–4 minutes, until soft, stirring occasionally. Add the rice and stir for 3–4 minutes, until the grains are evenly coated in oil. Add 5 tablespoons of the wine and then the stock, a little at a time, stirring over low heat and letting the rice absorb the liquid before adding more.

**5** Take a trout fillet, place a spoonful of risotto at one end and roll up. Wrap each fillet in a slice of prosciutto and place in a lightly greased ovenproof dish.

**6** Spoon any remaining risotto around the fish fillets and sprinkle on the rest of the wine. Bake the rolls for 15–20 minutes, until the fish is cooked and tender. Spoon the risotto onto a platter, top with the trout rolls and garnish with some fat capers. Serve immediately.

**1** First, make the risotto. Heat the oil in a heavy saucepan or deep-frying pan and stir-fry the shrimp very briefly until flecked with pink. Lift out using a slotted spoon and transfer to a plate. Set aside.

**3** Drain the mushrooms, reserving the liquid, and cut the larger ones in half. Toward the end of cooking, stir the mushrooms into the risotto with 1 tablespoon of the reserved mushroom liquid. If the rice is not yet *al dente*, add a little more stock or mushroom liquid and cook for 2–3 more minutes. Season to taste with salt and pepper.

**4** Remove the pan from heat and stir in the shrimp. Preheat the oven to 375°F.

### COOK'S TIP
Make sure you use proper risotto rice, such as arborio or carnaroli, for this recipe. Short-grain rice will not give the right consistency.

### NUTRITIONAL NOTES
*Per portion:*

| | |
|---|---|
| Energy | 245cals |
| Total fat | 5g |
| Saturated fat | 1.1g |
| Cholesterol | 63.8mg |
| Fiber | 0.3g |

# VEGETARIAN
# DISHES
## AND
# VEGETABLES

VEGETARIAN *dishes and vegetables*
*play an important part in a* LOW-FAT
*diet, providing nutritious and filling dishes
made from* FRESH INGREDIENTS
*that the whole family will enjoy. Many of the
dishes are* SIMPLE *but substantial and
enticing, including* HERB POLENTA *with
Grilled Tomatoes, Red Bell Pepper Risotto,
Stuffed Eggplant and* CAPONATA.

# HERB POLENTA WITH GRILLED TOMATOES

Golden polenta flavored with fresh summer herbs and served with sweet grilled tomatoes make up this tasty Italian dish, ideal for lunch or supper.

### INGREDIENTS

*1¹/₂ cups polenta*
*3 cups stock or water*
*1 teaspoon salt*
*1 tablespoon butter*
*5 tablespoons mixed chopped*
*fresh parsley, chives and basil,*
*plus extra to garnish*
*2 teaspoons olive oil*
*4 large plum or beefsteak tomatoes, halved*
*salt and freshly ground black pepper*

### SERVES 6

**1** Prepare the polenta in advance: place the stock or water in a saucepan with the salt, and bring to a boil.

**2** Reduce the heat and gradually add the polenta, stirring constantly to ensure that it doesn't form any lumps.

### NUTRITIONAL NOTES
*Per portion:*

| | |
|---|---|
| Energy | 185cals |
| Total fat | 4.7g |
| Saturated fat | 2g |
| Cholesterol | 7mg |
| Fiber | 0.4g |

**3** Stir constantly over medium heat for 5 minutes, until the polenta begins to thicken and comes away from the sides of the pan.

**4** Remove the pan from heat and stir in the butter, herbs and black pepper.

**5** Transfer the polenta mixture to a wide, lightly greased dish or pan and spread it out evenly. Let it sit until it is completely cool and has set.

**6** Turn the polenta out onto a board and cut it into squares or stamp out rounds with a large cookie cutter. Lightly brush the squares or rounds with oil.

**7** Lightly brush the tomatoes with oil and sprinkle with salt and pepper.

**8** Cook the tomatoes and polenta on a medium hot grill for 5 minutes, turning once. Serve hot, garnished with fresh herbs.

### VARIATION
Any mixture of fresh herbs can be used, or try using just basil or chives alone, for a really distinctive flavor.

# POLENTA WITH MUSHROOMS

—

**This low-fat Italian dish is delicious made with a mixture of fresh wild and cultivated mushrooms. Serve with a mixed green salad for a delicious meal.**

### INGREDIENTS

*2 tablespoons dried porcini mushrooms
(omit if using wild mushrooms)
4 teaspoons olive oil
1 small onion, finely chopped
1½ pounds mushrooms, wild or
cultivated, or a combination of both
2 garlic cloves, finely chopped
3 tablespoons chopped fresh parsley
3 tomatoes, skinned and diced
1 tablespoon tomato paste
¾ cup warm water
¼ teaspoon fresh thyme leaves, or
1 large pinch of dried thyme
1 bay leaf
2½ cups polenta
salt and freshly ground black pepper
fresh parsley sprigs, to garnish*

### SERVES 6

**1** Soak the dried mushrooms, if using, in a small bowl of warm water for about 20 minutes. Remove the mushrooms with a slotted spoon and rinse them well in several changes of cold water. Set aside. Filter the soaking water through a layer of absorbent paper towels placed in a sieve and reserve.

**2** In a large frying pan, heat the oil and sauté the onion over low heat until soft and golden.

**3** Clean the fresh mushrooms by wiping them with a damp cloth. Cut into slices. When the onion is soft, add the mushrooms to the pan. Stir over medium to high heat until they release their liquid. Add the garlic, parsley and diced tomatoes. Cook for 4–5 minutes, stirring occasionally.

**4** Soften the tomato paste in the warm water (use only ½ cup water if using dried mushrooms). Add to the pan with the herbs. Add the dried mushrooms and soaking liquid, if using, and season with salt and pepper.

**5** Reduce the heat to low and cook for 15–20 minutes, stirring occasionally. Remove the pan from heat and set the sauce aside.

**6** Bring 6¼ cups water to a boil in a large, heavy saucepan. Add 1 tablespoon salt.

**7** Reduce the heat to a simmer and begin to add the polenta in a fine rain. Stir with a whisk until the polenta has all been incorporated.

**8** Switch to a long-handled wooden spoon and continue to stir the polenta over low to medium heat until it is a thick mass and pulls away from the sides of the pan. This may take 25–50 minutes, depending on the type of polenta used. For best results, never stop stirring the polenta until you remove it from heat.

**9** When the polenta has almost finished cooking, gently reheat the mushroom sauce until piping hot.

**10** To serve, spoon the polenta onto a warmed serving platter. Make a well in the center. Spoon some of the mushroom sauce into the well, and garnish with fresh parsley sprigs.

**11** Serve immediately, passing the remaining mushroom sauce in a separate bowl.

### NUTRITIONAL NOTES
*Per portion:*

| | |
|---|---|
| Energy | 244cals |
| Total fat | 3.5g |
| Saturated fat | 0.6g |
| Cholesterol | 0mg |
| Fiber | 1.5g |

# BAKED CHEESE POLENTA WITH TOMATO SAUCE

Polenta, or cornmeal, is a staple food in Italy. It is cooked in a similar way to porridge, and eaten soft, or set, cut into shapes, then baked or grilled. Serve with crusty Italian bread.

### INGREDIENTS

*1 teaspoon salt*
*2 1/4 cups quick-cook polenta*
*1 teaspoon paprika*
*1/2 teaspoon ground nutmeg*
*1 teaspoon olive oil*
*1 large onion, finely chopped*
*2 garlic cloves, crushed*
*2 14-ounce cans chopped tomatoes*
*1 tablespoon tomato paste*
*1 teaspoon sugar*
*salt and freshly ground black pepper*
*1/2 cup Gruyère, grated*

### SERVES 6

**1** Preheat the oven to 400°F. Line a baking pan (11 × 7 inches) with plastic wrap. Bring 4 cups water to a boil in a saucepan with the salt.

**2** Pour in the polenta in a steady stream and cook for 5 minutes, stirring continuously. Beat in the paprika and nutmeg, then pour the mixture into the prepared pan and smooth the surface. Let cool.

**3** Heat the oil in a nonstick saucepan and cook the onion and garlic until soft, stirring occasionally. Stir in the tomatoes, tomato paste, sugar and seasoning. Bring to a boil, reduce the heat and simmer for 20 minutes, stirring occasionally.

### NUTRITIONAL NOTES
*Per portion:*

| | |
|---|---|
| Energy | 219cals |
| Total fat | 5g |
| Saturated fat | 2g |
| Cholesterol | 0mg |
| Fiber | 1g |

**4** Turn the cooled polenta out onto a cutting board, and cut evenly into 2-inch squares.

**5** Place half the polenta squares in a greased ovenproof dish. Spoon on half the tomato sauce, and sprinkle half the cheese on. Repeat the layers. Bake for about 25 minutes, until golden. Serve.

# RED BELL PEPPER RISOTTO

**This delicious Italian risotto is a flavorful and low-fat supper or main-course dish, ideally served with fresh Italian bread.**

### INGREDIENTS

*3 large red bell peppers*
*2 teaspoons olive oil*
*3 large garlic cloves,*
*thinly sliced*
*1 1/2 14-ounce cans chopped tomatoes*
*2 bay leaves*
*5–6 1/4 cups vegetable stock*
*2 1/2 cups arborio rice or brown rice*
*6 fresh basil leaves, snipped*
*salt and freshly ground black pepper*

### SERVES 4

**3** Pour the vegetable stock into a separate large, heavy saucepan and heat it to the simmering point. Stir the rice into the vegetable mixture and cook for about 2 minutes, then add two or three ladlefuls of the hot stock. Cook, stirring occasionally, until all the stock has been absorbed into the rice.

### NUTRITIONAL NOTES
*Per portion:*

| | |
|---|---|
| Energy | 306cals |
| Total fat | 3.7g |
| Saturated fat | 0.7g |
| Cholesterol | 0mg |
| Fiber | 2.7g |

**4** Continue to add stock in this way, making sure each addition has been absorbed before adding the next. When the rice is tender, season with salt and pepper. Remove the pan from heat, cover and let stand for 10 minutes. Remove and discard the bay leaves, then stir in the basil. Serve.

**1** Preheat the broiler. Put the peppers in a broiler pan and broiler until the skins are blackened and blistered all over. Put the peppers in a bowl, cover with several layers of damp absorbent paper towels and let sit for 10 minutes. Peel off and discard the skins, then slice the peppers, discarding the cores and seeds. Set aside.

**2** Heat the oil in a wide, shallow saucepan. Add the garlic and tomatoes and cook over low heat for 5 minutes, stirring occasionally, then add the prepared pepper slices and the bay leaves. Stir well and cook gently for 15 minutes, stirring occasionally.

# MILANESE RISOTTO

This traditional Italian risotto is deliciously flavored with garlic, shavings of Parmesan and fresh parsley to create a filling and flavorful low-fat dish.

### INGREDIENTS
*2 garlic cloves, crushed*
*1/4 cup chopped fresh parsley*
*finely grated zest of 1 lemon*

### FOR THE RISOTTO
*1 teaspoon (or 1 envelope) saffron threads*
*1/2 ounce butter*
*1 large onion, finely chopped*
*1 1/2 cups arborio rice*
*2/3 cup dry white wine*
*4 cups hot vegetable stock*
*salt and freshly ground black pepper*
*1/2 ounce shaved fresh Parmesan cheese,*
*to serve*

### SERVES 4

**3** Stir in the rice and cook it for about 2 minutes, until it becomes translucent. Add the wine and saffron mixture and cook, stirring, for several minutes, until all the wine is absorbed.

**4** Add 2 1/2 cups of the stock and simmer gently until the stock is absorbed, stirring frequently.

**5** Gradually add more stock, a ladleful at a time, until the rice is tender, stirring frequently. (The rice might be tender and creamy before you've added all the stock, so add it slowly toward the end.)

**6** Season the risotto with salt and pepper and transfer to a serving dish. Serve, scattered with shavings of Parmesan cheese and the garlic and parsley mixture.

### NUTRITIONAL NOTES
*Per portion:*

| | |
|---|---|
| Energy | 258cals |
| Total fat | 5g |
| Saturated fat | 2.6g |
| Cholesterol | 9.9mg |
| Fiber | 1.3g |

**1** Combine the garlic, parsley and lemon zest in a bowl. Set aside.

**2** To make the risotto, put the saffron in a small bowl with 1 tablespoon boiling water and let stand while the saffron infuses. Melt the butter in a heavy saucepan and gently sauté the onion for 5 minutes, until softened and golden, stirring occasionally.

# RISOTTO WITH MUSHROOMS AND PARMESAN

A classic Italian risotto of mixed mushrooms, herbs and fresh Parmesan cheese, made using long-grain brown rice. Serve simply, with a mixed green salad tossed in a fat-free dressing.

**2** Stir the stock and the porcini liquid into the rice mixture. Bring to a boil, reduce the heat and simmer, uncovered, for about 20 minutes or until most of the liquid is absorbed, stirring frequently.

**3** Add the porcini and fresh mushrooms, stir, and cook for another 10–15 minutes, until the rice is tender and the liquid absorbed, stirring frequently.

**4** Season with salt and pepper to taste, stir in the chopped parsley and grated Parmesan and serve immediately.

### INGREDIENTS

*2 teaspoons olive oil*
*4 shallots, finely chopped*
*2 garlic cloves, crushed*
*2 tablespoons dried porcini mushrooms,*
*soaked in 2/3 cup hot water for 20 minutes*
*1 1/3 cups long-grain brown rice*
*3 3/4 cups well-flavored vegetable stock*
*6 cups mixed mushrooms, such as closed*
*cup, chestnut and field mushrooms, sliced*
*if large*
*2–3 tablespoons chopped fresh*
*flat-leaf parsley*
*1 ounce grated fresh Parmesan cheese*
*salt and freshly ground black pepper*

### SERVES 4

**1** Heat the oil in a large saucepan, add the shallots and garlic and cook gently for 5 minutes, stirring. Drain the porcini, reserving their liquid, and chop roughly. Set aside. Add the brown rice to the shallot mixture and stir to coat the grains in oil.

### NUTRITIONAL NOTES
*Per portion:*

| Energy | 233cals |
| --- | --- |
| Total fat | 4.8g |
| Saturated fat | 1.5g |
| Cholesterol | 4mg |
| Fiber | 1.9g |

# STUFFED EGGPLANT

This typical dish from the Ligurian region of Italy is spiked with paprika and allspice, a legacy
from the days when spices from the East came into northern Italy via the port of Genoa.

### INGREDIENTS

*2 eggplant, about 8 ounces each,*
*stems removed*
*10 ounces potatoes, peeled and diced*
*1 tablespoon olive oil*
*1 small onion, finely chopped*
*1 garlic clove, finely chopped*
*good pinch of ground allspice and paprika*
*2 tablespoons skim milk*
*1 ounce grated fresh Parmesan cheese*
*1 tablespoon fresh white bread crumbs*
*salt and freshly ground black pepper*
*fresh mint sprigs, to garnish*
*salad greens, to serve*

### SERVES 6

**1** Bring a large saucepan of lightly salted
water to a boil. Add the whole eggplant
and cook for 5 minutes, turning
frequently. Remove with a slotted spoon
and set aside. Add the diced potatoes to
the pan and boil for about 15 minutes or
until cooked.

**2** Meanwhile, cut the eggplant in half
lengthwise and gently scoop out the flesh
with a small sharp knife and a spoon,
leaving ¼-inch of the shell intact. Select
a baking dish that will hold the eggplant
shells snugly in a single layer. Brush it
lightly with oil. Put the shells in the
baking dish and chop the eggplant flesh
roughly. Set aside.

**3** Heat the oil in a frying pan, add the
onion and cook gently, stirring frequently,
until softened. Add the chopped eggplant
flesh and the garlic. Cook, stirring
frequently, for 6–8 minutes. Transfer
to a bowl and set aside. Preheat the
oven to 375°F.

**4** Drain and mash the potatoes. Add to
the eggplant mixture with the ground
spices and milk. Set aside 1 tablespoon
of the Parmesan cheese and add the
rest to the eggplant mixture, stirring
in salt and pepper to taste.

### NUTRITIONAL NOTES
*Per portion:*

| | |
|---|---|
| Energy | 130cals |
| Total fat | 5g |
| Saturated fat | 1.5g |
| Cholesterol | 5.1mg |
| Fiber | 3.3g |

**5** Spoon the mixture into the eggplant
shells. Mix the bread crumbs with the
reserved Parmesan cheese and sprinkle
the mixture evenly on the eggplant. Bake
for 30–40 minutes, until the topping is
crisp. Garnish with mint sprigs and serve
with salad greens.

# ITALIAN STUFFED BELL PEPPERS

—

**These flavorful Italian stuffed peppers are easy to make for a light
and healthy lunch or supper.**

### INGREDIENTS

*2 teaspoons olive oil*
*1 red onion, sliced*
*1 zucchini, diced*
*4 ounces mushrooms, sliced*
*1 garlic clove, crushed*
*14-ounce can chopped tomatoes*
*1 tablespoon tomato paste*
*1 ounce pine nuts (optional)*
*2 tablespoons chopped fresh basil*
*4 large yellow bell peppers*
*1/4 cup finely grated fresh Parmesan or*
*Fontina cheese (optional)*
*salt and freshly ground black pepper*
*fresh basil leaves, to garnish*

### SERVES 4

**1** Preheat the oven to 350°F. Heat the oil in a saucepan, add the onion, zucchini, mushrooms and garlic and cook gently for 3 minutes, stirring the mixture occasionally.

### NUTRITIONAL NOTES

*Per portion:*

| | |
|---|---|
| Energy | 70cals |
| Total fat | 2.5g |
| Saturated fat | 0.4g |
| Cholesterol | 0mg |
| Fiber | 2.4g |

**2** Stir in the tomatoes and tomato paste, then bring to a boil and simmer, uncovered, for 10–15 minutes, stirring occasionally, until thickened slightly. Remove the pan from heat and stir in the pine nuts, if using, chopped basil and seasoning. Set aside.

**3** Cut the peppers in half lengthwise and deseed them. Blanch the pepper halves in a saucepan of boiling water for about 3 minutes. Drain.

**4** Place the peppers cut-side up in a shallow ovenproof dish and fill with the vegetable mixture.

**5** Cover the dish with aluminum foil and bake for 20 minutes. Uncover, sprinkle each pepper half with a little grated cheese, if using, and bake, uncovered, for another 5–10 minutes. Garnish with fresh basil leaves and serve.

# MEDITERRANEAN VEGETABLES WITH CHICKPEAS

The flavors of the Mediterranean are captured in this delicious low-fat vegetable dish, ideal for
an appetizer or lunch, served with fresh crusty bread.

### INGREDIENTS

*1 onion, sliced*
*2 leeks, sliced*
*2 garlic cloves, crushed*
*1 red bell pepper, deseeded and sliced*
*1 green bell pepper, deseeded*
*and sliced*
*1 yellow bell pepper, deseeded*
*and sliced*
*12 ounces zucchini, sliced*
*3 cups mushrooms, sliced*
*14-ounce can chopped tomatoes*
*2 tablespoons ruby port or red wine*
*2 tablespoons tomato paste*
*1 tablespoon ketchup (optional)*
*14-ounce can chickpeas*
*1 cup pitted black olives*
*3 tablespoons chopped fresh mixed herbs*
*salt and freshly ground black pepper*
*chopped fresh mixed herbs, to garnish*

### SERVES 6

**1** Put the onion, leeks, garlic, red,
yellow and green peppers, zucchini
and mushrooms into a large saucepan.

### COOK'S TIP

For the best Mediterranean flavor, try
to include fresh basil and oregano in the
mixed herbs used in this recipe.

**2** Add the tomatoes, port or red wine,
tomato paste and ketchup, if using, to
the saucepan and combine all the
ingredients well.

**3** Rinse and drain the chickpeas and add
to the pan. Stir to mix.

**4** Cover, bring to a boil, then reduce the
heat and simmer the mixture gently for
20–30 minutes, until the vegetables are
cooked and tender but not overcooked,
stirring occasionally.

**5** Remove the lid of the saucepan and
increase the heat slightly for the last
10 minutes of the cooking time, to
thicken the sauce, if desired.

**6** Stir in the olives, herbs and seasoning.
Serve either hot or cold, garnished with
chopped mixed herbs.

### NUTRITIONAL NOTES
*Per portion:*

| | |
|---|---|
| Energy | 55cals |
| Total fat | 4.56g |
| Saturated fat | 0.67g |
| Cholesterol | 0mg |
| Fiber | 6.98g |

# ROSEMARY ROAST POTATOES

These tasty Italian-style roast potatoes use much less fat than traditional roast potatoes, and because they still have their skins they not only absorb less oil but also have more flavor.

### INGREDIENTS
*2¹/4 pounds small red potatoes*
*2 teaspoons walnut or sunflower oil*
*2 tablespoons fresh rosemary leaves*
*salt and paprika*

### SERVES 4

**1** Preheat the oven to 475°F. Leave the potatoes whole with the peel on or, if large, cut in half. Place the potatoes in a large saucepan of cold water and bring to a boil. Drain well.

**2** Drizzle the walnut or sunflower oil on the potatoes and shake the pan to coat them evenly.

**3** Transfer the potatoes to a shallow roasting pan. Sprinkle with rosemary, salt and paprika. Roast for 30 minutes or until cooked and crisp. Serve hot.

### NUTRITIONAL NOTES
*Per portion:*

| | |
|---|---|
| Energy | 205cals |
| Total fat | 2.22g |
| Saturated fat | 0.19g |
| Cholesterol | 0mg |
| Fiber | 3.25g |

# BAKED ZUCCHINI IN PASSATA

Sliced zucchini, oven-baked with onions, passata and fresh thyme, make a delicious, virtually fat-free vegetable dish.

### INGREDIENTS
*1 teaspoon olive oil*
*3 large zucchini, thinly sliced*
*¹/2 small red onion, finely chopped*
*1¹/4 cups passata*
*2 tablespoons chopped fresh thyme*
*garlic salt and freshly ground black pepper*
*fresh thyme sprigs, to garnish*

### SERVES 4

### NUTRITIONAL NOTES
*Per portion:*

| | |
|---|---|
| Energy | 49cals |
| Total fat | 1.43g |
| Saturated fat | 0.22g |
| Cholesterol | 0mg |
| Fiber | 1.73g |

**1** Preheat the oven to 375°F. Brush an ovenproof dish with the olive oil.

**2** Arrange half the zucchini and onion in the dish.

**3** Spoon half the passata onto the vegetables and sprinkle with some of the fresh thyme, then season to taste with garlic salt and pepper.

**4** Arrange the remaining zucchini and onion in the dish on top of the passata, then season to taste with more garlic salt and pepper. Spoon on the remaining passata and spread evenly.

**5** Cover the dish with aluminum foil, then bake for 40–45 minutes or until the zucchini are tender. Garnish with sprigs of fresh thyme and serve hot.

# ROASTED MEDITERRANEAN VEGETABLES

—

**Mixed Mediterranean vegetables are oven-roasted in olive oil with garlic and rosemary in this really colorful and appetizing low-fat dish. The flavor is also wonderfully intense.**

### INGREDIENTS
*1 red bell pepper*
*1 yellow bell pepper*
*2 Spanish onions*
*2 large zucchini*
*1 large eggplant or 4 baby eggplant, trimmed*
*1 fennel bulb, thickly sliced*
*2 beefsteak tomatoes*
*8 large garlic cloves*
*1½ tablespoons olive oil*
*fresh rosemary sprigs*
*freshly ground black pepper*
*lemon wedges and black olives, to garnish (optional)*

**SERVES 6**

**3** Preheat the oven to 425°F. Spread the peppers, onions, zucchini, eggplant and fennel in a lightly greased shallow ovenproof dish or roasting pan or, if desired, arrange in rows to make a colorful design.

**4** Cut each tomato in half and place, cut-side up, with the vegetables.

**5** Tuck the garlic cloves in among the vegetables, then brush all the vegetables with the olive oil. Place some sprigs of rosemary among the vegetables and grind on some black pepper, particularly on the tomatoes.

**6** Roast for 20–25 minutes, turning the vegetables halfway through the cooking time. Serve from the dish or on a flat platter, garnished with lemon wedges. Sprinkle on a few black olives just before serving, if desired.

### NUTRITIONAL NOTES
*Per portion:*

| | |
|---|---|
| Energy | 72cals |
| Total fat | 4g |
| Saturated fat | 0.6g |
| Cholesterol | 0mg |
| Fiber | 2.3g |

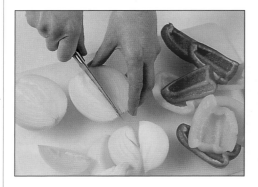

**1** Halve and seed the peppers, then cut them into large chunks. Peel the onions and cut into thick wedges.

**2** Cut the zucchini and eggplant into large chunks.

# BELL PEPPER GRATIN

Serve this simple but delicious Italian dish as a low-fat appetizer or snack with a small mixed green or arugula salad and some good crusty bread to mop up the juices from the peppers.

**3** Use a little of the olive oil to grease a small baking dish. Arrange the pepper strips in the dish.

**4** Sprinkle the garlic, capers, olives and chopped herbs on top. Season with salt and pepper. Sprinkle on the fresh white bread crumbs and drizzle with the remaining olive oil. Bake for about 20 minutes, until the bread crumbs have browned. Garnish with fresh herbs and serve immediately.

### INGREDIENTS

*2 red bell peppers*
*1 tablespoon extra virgin olive oil*
*1 garlic clove, finely chopped*
*1 teaspoon drained bottled capers*
*8 pitted black olives, roughly chopped*
*1 tablespoon chopped fresh oregano*
*1 tablespoon chopped fresh flat-leaf parsley*
*1/4 cup fresh white bread crumbs*
*salt and freshly ground black pepper*
*fresh herbs, to garnish*

### SERVES 4

**1** Preheat the oven to 400°F. Place the peppers on a broiler rack and cook under a hot broiler. Turn occasionally until they are blackened and blistered all over. Remove from heat and place in a plastic bag. Seal and let cool.

**2** When cool, peel the peppers. (Don't skin them under the tap, as the water would wash away some of the delicious smoky flavor.) Halve and remove and discard the seeds, then cut the flesh into large strips.

### NUTRITIONAL NOTES
*Per portion:*

| | |
|---|---|
| Energy | 72cals |
| Total fat | 3.4g |
| Saturated fat | 0.5g |
| Cholesterol | 0mg |
| Fiber | 0.9g |

# FENNEL GRATIN

**This is one of the best ways to eat fresh fennel as a snack or vegetable accompaniment.**

### INGREDIENTS
*2 fennel bulbs, about 1¹/2 pounds total*
*1¹/4 cups skim milk*
*1 tablespoon butter*
*1 tablespoon all-purpose flour*
*scant ¹/2 cup dry white bread crumbs*
*1¹/2 ounces Gruyère, grated*
*salt and freshly ground black pepper*

### SERVES 6

**1** Preheat the oven to 475°F. Discard the stems and root ends from the fennel. Slice the fennel into quarters and place in a large saucepan. Pour in the milk, bring to a boil, then simmer for 10–15 minutes, until tender.

**2** Grease a small baking dish. Remove the fennel pieces with a slotted spoon, reserving the milk. Arrange the fennel pieces in the dish.

**3** Melt the butter in a small saucepan and add the flour. Stir well, then gradually whisk in the reserved milk. Cook the sauce until thickened, stirring.

**4** Pour the sauce over the fennel pieces, sprinkle with the bread crumbs and Gruyère. Season and bake for about 20 minutes, until browned. Serve.

### VARIATION
Instead of the Gruyère, Parmesan, Pecorino, aged Cheddar or any other strong cheese would work perfectly.

### NUTRITIONAL NOTES
*Per portion:*

| | |
|---|---|
| Energy | 89cals |
| Total fat | 4.8g |
| Saturated fat | 2.9g |
| Cholesterol | 8.24mg |
| Fiber | 2.5g |

# ITALIAN SWEET-AND-SOUR ONIONS

**Onions are naturally sweet, and when they are cooked at a high temperature the sweetness intensifies. Serve these delicious onions with cooked lean meat or cooked fresh vegetables.**

### INGREDIENTS
*2 tablespoons butter*
*5 tablespoons sugar*
*¹/2 cup white wine vinegar*
*2 tablespoons balsamic vinegar*
*1¹/2 pounds small pickling onions, peeled*
*salt and freshly ground black pepper*

### SERVES 6

### COOK'S TIP
This recipe also looks delicious when made with either yellow or red onions, cut into slices. Cooking times vary, depending on the size of the pieces.

**1** Melt the butter in a large saucepan over low heat. Add the sugar and cook until it begins to dissolve, stirring constantly.

**2** Add the vinegars to the pan with the onions and heat gently. Season, cover and cook over medium heat for 20–25 minutes, stirring occasionally, until the onions are soft when pierced with a knife. Serve hot.

### NUTRITIONAL NOTES
*Per portion:*

| | |
|---|---|
| Energy | 106cals |
| Total fat | 3.6g |
| Saturated fat | 2.2g |
| Cholesterol | 9.5mg |
| Fiber | 1.3g |

# ZUCCHINI AND ASPARAGUS PARCELS

To appreciate the aroma, these Italian-style zucchini and asparagus-filled paper parcels should
be broken open at the table. They make a tasty and low-fat vegetable accompaniment.

### INGREDIENTS
*2 zucchini*
*1 leek*
*8 ounces young asparagus, trimmed*
*4 tarragon sprigs*
*4 whole garlic cloves, unpeeled*
*1 egg, beaten, to glaze*
*salt and freshly ground black pepper*

### SERVES 4

**1** Preheat the oven to 400°F. Using a
potato peeler, carefully slice the zucchini
lengthwise into thin strips.

**2** Cut the leek into very fine julienne
strips and cut the asparagus evenly into
2-inch lengths.

**3** Cut out four sheets of waxed paper
measuring 12 × 15 inches and fold each
one in half. Draw a large curve to make a
heart shape when unfolded. Cut along the
inside of the line and open out.

**4** Divide the zucchini, leek and
asparagus evenly between each paper
heart, positioning the filling on one side
of the fold line, then top each portion with
a sprig of tarragon and an unpeeled garlic
clove. Season to taste.

**5** Brush the edges of the paper lightly
with the beaten egg and fold over.

**6** Twist the edges of the paper together
so that each parcel is completely sealed.
Lay the parcels on a baking sheet.

**7** Bake in the preheated oven for
10 minutes. Serve the parcels immediately.

### NUTRITIONAL NOTES
*Per portion:*

| | |
|---|---|
| Energy | 110cals |
| Total fat | 2.29g |
| Saturated fat | 0.49g |
| Cholesterol | 48mg |
| Fiber | 6.73g |

# GREEN BEANS WITH TOMATOES

This is a real Italian summer favorite using the best ripe plum tomatoes and green beans. It is ideal served as an accompaniment or with fresh Italian bread for a tasty lunch or supper dish.

### INGREDIENTS

*1 tablespoon olive oil*

*1 large onion, thinly sliced*

*2 garlic cloves, finely chopped*

*6 large ripe plum tomatoes, peeled, deseeded and coarsely chopped*

*2/3 cup dry white wine*

*1 pound green beans, sliced in half lengthwise*

*16 pitted black olives*

*2 teaspoons lemon juice*

*salt and freshly ground black pepper*

*SERVES 4*

**1** Heat the oil in a large frying pan. Add the onion and garlic and cook for about 5 minutes, until the onion is softened but not brown, stirring occasionally.

**2** Add the chopped tomatoes, white wine, beans, olives and lemon juice and cook over low heat for another 20 minutes, stirring occasionally, until the sauce is thickened and the beans are tender. Season with salt and pepper to taste and serve immediately.

### COOK'S TIP

Green beans need little preparation—you simply trim them. When choosing, make sure that the beans snap easily—this is a sure sign of freshness.

### NUTRITIONAL NOTES

*Per portion:*

| | |
|---|---|
| Energy | 69cals |
| Total fat | 2.7g |
| Saturated fat | 0.4g |
| Cholesterol | 0mg |
| Fiber | 2.4g |

### VARIATION

Any leftovers of this dish are delicious eaten cold, as a salad, with plenty of crusty Italian bread to mop up the juices.

# CAPONATA

This dish is a quintessential part of Sicilian antipasti and is a rich, spicy mixture of eggplant, tomatoes, capers and celery. Serve with warm crusty bread and olives.

**3** Cover the surface of the vegetables with a circle of waxed paper and simmer for 8–10 minutes. Remove and discard the paper.

**4** Add the capers and olives to the pan, then season to taste with salt and combine.

**5** Spoon the caponata into a bowl, garnish with chopped fresh parsley and serve at room temperature.

### INGREDIENTS

*4 teaspoons olive oil*
*1 large onion, sliced*
*2 celery stalks, sliced*
*1 pound eggplant, diced*
*5 ripe tomatoes, chopped*
*1 garlic clove, crushed*
*3 tablespoons red wine vinegar*
*1 tablespoon sugar*
*2 tablespoons capers*
*12 olives*
*pinch of salt*
*1/4 cup chopped fresh parsley, to garnish*

SERVES 4

**1** Heat half the oil in a large heavy saucepan. Add the onion and celery and cook over low heat for 3–4 minutes to soften, stirring occasionally.

**2** Add the remainder of the oil with the eggplant and stir to mix. Cook until the eggplant begins to color, stirring occasionally, then stir in the tomatoes, garlic, vinegar and sugar.

### NUTRITIONAL NOTES
*Per portion:*

| | |
|---|---|
| Energy | 81cals |
| Total fat | 4.7g |
| Saturated fat | 0.7g |
| Cholesterol | 0mg |
| Fiber | 2.9g |

# KOHLRABI STUFFED WITH BELL PEPPERS

The slightly sharp flavor of the peppers is an excellent foil to the more earthy flavor of the kohlrabi in this delicious low-fat Italian-style vegetable dish.

### INGREDIENTS

*4 small kohlrabies, 6–8 ounces each*
*about 1²/₃ cups hot vegetable stock*
*1 tablespoon sunflower oil*
*1 onion, chopped*
*1 small red bell pepper, deseeded and sliced*
*1 small green bell pepper, deseeded and sliced*
*salt and freshly ground black pepper*
*fresh flat-leaf parsley, to garnish*
*(optional)*

### SERVES 4

**1** Preheat the oven to 350°F. Trim the kohlrabies and arrange in an ovenproof dish.

**2** Pour in enough stock to come about halfway up the vegetables. Cover and braise for about 30 minutes, until tender. Transfer to a plate and let cool, reserving the stock.

**3** Heat the oil in a frying pan and sauté the onion over low heat for 3–4 minutes, stirring occasionally. Add the peppers and cook for another 2–3 minutes, until the onion is lightly browned, stirring the vegetables occasionally.

**4** Add the reserved vegetable stock and a little seasoning and let simmer, uncovered, over medium heat, until the stock has almost all evaporated, stirring occasionally.

**5** Scoop out the insides of the kohlrabies and chop roughly. Stir into the onion and pepper mixture and adjust the seasoning to taste. Arrange the kohlrabi shells in a shallow ovenproof dish.

**6** Spoon the pepper filling into the kohlrabi shells. Place in the oven for 5–10 minutes to heat through and then serve, garnished with a sprig of flat-leaf parsley, if desired.

### NUTRITIONAL NOTES

*Per portion:*

| | |
|---|---|
| Energy | 112cals |
| Total fat | 4.63g |
| Saturated fat | 0.55g |
| Cholesterol | 0mg |
| Fiber | 5.8g |

# ZUCCHINI WITH ONION AND GARLIC

Use good-quality olive oil and sunflower oil for this dish. The olive oil gives the dish a delicious fragrance without overpowering the zucchini, making this an ideal vegetable side dish.

### INGREDIENTS

*2 teaspoons olive oil*
*2 teaspoons sunflower oil*
*1 large onion, chopped*
*1 garlic clove, crushed*
*4–5 zucchini, cut into*
*1/2-inch slices*
*2/3 cup vegetable stock*
*1/2 teaspoon chopped fresh oregano*
*salt and freshly ground black pepper*
*chopped fresh parsley,*
*to garnish*

### SERVES 4

**1** Heat the olive and sunflower oils in a large frying pan and sauté the onion with the garlic over medium heat for 5–6 minutes, stirring occasionally, until the onion has softened and is beginning to brown.

**2** Add the sliced zucchini and fry for about 4 minutes, until they begin to be flecked with brown, stirring frequently.

**3** Stir in the stock, oregano and seasoning and simmer gently for 8–10 minutes or until the liquid has almost evaporated, stirring occasionally.

**4** Spoon the zucchini into a warmed serving dish, sprinkle with chopped parsley and serve.

### NUTRITIONAL NOTES
*Per portion:*

| | |
|---|---|
| Energy | 47cals |
| Total fat | 4.1g |
| Saturated fat | 0.5g |
| Cholesterol | 0mg |
| Fiber | 0.5g |

# ZUCCHINI IN CITRUS SAUCE

These tender baby zucchini served in a virtually fat-free citrus sauce make this a tasty and low-fat accompaniment to grilled or broiled fish fillets.

### INGREDIENTS
*12 ounces baby zucchini*
*4 scallions, thinly sliced*
*1-inch piece fresh ginger root, peeled*
*and grated*
*2 tablespoons white wine vinegar*
*1 tablespoon light soy sauce*
*1 teaspoon light brown sugar*
*3 tablespoons vegetable stock*
*finely grated zest and juice of 1/2 lemon*
*and 1/2 orange*
*1 teaspoon cornstarch*

### SERVES 4

**1** Place the zucchini in a saucepan of lightly salted boiling water and cook for 3–4 minutes or until just tender. Drain well and return to the pan. Set aside.

**2** Meanwhile, put all the remaining ingredients, except the cornstarch, into a saucepan and bring to a boil, stirring occasionally. Simmer for 3 minutes.

**3** Blend the cornstarch with 2 teaspoons cold water in a small bowl and stir into the sauce. Bring the sauce to a boil, stirring continuously, until the sauce has thickened.

**4** Pour the sauce over the zucchini in the pan and heat gently, shaking the pan to coat them evenly. Transfer to a warmed serving dish and serve.

### COOK'S TIP
If baby zucchini are unavailable, you can use larger ones, but they should be cooked whole so that they don't absorb too much water. After cooking, halve them lengthwise and cut them into 4-inch lengths.

### NUTRITIONAL NOTES
*Per portion:*

| | |
|---|---|
| Energy | 33cals |
| Total fat | 2.18g |
| Saturated fat | 0.42g |
| Cholesterol | 0.09mg |
| Fiber | 0.92g |

# POTATO GNOCCHI

Gnocchi are little Italian dumplings made either with mashed potatoes and flour, as here, or with semolina. They should be light in texture, and must not be overworked while being made.

### INGREDIENTS

*2¼ pounds waxy potatoes, scrubbed*
*2–2½ cups all-purpose flour*
*1 egg*
*pinch of grated nutmeg*
*2 tablespoons butter*
*salt*
*a little grated fresh Parmesan cheese,*
*to serve (optional)*

### SERVES 6

**1** Place the unpeeled potatoes in a large saucepan of salted water. Bring to a boil and cook until the potatoes are tender but not falling apart. Drain. Peel as soon as possible, while the potatoes are still hot.

**2** On a work surface, spread out a layer of flour. Mash the hot potatoes with a food mill, dropping them onto the flour. Sprinkle with about half of the remaining flour. Mix the flour very lightly into the potatoes.

## NUTRITIONAL NOTES
*Per portion:*

| | |
|---|---|
| Energy | 256cals |
| Total fat | 4.6g |
| Saturated fat | 2.4g |
| Cholesterol | 37.8mg |
| Fiber | 2.6g |

**3** Break the egg into the mixture, add the nutmeg and knead lightly, drawing in more flour as necessary. When the dough is light to the touch and no longer moist or sticky, it is ready to be rolled. Do not overwork or the gnocchi will be heavy.

**4** Divide the dough into four parts. On a lightly floured board, form each part into a roll about ¾ inches in diameter, taking care not to over handle the dough. Cut the rolls crosswise into pieces about ¾ inches long.

**5** Hold an ordinary table fork with long tines sideways, leaning on the board. One by one, press and roll the gnocchi lightly along the tines of the fork toward the points, making ridges on one side and a depression from your thumb on the other.

**6** Bring a large saucepan of water to a fast boil. Add salt and drop in about half the gnocchi.

**7** When they rise to the surface, after 3–4 minutes, the gnocchi are done. Scoop them out, let drain and place in a warmed serving bowl. Dot with butter. Keep warm while the remaining gnocchi are boiling.

**8** As soon as they are cooked, toss the drained gnocchi with the butter, sprinkle with a little grated Parmesan, if using, and serve.

### VARIATION

Green gnocchi are made in exactly the same way as potato gnocchi, with the addition of fresh or frozen spinach. Use 1½ pounds fresh spinach, or 14 ounces frozen spinach. Mix with the potato and the flour in Step 2. Almost any pasta sauce is suitable for serving with gnocchi; they are particularly good with Gorgonzola sauce, or simply drizzled with a little olive oil. Gnocchi can also be served in clear soup.

# MEAT AND POULTRY PASTA DISHES

*Freshly cooked* PASTA *topped or tossed with a tasty* FAT-FREE *or low-fat sauce made with* MEAT *or poultry and served with crusty Italian* BREAD *or a salad makes for an appealing meal for all to* ENJOY. *Choose from a* VARIETY *of fat-free and low-fat Italian recipes all packed full of* FLAVOR, *including low-free versions of classic dishes such as Spaghetti* BOLOGNESE, *Lasagne and Spaghetti alla* CARBONARA.

# SPAGHETTI BOLOGNESE

A very popular Italian dish, this tasty spaghetti Bolognese is full of flavor and low in fat too.

### INGREDIENTS

*1 onion, chopped*
*2–3 garlic cloves, crushed*
*1¹/4 cups beef or chicken stock*
*1 pound extra-lean ground turkey or beef*
*2 14-ounce cans chopped tomatoes*
*1 teaspoon dried basil*
*1 teaspoon dried oregano*
*¹/4 cup tomato paste*
*1 pound button mushrooms,*
*quartered and sliced*
*²/3 cup red wine*
*1 pound dried spaghetti*
*salt and freshly ground black pepper*

### SERVES 8

**1** Put the chopped onion and garlic into a nonstick saucepan with half of the stock. Bring to a boil and cook for 5 minutes, until the onion is tender and the stock has reduced completely, stirring occasionally.

### NUTRITIONAL NOTES
*Per portion:*

| | |
|---|---|
| Energy | 321cals |
| Total fat | 4.1g |
| Saturated fat | 1.3g |
| Cholesterol | 33mg |
| Fiber | 2.7g |

**2** Add the turkey or beef and cook for 5 minutes, breaking up the meat with a fork. Add the tomatoes, herbs and tomato paste, bring to a boil, then cover, reduce the heat and simmer for 1 hour, stirring occasionally.

### COOK'S TIP
Sautéing vegetables in stock rather than oil is an easy way of cutting down on calories and fat. Choose fat-free stock to reduce them even more.

**3** Meanwhile, cook the mushrooms with the wine for 5 minutes in a nonstick saucepan or until the wine has evaporated, stirring occasionally. Add the mushrooms to the meat with salt and pepper to taste and stir to mix.

**4** Meanwhile, cook the pasta in a large saucepan of boiling salted water for 8–12 minutes, until tender or *al dente*. Drain thoroughly. Serve the cooked spaghetti topped with the meat sauce.

# PIPE RIGATE WITH SPICY MEAT SAUCE

Fresh chili-flavored cooked ground meat combines well with pasta to create
a flavorful and filling low-fat Italian dish.

### INGREDIENTS

*1 pound extra-lean ground beef or turkey*
*1 onion, finely chopped*
*2–3 garlic cloves, crushed*
*1–2 fresh red chiles,*
*deseeded and finely chopped*
*14-ounce can chopped tomatoes*
*3 tablespoons tomato paste*
*1 teaspoon dried mixed herbs*
*4 cups dried pipe rigate*
*14-ounce can red kidney beans, drained*
*salt and freshly ground black pepper*

### SERVES 6

**1** Cook the ground beef or turkey in a nonstick saucepan, breaking up any large pieces with a wooden spoon, until browned all over.

**2** Stir in the onion, garlic and chile, cover the pan with a lid and cook gently for 5 minutes.

### NUTRITIONAL NOTES
#### Per portion:

| | |
|---|---|
| Energy | 246cals |
| Total fat | 1.8g |
| Saturated fat | 0.4g |
| Cholesterol | 38.5mg |
| Fiber | 6g |

**3** Stir in the tomatoes, tomato paste, herbs, 1³/₄ cups water and seasoning. Bring to a boil, then reduce the heat and simmer for 1¹/₂ hours, stirring occasionally. Remove the pan from heat and let cool slightly.

**4** Meanwhile, cook the pasta in a large saucepan of boiling, salted water until tender or *al dente*. Drain thoroughly. Meanwhile, skim off and discard any fat from the surface of the meat. Add the red kidney beans and cook for 5–10 minutes, until piping hot, stirring occasionally. Pour the sauce over the cooked pasta, and serve.

# SPAGHETTI WITH MEATBALLS

—

**Italian-style meatballs simmered in a sweet and spicy tomato sauce are truly delicious served with spaghetti, and make an ideal low-fat dish for all the family to enjoy.**

**4** Place the meatballs on a tray and chill in the refrigerator for about 30 minutes.

**5** Heat the oil in a large nonstick frying pan. Cook the meatballs in batches until browned all over. Set aside.

**6** Pour the passata and stock into a large saucepan. Heat gently, then add the remaining chiles and the sugar, with salt and pepper to taste. Add the meatballs to the passata mixture, then bring to a boil. Reduce the heat, cover and simmer for 20 minutes, stirring occasionally.

**7** Cook the pasta in a large saucepan of boiling salted water, according to the package instructions, until it is tender or *al dente*. Drain well and put it in a warmed large bowl. Pour the sauce onto the pasta and toss gently to mix. Sprinkle with the remaining parsley and serve with grated Parmesan passed separately.

## INGREDIENTS

*12 ounces extra-lean ground beef*
*1 egg*
*1/4 cup roughly chopped fresh flat-leaf parsley*
*1/2 teaspoon crushed dried red chiles*
*1 thick slice of white bread, crusts removed*
*2 tablespoons skim milk*
*1 tablespoon olive oil*
*1 1/4 cups passata*
*1 2/3 cups vegetable stock*
*1 teaspoon sugar*
*1 pound dried spaghetti*
*salt and freshly ground black pepper*
*1 1/2 ounces grated fresh Parmesan cheese, to serve*

### SERVES 8

**1** Put the ground beef in a large bowl. Add the egg, half the parsley and half the crushed chiles. Season with plenty of salt and pepper. Mix well.

**2** Tear the bread into small pieces and place in a small bowl. Moisten with the milk. Let soak for a few minutes, then squeeze out and discard the excess milk and crumble the bread onto the meat mixture. Combine everything with a wooden spoon, then use your hands to squeeze and knead the mixture so that it becomes smooth and sticky.

**3** Wash your hands, rinse them under the cold tap, then pick up small pieces of the mixture and roll them between your palms to make 40–60 small balls.

### NUTRITIONAL NOTES
*Per portion:*

| | |
|---|---|
| Energy | 148cals |
| Total fat | 5.0g |
| Saturated fat | 1.9g |
| Cholesterol | 44.8mg |
| Fiber | 0.9g |

# SPAGHETTI WITH SPICY GROUND BEEF SAUCE

This is a delicious spicy version of spaghetti Bolognese, which is not an authentic Italian dish.
It was "invented" by Italian émigrés in America in the 1960s in response to popular demand.

### INGREDIENTS

*2 teaspoons olive oil*
*1 onion, finely chopped*
*1 garlic clove, crushed*
*1 teaspoon dried mixed herbs*
*1/4 teaspoon cayenne pepper*
*1 pound extra-lean ground beef*
*14-ounce can chopped*
  *Italian plum tomatoes*
*3 tablespoons ketchup*
*1 tablespoon sun-dried tomato paste*
*1 teaspoon Worcestershire sauce*
*1 teaspoon dried oregano*
*scant 2 cups beef or vegetable stock*
*3 tablespoons red wine*
*1 pound dried spaghetti*
*salt and freshly ground black pepper*
*1 ounce grated fresh Parmesan cheese,*
  *to serve (optional)*

### SERVES 6

**2** Stir in the tomatoes, ketchup, sun-dried tomato paste, Worcestershire sauce, oregano and plenty of ground black pepper. Pour in the stock and red wine and bring to a boil, stirring. Cover the pan, reduce the heat and let the sauce simmer for 30 minutes, stirring occasionally.

**3** Meanwhile, cook the pasta in a large saucepan of boiling salted water, according to the package instructions, until tender or *al dente*. Drain, and divide among warmed bowls. Taste the meat sauce and add a little salt if necessary, then spoon it on top of the pasta and sprinkle with a little grated Parmesan, if using. Serve immediately.

### NUTRITIONAL NOTES
*Per portion:*

| | |
|---|---|
| Energy | 207cals |
| Total fat | 4.9g |
| Saturated fat | 1.5g |
| Cholesterol | 39.1mg |
| Fiber | 1.8g |

**1** Heat the oil in a medium saucepan, add the onion and garlic and cook over low heat, stirring frequently, for about 5 minutes, until softened. Stir in the mixed herbs and cayenne and cook for another 2–3 minutes. Add the ground beef and cook gently for about 5 minutes, stirring frequently and breaking up any lumps in the meat with a wooden spoon.

# LASAGNE

This is a delicious low-fat version of the classic Italian lasagne, ideal served with a mixed salad and crusty bread for an appetizing supper with friends.

### INGREDIENTS

*1 large onion, chopped*
*2 garlic cloves, crushed*
*1¼ pounds extra-lean ground beef*
*or turkey*
*1 pound passata*
*1 teaspoon dried mixed herbs*
*8 ounces frozen spinach, defrosted*
*7 ounces lasagne verdi*
*7 ounces low-fat cottage cheese*
*mixed salad, to serve*

### FOR THE SAUCE

*1 ounce low-fat margarine*
*1 ounce all-purpose flour*
*1¼ cups skim milk*
*¼ teaspoon ground nutmeg*
*1 ounce grated fresh Parmesan cheese*
*salt and freshly ground black pepper*

### SERVES 8

**1** Put the onion, garlic and ground meat in a nonstick saucepan. Cook quickly for 5 minutes, stirring with a wooden spoon to separate the pieces, until the meat is lightly browned all over.

### COOK'S TIP

Make sure you use the type of lasagne that does not require any pre-cooking for this recipe.

**2** Add the passata, herbs and seasoning and stir to mix. Bring to a boil, cover, then reduce the heat and simmer for about 30 minutes, stirring occasionally.

**3** Make the sauce: put all the sauce ingredients, except the Parmesan cheese, into a saucepan. Cook until the sauce thickens, whisking continuously until bubbling and smooth. Turn the heat off. Adjust the seasoning to taste, add the Parmesan cheese to the sauce and stir to mix.

### NUTRITIONAL NOTES

*Per portion:*

| | |
|---|---|
| Energy | 244cals |
| Total fat | 4.8g |
| Saturated fat | 1.9g |
| Cholesterol | 37.9mg |
| Fiber | 2g |

**4** Preheat the oven to 375°F. Lay the spinach leaves out on sheets of absorbent paper towels and pat them until they are dry.

**5** Layer the meat mixture, lasagne, cottage cheese and spinach in an 8-cup ovenproof dish, starting and ending with a layer of meat.

**6** Spoon the sauce on top to cover the meat completely and bake for 40–50 minutes or until bubbling. Serve with a mixed salad.

# TAGLIATELLE WITH MEAT SAUCE

—

**This recipe is an authentic meat sauce—ragù—from the city of Bologna in Emilia-Romagna. It is quite rich and very delicious, and is always served with tagliatelle, never with spaghetti.**

### INGREDIENTS
*1 pound dried tagliatelle*
*salt and freshly ground black pepper*
*grated fresh Parmesan cheese,*
*to serve (optional)*

### FOR THE BOLOGNESE MEAT SAUCE
*1 onion*
*2 carrots*
*2 celery stalks*
*2 garlic cloves*
*1 tablespoon olive oil*
*4 ounces lean bacon, diced*
*9 ounces extra-lean ground beef*
*9 ounces extra-lean ground pork*
*1/2 cup dry white wine*
*2 14-ounce cans crushed*
*Italian plum tomatoes*
*2–3 cups beef stock*

### SERVES 8

**1** Make the meat sauce. Chop all the fresh vegetables finely. Heat the oil in a large frying pan or saucepan. Add the chopped vegetables and the bacon and cook over medium heat, stirring frequently, for 10 minutes or until the vegetables have softened.

**2** Add the ground beef and pork, reduce the heat and cook gently for 10 minutes, stirring frequently and breaking up any lumps in the meat with a wooden spoon.

**3** Stir in salt and pepper to taste, then add the wine and stir again. Simmer for about 5 minutes or until reduced.

**4** Add the tomatoes and 1 cup of the stock and bring to a boil. Stir the sauce well, then reduce the heat. Half cover the pan with a lid and let simmer very gently for 2 hours. Stir occasionally and add more stock as it becomes absorbed.

**5** Simmer the sauce, without a lid, for another 30 minutes, stirring frequently. Meanwhile, cook the pasta in a large saucepan of boiling salted water, according to the package instructions, until tender or *al dente*. Taste the sauce and adjust the seasoning. Drain the cooked pasta and transfer it to a warmed bowl. Pour the meat sauce onto the pasta and toss well. Serve immediately, sprinkled with grated Parmesan, if using.

### NUTRITIONAL NOTES
*Per portion:*

| | |
|---|---|
| Energy | 185cals |
| Total fat | 5g |
| Saturated fat | 1.7g |
| Cholesterol | 36.3mg |
| Fiber | 1.8g |

# LAMB AND SWEET BELL PEPPER SAUCE

This simple sauce is a specialty of the Abruzzo-Molise region of Italy, east of Rome, where it is traditionally served with *maccheroni alla chitarra*—square-shaped long macaroni.

**2** Sprinkle in the garlic and add the bay leaves, then pour in the wine and let it bubble until reduced.

### INGREDIENTS

*1 tablespoon olive oil*
*9 ounces boneless lean lamb fillet, diced quite small*
*2 garlic cloves, finely chopped*
*2 bay leaves, torn*
*1 cup dry white wine*
*4 ripe Italian plum tomatoes, skinned and chopped*
*2 large red bell peppers, deseeded and diced*
*1 pound dried spaghetti*
*salt and freshly ground black pepper*

### SERVES 6

**1** Heat the oil in a medium frying pan or saucepan, add the lamb and a little salt and pepper. Cook over medium to high heat for about 10 minutes, stirring frequently, until browned all over.

**3** Add the tomatoes and peppers and stir to mix. Season again. Cover with the lid, bring to a boil, then reduce the heat and simmer gently for 45–55 minutes or until the lamb is very tender. Stir occasionally during cooking and add a little water if the sauce becomes too dry. Meanwhile, cook the pasta in a large saucepan of boiling salted water, according to the package instructions, until tender or *al dente*. Drain well. Remove and discard the bay leaves from the lamb sauce before serving it with the cooked pasta.

### NUTRITIONAL NOTES

*Per portion:*

| | |
|---|---|
| Energy | 179cals |
| Total fat | 5g |
| Saturated fat | 1.8g |
| Cholesterol | 28mg |
| Fiber | 1.4g |

### COOK'S TIP

You can make your own fresh *maccheroni alla chitarra* or buy the dried pasta at an Italian specialty store. Alternatively, this sauce is just as good served with ordinary spaghetti or long or short macaroni.

### VARIATION

The peppers don't have to be red. Use yellow, orange or green if you prefer, either one color or a mixture.

# TAGLIOLINI WITH MEATY TOMATO SAUCE

Serve cooked tagliolini or tagliarini with this delicious meat-flavored tomato sauce for an
appetizing main course or supper.

### INGREDIENTS

*1 small onion*
*1 small carrot*
*2 celery stalks*
*2 garlic cloves*
*1 small handful of fresh flat-leaf parsley*
*2 ounces lean ham or bacon, finely chopped*
*4–6 tablespoons dry white wine,*
*or more to taste*
*1 1/4 pounds ripe Italian plum*
*tomatoes, chopped*
*12 ounces dried tagliolini or tagliarini*
*salt and freshly ground black pepper*
*fresh flat-leaf parsley sprigs, to garnish*

### SERVES 4

**1** Chop the onion, carrot and celery finely
in a food processor. Add the garlic cloves
and parsley and process until finely
chopped. Alternatively, chop everything
by hand.

**2** Put the chopped vegetable mixture in a
medium shallow saucepan or skillet with
the ham or bacon and cook, stirring, over
low heat, for about 5 minutes. Add the
wine, with salt and pepper to taste, and
simmer for 5 minutes, then stir in the
tomatoes. Bring to a boil, reduce the heat
and simmer for 40 minutes, stirring
occasionally and adding a little hot water
if the sauce seems too dry.

**3** Have ready a large sieve placed over a
large bowl. Carefully pour in the sauce
and press it through the sieve with the
back of a metal spoon, leaving behind the
tomato skins and any tough pieces of
vegetable that won't go through. Discard
the contents of the sieve.

**4** Return the sauce to the rinsed-out
saucepan and heat it through, adding a
little more wine or hot water if it is too
thick. Taste the sauce and adjust the
seasoning. Meanwhile, cook the pasta in
a large saucepan of boiling salted water,
according to the package instructions,
until tender or *al dente*. Drain thoroughly.
Toss the cooked pasta with the tomato
sauce and serve immediately, garnished
with fresh parsley sprigs.

### NUTRITIONAL NOTES
*Per portion:*

| | |
|---|---|
| Energy | 187cals |
| Total fat | 3.3g |
| Saturated fat | 1g |
| Cholesterol | 8.8mg |
| Fiber | 2.7g |

# RIGATONI WITH PORK

This is an excellent and very tasty, low-fat meat sauce made using lean ground pork rather than the more usual ground beef. You could serve it with tagliatelle or spaghetti instead of rigatoni.

### INGREDIENTS
*1 small onion*
*1/2 carrot*
*1/2 celery stalk*
*2 garlic cloves*
*1 tablespoon olive oil*
*5 ounces extra-lean ground pork*
*1/4 cup dry white wine*
*14-ounce can chopped Italian plum tomatoes*
*a few fresh basil leaves, plus extra basil leaves, to garnish*
*3 1/2 cups dried rigatoni*
*salt and freshly ground black pepper*
*freshly shaved Parmesan cheese, to serve (optional)*

### SERVES 4

**1** Chop the fresh vegetables and garlic finely, in a food processor or by hand. Heat the oil in a large frying pan or saucepan until just sizzling, add the vegetables and cook over medium heat, stirring frequently, for 3–4 minutes.

### VARIATION
To give the sauce a more intense flavor, soak 1/2 ounce dried porcini mushrooms in 3/4 cup warm water for 15–20 minutes, then drain, chop and add with the meat.

**2** Add the ground pork and cook gently for 2–3 minutes, breaking up any lumps in the meat with a wooden spoon.

**3** Reduce the heat and cook for another 2–3 minutes, stirring frequently, then stir in the wine. Mix in the tomatoes, whole basil leaves, salt to taste and plenty of pepper. Bring to a boil, then reduce the heat, cover and simmer for 40 minutes, stirring occasionally.

**4** Cook the pasta in a large saucepan of boiling salted water, according to the package instructions, until tender or *al dente*. Just before draining it, add a ladleful or two of the cooking water to the sauce. Stir well, then taste the sauce and adjust the seasoning.

**5** Drain the pasta, add it to the pan of sauce and toss well. Serve immediately, sprinkled with the basil leaves and shaved Parmesan, if using.

### NUTRITIONAL NOTES
*Per portion:*

| | |
|---|---|
| Energy | 70cals |
| Total fat | 2.5g |
| Saturated fat | 0.4g |
| Cholesterol | 0mg |
| Fiber | 2.4g |

# TAGLIATELLE WITH MILANESE SAUCE

Tagliatelle is served with a tasty, low-fat version of the classic Milanese sauce to create this flavorful dish, ideal for a family meal.

### INGREDIENTS

*1 onion, finely chopped*
*1 celery stalk, finely chopped*
*1 red bell pepper, deseeded*
*and diced*
*1–2 garlic cloves, crushed*
*2/3 cup vegetable*
*or chicken stock*
*14-ounce can tomatoes*
*1 tablespoon tomato paste*
*2 teaspoons sugar*
*1 teaspoon dried*
*mixed herbs*
*12 ounces tagliatelle*
*4 ounces button or small cap*
*mushrooms, sliced*
*1/4 cup dry white wine*
*4 ounces lean cooked ham,*
*coarsely diced*
*salt and freshly ground black pepper*
*1 tablespoon chopped fresh parsley,*
*to garnish*

### SERVES 4

**1** Put the onion, celery, red pepper and garlic into a saucepan.

**2** Add the stock, bring to a boil and cook for 5 minutes or until tender, stirring occasionally.

**3** Add the tomatoes, tomato paste, sugar and dried herbs. Season with salt and pepper.

**4** Bring to a boil, then reduce the heat and simmer for 30 minutes, stirring occasionally, until the sauce is thick.

**5** Cook the pasta in a large saucepan of boiling salted water, according to the package instructions, until tender or *al dente*. Drain thoroughly.

**6** Meanwhile, put the mushrooms into a small saucepan with the white wine, cover and cook for 3–4 minutes, until the mushrooms are tender and all the wine has been absorbed, stirring occasionally.

**7** Stir the mushrooms and ham into the tomato sauce and reheat gently over low heat until piping hot.

**8** Transfer the pasta to a warmed serving dish and spoon the sauce on top. Garnish with chopped parsley and serve.

### NUTRITIONAL NOTES
*Per portion:*

| | |
|---|---|
| Energy | 405cals |
| Total fat | 3.5g |
| Saturated fat | 0.8g |
| Cholesterol | 17mg |
| Fiber | 4.5g |

### COOK'S TIP
To reduce the calorie and fat content even more, omit the ham and use corn kernels or cooked broccoli florets instead.

# SPAGHETTI ALLA CARBONARA

—

This is a low-fat variation of the classic Italian dish, using lean bacon and low-fat cream cheese.
Serve with a few Parmesan cheese shavings.

**2** Add the wine and boil rapidly until reduced by half. Whisk in the cheese and season to taste with salt and pepper.

**3** Meanwhile, cook the spaghetti in a large saucepan of boiling, salted water for 10–12 minutes, until tender or *al dente*. Drain thoroughly.

**4** Return the cooked spaghetti to the pan with the sauce and parsley, toss well and serve immediately topped with a few thin shavings of Parmesan cheese.

### INGREDIENTS

*5 ounces lean bacon*
*1 onion, chopped*
*1–2 garlic cloves, crushed*
*2/3 cup chicken stock*
*2/3 cup dry white wine*
*7 ounces low-fat cream cheese*
*1 pound chili and garlic-flavored dried spaghetti*
*2 tablespoons chopped fresh parsley*
*salt and freshly ground black pepper*
*1/2 ounce shaved fresh Parmesan cheese, to serve*

**SERVES 4**

**1** Cut the bacon into ½-inch strips. Fry quickly in a nonstick frying pan for 2–3 minutes, stirring. Add the onion, garlic and stock to the pan. Bring to a boil, cover, then reduce the heat and simmer for about 5 minutes, until tender.

### NUTRITIONAL NOTES
*Per portion:*

| | |
|---|---|
| Energy | 428cals |
| Total fat | 4.6g |
| Saturated fat | 1.6g |
| Cholesterol | 9.96mg |
| Fiber | 3g |

# PAPPARDELLE WITH RABBIT SAUCE

—

**This delicious low-fat pasta dish comes from the north of Italy, where rabbit sauces for pasta are very popular. Serve with crusty fresh bread and a mixed green salad for a filling meal.**

### INGREDIENTS

*1/4 cup dried porcini mushrooms*
*3/4 cup warm water*
*1 small onion*
*1/2 carrot*
*1/2 celery stalk*
*2 bay leaves*
*1 tablespoon olive oil*
*1 1/2 ounces lean bacon, chopped*
*1 tablespoon roughly chopped fresh*
*flat-leaf parsley, plus extra to garnish*
*12 ounces boneless lean rabbit meat*
*6 tablespoons dry white wine*
*7-ounce can chopped Italian plum*
*tomatoes or scant 1 cup passata*
*1 pound dried pappardelle*
*salt and freshly ground black pepper*

### SERVES 6

**1** Put the dried mushrooms in a bowl, pour on the warm water and let soak for 15–20 minutes. Finely chop the fresh vegetables. Make a tear in each bay leaf, so they release their flavor.

**2** Heat the oil in a frying pan or medium saucepan. Add the vegetables, bacon and parsley and cook for about 5 minutes, stirring occasionally.

**3** Add the pieces of rabbit and fry on both sides for 3–4 minutes, stirring frequently. Pour in the wine and let it bubble and reduce for a few minutes, then add the tomatoes or passata. Drain the mushrooms and pour the soaking liquid into the pan. Chop the mushrooms and add them to the pan with the bay leaves and salt and pepper to taste. Stir well, cover, bring to a boil, then reduce the heat and simmer for 35–40 minutes, until the rabbit is tender, stirring occasionally.

**4** Remove from heat and lift out the rabbit with a slotted spoon. Cut into bite-size chunks and stir into the sauce. Remove the bay leaves. Add more salt and pepper, if needed. Cook the pasta in a large saucepan of boiling salted water, according to the package instructions, until tender or *al dente*. Meanwhile, reheat the sauce until piping hot. Drain the pasta and toss with the sauce in a warmed bowl. Serve immediately, sprinkled with parsley.

### NUTRITIONAL NOTES
*Per portion:*

| | |
|---|---|
| Energy | 166cals |
| Total fat | 4.7g |
| Saturated fat | 1.4g |
| Cholesterol | 33.9mg |
| Fiber | 1.4g |

# FISH AND SHELLFISH PASTA DISHES

*The wide variety of different SHAPES, sizes and FLAVORS of fresh and dried pasta creates a wonderful basis for many delicious and NUTRITIOUS fat-free and low-fat Italian fish and shellfish PASTA dishes. We include a tempting selection of no-fuss recipes, using a variety of FISH and SHELLFISH, to please every palate. Choose from Farfalle with TUNA, Smoked Trout Cannelloni, Tagliatelle with Scallops and Vermicelli with CLAM Sauce.*

# FUSILLI WITH SMOKED TROUT

—

Fusilli pasta is served with a delicious smoked trout and vegetable sauce in this flavorful lunch
or supper dish. Smoked salmon may be used instead of the trout, for a tasty change.

## INGREDIENTS

*2 carrots, cut into julienne sticks*
*1 leek, cut into julienne sticks*
*2 celery stalks, cut into*
*julienne sticks*
*2/3 cup vegetable or fish stock*
*8 ounces smoked trout fillets,*
*skinned and cut into strips*
*7 ounces low-fat cream cheese*
*2/3 cup medium sweet*
*white wine or fish stock*
*1 tablespoon chopped fresh dill or fennel*
*8 ounces dried fusilli lunghi*
*salt and freshly ground black pepper*
*fresh dill sprigs, to garnish*

**SERVES 6**

**1** Put the carrots, leek and celery into a
saucepan with the vegetable or fish stock.
Bring to a boil and cook quickly for
4–5 minutes, until the vegetables are
tender and most of the stock has
evaporated, stirring occasionally. Turn
the heat off and stir in the smoked trout.
Set aside.

**2** To make the sauce, put the cream
cheese and wine or fish stock into a
saucepan and cook, whisking until
smooth. Season. Stir in the dill or fennel.

**3** Meanwhile, cook the pasta in a large
saucepan of boiling salted water
according to the instructions, until tender
or *al dente*. Drain thoroughly. Return to
the pan, add the sauce, toss and transfer
to a serving bowl. Top with the vegetables
and trout. Serve garnished with dill sprigs.

## NUTRITIONAL NOTES

*Per portion:*

| | |
|---|---|
| Energy | 234cals |
| Total fat | 3.7g |
| Saturated fat | 1.3g |
| Cholesterol | 40mg |
| Fiber | 1.7g |

# PASTA WITH TOMATO AND TUNA

Pasta shells are topped with a tasty tuna and tomato sauce in this delicious, low-fat Italian-style pasta dish.

**3** Meanwhile, cook the pasta in a large saucepan of boiling, salted water according to the package instructions, until tender or *al dente*. Drain thoroughly and transfer to a warm serving dish.

**4** Flake the tuna into large chunks and add to the sauce with the capers. Cook gently for 1–2 minutes, stirring, then pour onto the pasta, toss gently and serve immediately.

### INGREDIENTS

*1 onion, finely chopped*
*1 celery stalk, finely chopped*
*1 red bell pepper, deseeded and diced*
*1 garlic clove, crushed*
*2/3 cup chicken stock*
*14-ounce can chopped tomatoes*
*1 tablespoon tomato paste*
*2 teaspoons sugar*
*1 tablespoon chopped fresh basil*
*1 tablespoon chopped fresh parsley*
*4 cups dried conchiglie*
*14-ounce can tuna in water, drained*
*2 tablespoons capers in vinegar, drained*
*salt and freshly ground black pepper*

### SERVES 6

**1** Put the onion, celery, red pepper and garlic into a saucepan. Add the stock, bring to a boil and cook for 5 minutes, until the stock has reduced significantly.

**2** Add the tomatoes, tomato paste, sugar and herbs. Season to taste with salt and pepper and bring to a boil. Reduce the heat and simmer for about 30 minutes, until thick, stirring occasionally.

### VARIATION
If fresh herbs are not available, use a 14-ounce can of chopped tomatoes with herbs and add 1–2 teaspoons dried mixed herbs, instead of the fresh herbs.

### NUTRITIONAL NOTES
*Per portion:*

| | |
|---|---|
| Energy | 369cals |
| Total fat | 2.1g |
| Saturated fat | 0.4g |
| Cholesterol | 34mg |
| Fiber | 4g |

# SAFFRON PAPPARDELLE

Serve this flavorful and low-fat Italian pasta dish with a mixed green salad and fresh Italian
bread for a wholesome and nutritious meal.

## INGREDIENTS

*large pinch of saffron threads*
*4 sun-dried tomatoes, chopped*
*1 teaspoon chopped fresh thyme*
*12 large fresh whole shrimp in their shells*
*8 ounces baby squid*
*8 ounces skinless monkfish fillet*
*2–3 garlic cloves, crushed*
*2 small onions, quartered*
*1 small bulb fennel, trimmed and sliced*
*2/3 cup white wine*
*8 ounces dried pappardelle*
*salt and freshly ground black pepper*
*2 tablespoons chopped fresh parsley,*
*to garnish*

## SERVES 4

**1** Put the saffron, sun-dried tomatoes and
thyme into a bowl with 1/4 cup hot water.
Let soak for 30 minutes.

### COOK'S TIP

Make sure you use the sun-dried
tomatoes for soaking in Step 1, rather
than the ones preserved in oil. Do not
try to substitute turmeric for the
saffron in this recipe; although the
colour will be similar, the flavor
will be quite different.

**2** Wash the shrimp and carefully remove
and discard the shells, but leave the
heads and tails intact. Pull the head from
the body of each squid and remove and
discard the quill. Cut the tentacles from
the head and rinse under cold water. Pull
off and discard the outer skin and cut the
flesh into 1/4-inch rings. Cut the monkfish
into 1-inch cubes. Set aside.

**3** Put the garlic, onions and fennel into a
pan with the wine. Cover and simmer for
5 minutes until tender. Stir occasionally.

### NUTRITIONAL NOTES

*Per portion:*

| | |
|---|---|
| Energy | 381cals |
| Total fat | 3.5g |
| Saturated fat | 0.6g |
| Cholesterol | 34mg |
| Fiber | 3.2g |

**4** Stir in the monkfish and the saffron
mixture. Cover and cook for 3 minutes,
then stir in the shrimp and squid. Cover
and cook gently for 1–2 minutes (do not
overcook). Season to taste.

**5** Meanwhile, cook the pasta in a large
saucepan of boiling, salted water
according to the package instructions,
until tender or *al dente*. Drain thoroughly.

**6** Divide the pasta among four serving
dishes and top with the sauce. Sprinkle
with parsley and serve immediately.

# FARFALLE WITH TUNA

This is a quick and simple dish that makes a good low-fat weekday supper if you have canned
tomatoes and tuna in the pantry. Serve with crusty fresh Italian bread.

**4** Meanwhile, cook the pasta in a large
saucepan of boiling salted water
according to the package instructions,
until tender or *al dente*.

**5** Drain the tuna and flake it with
a fork. Add to the sauce with about
1/4 cup of the pasta water and stir to mix.
Adjust the seasoning to taste.

**6** Drain the pasta well and transfer it to
a warmed serving bowl. Pour the sauce
on top and toss to mix. Serve immediately,
garnished with oregano.

### INGREDIENTS
*1 tablespoon olive oil*
*1 small onion, finely chopped*
*1 garlic clove, finely chopped*
*14-ounce can chopped Italian*
*plum tomatoes*
*3 tablespoons dry white wine*
*8–10 pitted black olives, sliced into rings*
*2 teaspoons chopped fresh oregano or*
*1 teaspoon dried oregano, plus extra fresh*
*oregano, to garnish*
*3 cups dried farfalle*
*6-ounce can tuna in water*
*salt and freshly ground black pepper*

### SERVES 4

**1** Heat the olive oil in a medium frying
pan or saucepan, and add the chopped
onion and garlic.

**2** Cook gently for 2–3 minutes,
until the onion is soft and golden,
stirring occasionally.

**3** Add the tomatoes and bring to a boil,
then add the white wine and simmer for a
minute or so. Stir in the olives and
oregano, with salt and pepper to taste,
then cover and cook for 20–25 minutes,
stirring occasionally.

### NUTRITIONAL NOTES
*Per portion:*

| | |
|---|---|
| Energy | 387cals |
| Total fat | 4.9g |
| Saturated fat | 0.8g |
| Cholesterol | 21.3mg |
| Fiber | 3.5g |

# MACARONI WITH BROCCOLI AND CAULIFLOWER

### This is a typical southern Italian dish, full of flavor and low in fat too. Without the anchovies, it can be served to vegetarians.

### INGREDIENTS

*6 ounces cauliflower florets, cut into*
*small sprigs*
*6 ounces broccoli florets, cut into*
*small sprigs*
*3 cups dried short-cut macaroni*
*1 tablespoon extra virgin olive oil*
*1 onion, finely chopped*
*2 tablespoons pine nuts (optional)*
*1 envelope of saffron powder, dissolved in*
*1 tablespoon warm water*
*1 tablespoon raisins*
*2 tablespoons sun-dried tomato paste*
*4 bottled or canned anchovies in olive oil,*
*drained and chopped*
*salt and freshly ground black pepper*
*grated fresh Pecorino cheese,*
*to serve (optional)*

### SERVES 4

**3** Meanwhile, heat the olive oil in a large frying pan or saucepan, add the onion and cook over low to medium heat, stirring frequently, for 2–3 minutes or until golden. Add the pine nuts, if using, the broccoli and cauliflower, and the saffron water. Add the raisins, sun-dried tomato paste and a couple of ladlefuls of the pasta cooking water until the mixture has the consistency of a sauce. Finally, add plenty of pepper.

**4** Stir well, cook for 1–2 minutes, then add the chopped anchovies. Drain the pasta and and the vegetable mixture. Toss well, then taste for seasoning and add salt if necessary. Serve the pasta immediately in four warmed bowls, sprinkled with freshly grated Pecorino, if using.

### NUTRITIONAL NOTES
*Per portion:*

| | |
|---|---|
| Energy | 339cals |
| Total fat | 5g |
| Saturated fat | 0.7g |
| Cholesterol | 0mg |
| Fiber | 4.5g |

**1** Cook the cauliflower in a large saucepan of boiling salted water for 3 minutes. Add the broccoli and boil for another 2 minutes. Remove the vegetables from the pan with a large slotted spoon, place on a plate and set aside.

**2** Add the pasta to the vegetable cooking water and bring back to a boil. Cook the pasta according to the package instructions, until it is tender or *al dente*.

# SMOKED TROUT CANNELLONI

Cannelloni are stuffed with a tasty smoked trout filling, topped with a low-fat cheese sauce and baked to create this appetizing Italian lunch or supper dish.

### INGREDIENTS
*1 large onion, finely chopped*
*1 garlic clove, crushed*
*1/4 cup vegetable stock*
*2 14-ounce cans chopped tomatoes*
*1/2 teaspoon dried mixed herbs*
*1 smoked trout, weighing about 14 ounces*
*3/4 cup frozen peas, thawed*
*1 1/2 cups fresh bread crumbs*
*16 cannelloni tubes*
*salt and freshly ground black pepper*
*mixed salad, to serve*

### FOR THE CHEESE SAUCE
*2 tablespoons low-fat margarine*
*1/4 cup all-purpose flour*
*1 1/2 cups skim milk*
*freshly grated nutmeg*
*1 1/2 tablespoons finely grated fresh Parmesan cheese*

### SERVES 6

**1** Simmer the onion, garlic and stock in a large covered saucepan for 3 minutes. Uncover and continue to cook, stirring occasionally, until reduced entirely.

### COOK'S TIP
Smoked trout can be bought already filleted or whole. If you buy fillets, you'll need 8 ounces fish.

**2** Stir in the tomatoes and herbs. Simmer uncovered for another 10 minutes or until very thick, stirring occasionally.

**3** Meanwhile, skin the smoked trout with a sharp knife. Carefully flake the flesh and discard all the bones. Mix with the tomato mixture, peas, bread crumbs, salt and pepper in a large bowl.

**4** Preheat the oven to 375°F. Spoon the filling into the cannelloni tubes and arrange in an ovenproof dish. Set aside.

**5** Make the sauce. Put the low-fat margarine, flour and milk into a saucepan and cook over medium heat, whisking until the sauce thickens. Simmer for 2–3 minutes, stirring continuously. Season to taste with salt, pepper and nutmeg.

**6** Pour the sauce over the cannelloni and sprinkle with the Parmesan cheese. Bake for 35–40 minutes or until the top is golden brown. Serve with a mixed salad.

### NUTRITIONAL NOTES
*Per portion:*

| | |
|---|---|
| Energy | 306cals |
| Total fat | 5g |
| Saturated fat | 1.3g |
| Cholesterol | 45.8mg |
| Fiber | 3g |

# SPAGHETTI WITH TUNA SAUCE

A speedy low-fat midweek meal, which can also be made with other pasta shapes, this tasty
Italian pasta dish is ideal for the whole family.

### INGREDIENTS

*8 ounces dried spaghetti, or 1 pound fresh*
*1 garlic clove, crushed*
*14-ounce can chopped tomatoes*
*15-ounce can tuna in water, drained*
*and flaked*
*1/2 teaspoon chili sauce (optional)*
*4 pitted black olives, chopped*
*salt and freshly ground black pepper*

### SERVES 4

**2** Add the garlic and tomatoes to the
saucepan and bring to a boil. Simmer,
uncovered, for 2–3 minutes, stirring the
mixture occasionally.

**3** Add the tuna, chili sauce, if using, the
olives and spaghetti. Heat gently until
hot, stirring. Add seasoning to taste and
serve hot.

**1** Cook the spaghetti in a large saucepan
of boiling salted water for 12 minutes or
until just tender or *al dente*. Drain well
and keep hot.

### COOK'S TIP

If fresh tuna is available, use 1 pound,
cut into small chunks, and add after
Step 2. Simmer for 6–8 minutes, then
add the chili sauce, olives and pasta.

### NUTRITIONAL NOTES

*Per portion:*

| Energy | 306cals |
| --- | --- |
| Total fat | 2.02g |
| Saturated fat | 0.37g |
| Cholesterol | 48.45mg |
| Fiber | 2.46g |

# PASTA WITH HERBED SCALLOPS

Low-fat sour cream, cooked with mustard, garlic, herbs and scallops, makes this deceptively creamy and delicious sauce ideal for serving with cooked pasta for a flavorful meal.

### INGREDIENTS

*1/2 cup low-fat sour cream*
*2 teaspoons whole-grain mustard*
*2 garlic cloves, crushed*
*2–3 tablespoons fresh lime juice*
*1/4 cup chopped fresh parsley*
*2 tablespoons snipped fresh chives*
*12 ounces dried black tagliatelle*
*12 large fresh scallops*
*1/4 cup white wine*
*2/3 cup fish stock*
*salt and freshly ground black pepper*
*lime wedges and fresh parsley sprigs,*
*to garnish*

### SERVES 4

**1** To make the sauce, combine the sour cream, mustard, garlic, lime juice, chopped parsley, chives and seasoning in a mixing bowl. Set aside.

**2** Cook the pasta in a large saucepan of boiling salted water according to the package instructions, until tender or *al dente*. Drain thoroughly and keep hot.

**3** Slice the scallops in half, horizontally. Keep any coral whole. Put the wine and fish stock into a saucepan and heat to the simmering point. Add the scallops and cook very gently for 3–4 minutes (but not for any longer or they will toughen).

**4** Remove the scallops, place on a plate and keep warm. Boil the wine and stock to reduce by half and then add the green sauce to the pan. Heat gently to warm through, stirring, then return the scallops to the pan and cook for 1 minute. Spoon the sauce over the cooked pasta and garnish with lime wedges and fresh parsley sprigs. Serve.

### NUTRITIONAL NOTES
*Per portion:*

| | |
|---|---|
| Energy | 368cals |
| Total fat | 4.01g |
| Saturated fat | 0.98g |
| Cholesterol | 99mg |
| Fiber | 1.91g |

# TAGLIATELLE WITH SCALLOPS

**Scallops and brandy add a taste of luxury to this appetizing pasta sauce, ideal as a supper dish.**

### INGREDIENTS
*7 ounces scallops, sliced*
*2 tablespoons all-purpose flour*
*1 tablespoon olive oil*
*2 scallions, cut into thin rings*
*1/2–1 small fresh red chile, deseeded and*
*very finely chopped*
*2 tablespoons finely chopped fresh*
*flat-leaf parsley*
*1/4 cup brandy*
*7 tablespoons fish stock*
*10 ounces fresh spinach-*
*flavored tagliatelle*
*salt and freshly ground black pepper*

*SERVES 4*

**1** Toss the scallops in the flour, shaking the excess. Bring a large saucepan of salted water to a boil for the pasta. Meanwhile, heat the oil in a frying pan. Add the scallions, chile and half the parsley and cook, stirring frequently, for 1–2 minutes over medium heat. Add the scallops and toss for 1–2 minutes.

**2** Pour the brandy over the scallops, then set it on fire. When the flames have died down, pour in the stock, season and stir. Simmer for 2–3 minutes, then cover and remove from heat. Cook the pasta according to the package instructions. Drain, add to the sauce and toss over medium heat until mixed. Serve immediately.

### NUTRITIONAL NOTES
*Per portion:*

| | |
|---|---|
| Energy | 372cals |
| Total fat | 4.8g |
| Saturated fat | 0.7g |
| Cholesterol | 0.0mg |
| Fiber | 2.2g |

# SPAGHETTI WITH SQUID AND PEAS

**In Tuscany, squid is often cooked with peas in a tomato sauce. This low-fat recipe is a tasty variation on the theme, and it works very well.**

### INGREDIENTS
*1 pound prepared squid*
*2 teaspoons olive oil*
*1 small onion, finely chopped*
*14-ounce can chopped Italian*
*plum tomatoes*
*1 garlic clove, finely chopped*
*1 tablespoon red wine vinegar*
*1 teaspoon sugar*
*2 teaspoons finely chopped fresh rosemary*
*1 cup frozen peas*
*10 ounces dried spaghetti*
*1 tablespoon chopped fresh*
*flat-leaf parsley*
*salt and freshly ground black pepper*

*SERVES 4*

**1** Cut the prepared squid into strips about 1/4-inch wide. Finely chop any tentacles. Set aside. Heat the oil in a frying pan, add the onion and cook gently, stirring, for about 5 minutes, until softened. Add the squid, tomatoes, garlic, vinegar and sugar and stir to mix.

### NUTRITIONAL NOTES
*Per portion:*

| | |
|---|---|
| Energy | 285cals |
| Total fat | 4g |
| Saturated fat | 0.4g |
| Cholesterol | 0.0mg |
| Fiber | 3g |

**2** Add the rosemary and seasoning. Bring to a boil, stirring, then cover, reduce the heat, and simmer for 20 minutes, stirring occasionally. Stir in the peas and cook for another 10 minutes. Cook the pasta according to the package instructions. Serve with the sauce and the parsley.

# HOT SPICY SHRIMP WITH CAMPANELLE

This low-fat shrimp sauce tossed with hot pasta creates an ideal Italian-style suppertime dish.
Add less or more chili seasoning depending on how hot you like your food.

### INGREDIENTS

*8 ounces cooked, peeled
jumbo shrimp
1–2 garlic cloves, crushed
finely grated zest of 1 lemon
1 tablespoon fresh lemon juice
1/4 teaspoon red chili paste or 1 large
pinch of chili powder
1 tablespoon light soy sauce
5 ounces lean bacon strips
1 shallot or small onion,
finely chopped
1/4 cup dry white wine
2 cups dried campanelle or
other dried pasta shapes
1/4 cup fish stock
4 firm ripe tomatoes, peeled,
deseeded and chopped
2 tablespoons chopped
fresh parsley
salt and freshly ground black pepper*

### SERVES 4

**1** In a glass bowl, mix the shrimp with the garlic, lemon zest and juice, then stir in the chili paste or powder and soy sauce.

**2** Season with salt and pepper, then cover and let marinate in a cool place for at least 1 hour.

**3** Broil the bacon strips under a hot broiler until cooked, then cut them into 1/4-inch dice. Set aside.

**4** Put the shallot or onion and white wine into a saucepan, bring to a boil, cover and cook for 2–3 minutes or until it is tender and the wine has reduced by half. Set aside.

**5** Meanwhile, cook the pasta in a large saucepan of boiling salted water according to the package instructions, until tender or *al dente*. Drain thoroughly and keep hot.

### COOK'S TIP

To save time later, the shrimp and marinade ingredients can be combined together. covered and chilled in the refrigerator overnight, until ready to use.

**6** Just before serving, put the shrimp with their marinade into a large frying pan, bring to a boil quickly and add the cooked bacon and fish stock. Heat through for 1 minute, stirring.

**7** Add to the hot pasta with the shallot or onion mixture, chopped tomatoes and parsley. Toss quickly to mix and serve immediately.

### NUTRITIONAL NOTES
*Per portion:*

| | |
|---|---|
| Energy | 214cals |
| Total fat | 3g |
| Saturated fat | 0.9g |
| Cholesterol | 37.5mg |
| Fiber | 1.4g |

# TRENETTE WITH SHELLFISH

—

Colorful and delicious, this typical pasta dish from the Genoese region of Italy is ideal for a low-fat lunch or supper. The sauce is quite runny, so serve it with spoons and crusty Italian bread.

### INGREDIENTS

*4 teaspoons olive oil*
*1 small onion, finely chopped*
*1 garlic clove, crushed*
*1/2 fresh red chile, deseeded and finely chopped*
*7-ounce can chopped Italian plum tomatoes*
*2 tablespoons chopped fresh flat-leaf parsley*
*1 pound fresh clams in their shells*
*1 pound fresh mussels in their shells*
*1/4 cup dry white wine*
*4 cups dried trenette*
*a few fresh basil leaves*
*2/3 cup cooked, peeled shrimp, thawed and thoroughly dried if frozen*
*salt and freshly ground black pepper*
*chopped fresh herbs, to garnish*

### SERVES 6

**1** Heat half the oil in a frying pan. Add the onion, garlic and chile and cook over medium heat for 1–2 minutes, stirring continuously. Stir in the tomatoes, half the parsley and pepper to taste. Bring to a boil, cover, reduce the heat and simmer for 15 minutes, stirring occasionally.

**2** Scrub the clams and mussels under cold running water. Discard any that are open or that do not close when sharply tapped against the work surface.

**3** In a large saucepan, heat the remaining oil. Add the clams and mussels, with the rest of the parsley and toss over high heat for a few seconds. Pour in the white wine, then cover tightly. Cook for about 5 minutes, shaking the pan frequently, until the clams and mussels have opened.

**4** Remove the pan from heat and transfer the clams and mussels to a bowl with a slotted spoon, discarding any shellfish that have failed to open.

### NUTRITIONAL NOTES
*Per portion:*

| | |
|---|---|
| Energy | 414cals |
| Total fat | 5g |
| Saturated fat | 0.7g |
| Cholesterol | 21mg |
| Fiber | 2.7g |

**5** Strain the cooking liquid into a measuring pitchers and set aside. Reserve a few clams and mussels in their shells for the garnish, then remove the rest from their shells.

**6** Cook the pasta in a large saucepan of boiling salted water, according to the package instructions, until tender or *al dente*. Meanwhile, add 1/2 cup of the seafood liquid to the tomato sauce. Bring to a boil over high heat, stirring. Reduce the heat, tear in the basil and add the shrimp with the shelled clams and mussels. Stir well, then adjust the seasoning to taste.

**7** Drain the pasta and transfer to a warmed bowl. Add the seafood sauce and toss well to combine. Serve sprinkled with chopped herbs and garnish each portion with the reserved clams and mussels.

# LINGUINE WITH CRAB

This pasta recipe comes from Rome. It makes a tasty low-fat first course served on its own, or it can be served for lunch or supper with crusty Italian bread.

## INGREDIENTS

*about 9 ounces shelled white crabmeat*
*1 tablespoon olive oil*
*1 small handful of fresh flat-leaf parsley,*
*roughly chopped, plus extra to garnish*
*1 garlic clove, crushed*
*12 ounces ripe Italian plum tomatoes,*
*skinned and chopped*
*4–6 tablespoons dry white wine*
*12 ounces dried linguine*
*salt and freshly ground black pepper*

### SERVES 4

**1** Put the crabmeat in a mortar and pound to a rough pulp with a pestle, or use a sturdy bowl and the end of a rolling pin. Set aside.

**2** Heat the oil in a large saucepan. Add the parsley and garlic, season to taste, and cook until the garlic begins to brown, stirring occasionally.

## NUTRITIONAL NOTES

### Per portion:

| | |
|---|---|
| Energy | 308cals |
| Total fat | 5g |
| Saturated fat | 0.7g |
| Cholesterol | 32.1mg |
| Fiber | 2.3g |

**3** Stir in the tomatoes, pounded crabmeat and wine, cover the pan, bring to a boil, then reduce the heat and simmer for 15 minutes, stirring occasionally.

**4** Meanwhile, cook the pasta in a large saucepan of boiling salted water, according to the package instructions, draining it the moment it is tender or *al dente*, and reserving a little of the cooking water. Return the pasta to the clean pan.

**5** Add the tomato and crab mixture to the pasta and toss to mix, adding a little cooking water if necessary. Adjust the seasoning to taste. Serve hot, in warmed bowls, sprinkled with chopped parsley.

### COOK'S TIP
Ask a fishmonger to remove the crabmeat from the shell, or buy dressed crab at the supermarket. Alternatively, use drained canned crabmeat.

# SPAGHETTI WITH CLAM SAUCE

This is one of Italy's most famous pasta dishes, sometimes translated as "white clam sauce" to distinguish it from that other classic, clams in tomato sauce.

### INGREDIENTS

*2¼ pounds fresh clams*
*1 tablespoon olive oil*
*3 tablespoons chopped fresh flat-leaf parsley*
*½ cup dry white wine*
*10 ounces dried spaghetti*
*2 garlic cloves*
*salt and freshly ground black pepper*

### SERVES 4

**1** Scrub the clams under cold running water, discarding any that are open or that do not close when sharply tapped against the work surface.

**2** Heat half the oil in a large saucepan, add the clams and 1 tablespoon of the parsley and cook over high heat for a few seconds. Pour in the wine, then cover tightly. Cook for about 5 minutes, shaking the pan frequently, until the clams have opened. Meanwhile, cook the pasta in a large saucepan of boiling salted water, according to the package instructions, until tender or *al dente*.

**3** Using a slotted spoon, transfer the clams to a bowl, discarding any that have failed to open. Strain the liquid and set it aside. Put eight clams to one side, then remove the rest from their shells.

**4** Heat the remaining oil in a clean saucepan. Cook the whole garlic cloves over medium heat until golden, crushing them with the back of a spoon. Remove the garlic with a slotted spoon and discard.

**5** Add the shelled clams to the pan, gradually add some of the strained liquid from the clams, then add plenty of pepper. Cook for 1–2 minutes, gradually adding more liquid as the sauce reduces. Add the remaining parsley and cook for 1–2 minutes, stirring occasionally.

**6** Drain the pasta, add it to the pan and toss well. Serve in individual dishes, scooping the shelled clams from the bottom of the pan and placing some of them on top of each serving. Garnish with the reserved clams in their shells and serve immediately.

### NUTRITIONAL NOTES
*Per portion:*

| | |
|---|---|
| Energy | 425cals |
| Total fat | 4.5g |
| Saturated fat | 0.4g |
| Cholesterol | 0mg |
| Fiber | 1.5g |

# VERMICELLI WITH CLAM SAUCE

This recipe originates from the city of Naples, where both fresh tomato sauce and seafood are traditionally served with vermicelli. The two are combined here in this tasty, low-fat dish.

### INGREDIENTS

*2 1/4 pounds fresh clams*
*1 cup dry white wine*
*2 garlic cloves, bruised*
*1 large handful of fresh flat-leaf parsley*
*2 teaspoons olive oil*
*1 small onion, finely chopped*
*8 ripe Italian plum tomatoes, peeled, deseeded and finely chopped*
*1/2–1 fresh red chile, deseeded and finely chopped*
*12 ounces dried vermicelli*
*salt and freshly ground black pepper*

### SERVES 4

**1** Scrub the clams thoroughly under cold running water and discard any that are open or that do not close when sharply tapped against the work surface.

**2** Pour the white wine into a large saucepan, add the bruised garlic cloves and half the parsley, then add the clams. Cover tightly with the lid and bring to a boil over high heat. Cook for about 5 minutes, shaking the pan frequently, until the clams have opened.

**3** Put the clams in a large colander set over a bowl and let the liquid drain through. Set the clams aside until cool enough to handle, then remove about two-thirds of them from their shells, tipping the clam liquor into the bowl of cooking liquid.

**4** Discard any clams that have failed to open. Set both shelled and unshelled clams aside, keeping the unshelled clams warm in a bowl covered with a lid. Reserve the cooking liquid and set aside.

**5** Heat the oil in a saucepan, add the onion and cook gently, stirring frequently, for about 5 minutes until softened. Add the tomatoes, then the clam liquid. Add the chile, season to taste, and stir.

**6** Bring to a boil, half cover, then simmer gently for 15–20 minutes, stirring occasionally. Meanwhile, cook the pasta in a large saucepan of boiling salted water, according to the package instructions. Chop the remaining parsley finely.

### NUTRITIONAL NOTES
*Per portion:*

| | |
|---|---|
| Energy | 536cals |
| Total fat | 4.7g |
| Saturated fat | 0.4g |
| Cholesterol | 0mg |
| Fiber | 2.4g |

**7** Add the shelled clams to the sauce, stir well and heat through very gently for 2–3 minutes, stirring occasionally.

**8** Drain the cooked pasta well and transfer it to a warmed bowl. Taste the clam and tomato sauce and adjust the seasoning, then pour the sauce over the pasta and toss everything together well. Garnish with the reserved clams in their shells, sprinkle the chopped parsley on the pasta and serve immediately.

# VEGETARIAN PASTA DISHES

*This appetizing* MEDLEY *of vegetarian pasta dishes brings together a wealth of* DELICIOUS *ingredients to create a collection of fat-free and low-fat recipes* PACKED *with goodness and the flavors of Italy for family and friends to* RELISH. *Select from recipes such as Tagliatelle with Sun-Dried* TOMATOES, *Mushroom Bolognese, Penne with Artichokes and* TAGLIATELLE *with Hazelnut Pesto.*

# CONCHIGLIE WITH TOMATOES AND ARUGULA

Cooked pasta shells, tossed together with lightly cooked tomatoes and fresh arugula, makes a
tasty low-fat dish that is ideal for a summer lunch or supper.

### INGREDIENTS
*4 cups dried conchiglie*
*1 pound ripe cherry tomatoes*
*3 ounces fresh arugula*
*1 tablespoon extra virgin olive oil*
*1/2 ounce fresh Parmesan cheese*
*salt and freshly ground black pepper*

### SERVES 4

**1** Cook the pasta in a large saucepan
of boiling salted water, according to the
package instructions, until tender or
*al dente*. Stir occasionally.

**2** While the pasta is cooking, halve the
cherry tomatoes. Trim, wash and dry
the arugula.

**3** Heat the oil in a large saucepan, add
the halved tomatoes and cook for barely
1 minute. The tomatoes should only just
heat through and not disintegrate.

**4** Meanwhile, cut the Parmesan cheese
into fine shavings, using a swivel
vegetable peeler.

---

### COOK'S TIP
This pasta dish relies for its success
on a salad green called arugula.
Available at most supermarkets, it is
easily grown in the garden or a window
box and tastes slightly peppery. When
you buy arugula, make sure
the leaves are very fresh with no sign
of wilting. Arugula does not keep
well unless it has been pre-packaged.
To keep it for a day or two, wrap it
in damp paper towels and store
in the refrigerator.

**5** Drain the pasta and tip it into the pan
with the tomatoes.

**6** Add the arugula and then carefully
stir to mix and heat through. Season
well with salt and pepper and serve
immediately, topped with a little shaved
Parmesan cheese.

---

### VARIATIONS
• You might like to try adding
1/4 teaspoon dried chile flakes and
2 finely chopped garlic cloves to
this dish. Simply add them to the oil
and sauté gently for a minute or so
before adding the tomatoes.
• Use a different type of pasta such
as fusilli instead of the conchiglie.
• Instead of the arugula, try
fresh watercress.

---

### NUTRITIONAL NOTES
*Per portion:*

| | |
|---|---|
| Energy | 329cals |
| Total fat | 5g |
| Saturated fat | 1.2g |
| Cholesterol | 2.3mg |
| Fiber | 3.5g |

# TAGLIATELLE WITH SUN-DRIED TOMATOES

Tagliatelle tossed in a delicious fresh and sun-dried tomato sauce is an ideal dish
for the whole family to enjoy.

### INGREDIENTS

*1 garlic clove, crushed*
*1 celery stalk, thinly sliced*
*1 cup sun-dried tomatoes, finely chopped*
*6 tablespoons red wine*
*8 plum tomatoes*
*12 ounces dried tagliatelle*
*salt and freshly ground black pepper*

### SERVES 4

**3** Add the plum tomatoes to the saucepan, stir to mix and simmer for another 5 minutes. Season to taste with salt and pepper.

**4** Meanwhile, cook the tagliatelle in a large saucepan of boiling salted water for 8–10 minutes or until tender or *al dente*. Drain well. Toss the cooked pasta with half the tomato sauce and serve on warmed plates, topped with the remaining tomato sauce.

**1** Put the garlic, celery, sun-dried tomatoes and wine into a saucepan. Cook gently for 15 minutes, stirring occasionally.

### NUTRITIONAL NOTES
*Per portion:*

| | |
|---|---|
| Energy | 357cals |
| Total fat | 2.32g |
| Saturated fat | 0.32g |
| Cholesterol | 0mg |
| Fiber | 5.09g |

### COOK'S TIP
Choose plain sun-dried tomatoes for this sauce, instead of those preserved in oil, which will increase the fat content of the dish.

**2** Meanwhile, plunge the plum tomatoes into a saucepan of boiling water for 1 minute, then into a saucepan of cold water. Drain, then peel and discard their skins. Halve the tomatoes, remove and discard the seeds and cores and roughly chop the flesh.

# SPAGHETTI WITH MIXED BEAN SAUCE

Mixed beans are flavored with fresh chile and garlic and cooked in a tomato sauce in this quick and easy pasta dish.

### INGREDIENTS

*1 onion, finely chopped*
*1–2 garlic cloves, crushed*
*1 large green chile, deseeded and finely chopped*
*2/3 cup vegetable stock*
*14-ounce can chopped tomatoes*
*2 tablespoons tomato paste*
*1/2 cup red wine*
*1 teaspoon dried oregano*
*7 ounces green beans, sliced*
*14-ounce can red kidney beans, drained*
*14-ounce can cannellini beans, drained*
*14-ounce can chickpeas, drained*
*1 pound dried spaghetti*
*salt and freshly ground black pepper*

### SERVES 6

**1** Put the onion, garlic and chile into a nonstick saucepan with the stock. Bring to a boil and cook for 5 minutes, until tender, stirring occasionally.

### NUTRITIONAL NOTES

*Per portion:*

| | |
|---|---|
| Energy | 431cals |
| Total fat | 3.6g |
| Saturated fat | 0.2g |
| Cholesterol | 0mg |
| Fiber | 9.9g |

**2** Stir in the tomatoes, tomato paste, wine, oregano and seasoning. Bring to a boil, cover, then reduce the heat and simmer for 20 minutes, stirring the mixture occasionally.

**3** Meanwhile, cook the green beans in a saucepan of boiling, salted water for 5–6 minutes, until tender. Drain the beans thoroughly.

**4** Add all the beans and the chickpeas to the sauce, stir to mix and simmer for another 10 minutes. Meanwhile, cook the spaghetti in a large saucepan of boiling salted water, according to the package instructions, until tender or *al dente*. Drain thoroughly. Transfer the pasta to a serving dish and top with the bean sauce. Serve immediately.

# TAGLIATELLE WITH BROCCOLI AND SPINACH

This is an excellent Italian vegetarian supper dish. It is nutritious, filling and low-fat and needs
no accompaniment. If desired, you can use tagliatelle flecked with herbs.

### INGREDIENTS
*2 heads of broccoli*
*1 pound fresh spinach, stems removed*
*freshly grated nutmeg*
*12 ounces dried egg tagliatelle*
*1 tablespoon extra virgin olive oil*
*juice of 1/2 lemon, or to taste*
*salt and freshly ground black pepper*
*1/2 ounce grated fresh Parmesan cheese,*
*to serve*

### SERVES 4

### NUTRITIONAL NOTES
*Per portion:*

| | |
|---|---|
| Energy | 288cals |
| Total fat | 4.9g |
| Saturated fat | 1g |
| Cholesterol | 1.9mg |
| Fiber | 4.5g |

**2** Add salt to the water in the steamer and
fill the steamer saucepan with boiling
water, then add the pasta and cook,
according to the package instructions,
until tender or *al dente*. Meanwhile, chop
the broccoli and spinach in the colander.

**3** Drain the pasta. Heat the oil in the
pasta pan, add the pasta and chopped
vegetables and toss over medium heat
until evenly mixed. Sprinkle in the
lemon juice and plenty of black pepper,
then taste and add more lemon juice, salt
and nutmeg. Serve immediately,
sprinkled with freshly grated Parmesan
and black pepper.

**1** Put the broccoli in the basket of a
steamer, cover and steam over a saucepan
of boiling water for 10 minutes. Add the
spinach to the broccoli, cover and steam
for 4–5 minutes or until both are tender.
Toward the end of the cooking time,
sprinkle the vegetables with freshly
grated nutmeg and salt and pepper to
taste. Transfer the vegetables to a
colander and set aside.

### VARIATION
If desired, add a sprinkling of
crushed dried chiles with the black
pepper in Step 3.

# PENNE WITH GREEN VEGETABLE SAUCE

**Lightly cooked fresh green vegetables are tossed with pasta to create this low-fat Italian dish, ideal for a light lunch or supper.**

### INGREDIENTS

*2 carrots*

*1 zucchini*

*3 ounces green beans*

*1 small leek, washed*

*2 ripe Italian plum tomatoes*

*1 handful of fresh flat-leaf parsley*

*1 tablespoon extra virgin olive oil*

*1/2 teaspoon sugar*

*1 cup frozen peas*

*3 cups dried penne*

*salt and freshly ground black pepper*

### SERVES 4

**1** Dice the carrots and the zucchini finely. Trim the green beans, then cut them into 3/4-inch lengths. Slice the leek thinly. Skin and dice the tomatoes. Finely chop the parsley and set aside.

**2** Heat the oil in a medium frying pan or saucepan. Add the carrots and leek. Sprinkle on the sugar and cook, stirring frequently, for about 5 minutes.

**3** Stir in the zucchini, green beans, peas and plenty of salt and pepper. Cover and cook over low to medium heat for 5–8 minutes, until the vegetables are tender, stirring occasionally.

**4** Meanwhile, cook the pasta in a large saucepan of boiling salted water, according to the package instructions, until it is tender or *al dente*. Drain the pasta well and keep it hot until it is ready to serve.

**5** Stir the parsley and chopped plum tomatoes into the vegetable mixture and adjust the seasoning to taste. Toss with the cooked pasta and serve immediately.

### NUTRITIONAL NOTES
*Per portion:*

| | |
|---|---|
| Energy | 328cals |
| Total fat | 4.5g |
| Saturated fat | 0.7g |
| Cholesterol | 0mg |
| Fiber | 5g |

# PAPPARDELLE AND SUMMER VEGETABLE SAUCE

A delicious low-fat sauce of tomatoes and fresh vegetables adds color and robust flavor to pasta in this tasty Italian-style dish.

### INGREDIENTS

*2 small red onions, peeled, root left intact*
*2/3 cup vegetable stock*
*1–2 garlic cloves, crushed*
*1/4 cup red wine*
*2 zucchini, cut into fingers*
*1 yellow bell pepper, deseeded and sliced*
*14-ounce can tomatoes*
*2 teaspoons chopped fresh thyme*
*1 teaspoon sugar*
*12 ounces dried pappardelle*
*salt and freshly ground black pepper*
*fresh thyme and 6 black olives, pitted and*
*roughly chopped, to garnish*

### SERVES 4

**1** Cut each onion into eight wedges through the root end, to hold them together during cooking. Put into a saucepan with the stock and garlic. Bring to a boil, cover, then reduce the heat and simmer for 5 minutes, until tender.

**2** Add the wine, zucchini, yellow pepper, tomatoes, chopped thyme and sugar. Season with salt and pepper and stir to mix. Bring to a boil and cook gently for 5–7 minutes, shaking the pan occasionally to coat the vegetables with the sauce. (Do not overcook the vegetables, as they are tastier if they are slightly crunchy.)

**3** Meanwhile, cook the pasta in a large saucepan of boiling salted water, according to the package instructions, until tender or *al dente*. Drain thoroughly.

### NUTRITIONAL NOTES
*Per portion:*

| | |
|---|---|
| Energy | 334cals |
| Total fat | 2.1g |
| Saturated fat | 0.3g |
| Cholesterol | 0mg |
| Fiber | 4g |

**4** Transfer the pasta to a warmed serving dish and top with the vegetables. Garnish with fresh thyme and chopped black olives and serve immediately.

# PASTA PRIMAVERA

You can use any mixture of fresh, young spring vegetables to make this delicately flavored
low-fat pasta dish, ideal for a quick and tasty supper.

### INGREDIENTS

*8 ounces thin asparagus spears,*
*chopped in half*
*4 ounces snowpeas, trimmed*
*4 ounces baby corn*
*8 ounces whole baby carrots, trimmed*
*1 small red bell pepper, deseeded*
*and chopped*
*8 scallions, sliced*
*8 ounces dried torchietti or other*
*pasta shapes*
*2/3 cup low-fat cottage cheese*
*2/3 cup low-fat yogurt*
*1 tablespoon lemon juice*
*1 tablespoon chopped fresh parsley*
*1 tablespoon snipped fresh chives*
*skim milk (optional)*
*salt and freshly ground black pepper*
*sun-dried tomato bread, to serve*

### SERVES 4

**1** Cook the asparagus spears in a
saucepan of boiling, salted water for
3–4 minutes. Add the snowpeas
halfway through the cooking time. Drain
and rinse both under cold water to stop
the cooking process. Set aside.

**2** Cook the baby corn, carrots, red pepper
and scallions in the same way in a
saucepan of boiling salted water until
tender. Drain, rinse and set aside.

**3** Meanwhile, cook the pasta in a
large saucepan of boiling salted water,
according to the package instructions,
until tender or *al dente*. Drain thoroughly
and keep hot.

### NUTRITIONAL NOTES
*Per portion:*

| | |
|---|---|
| Energy | 320cals |
| Total fat | 3.1g |
| Saturated fat | 0.4g |
| Cholesterol | 3mg |
| Fiber | 6.2g |

**4** Put the cottage cheese, yogurt, lemon
juice, parsley, chives and seasoning into a
blender or food processor and blend until
smooth. Thin the sauce with a little milk,
if necessary. Put the sauce into a large
saucepan with the cooked pasta and
vegetables, heat gently and toss carefully
to mix. Serve immediately with sun-dried
tomato breadsticks.

# LENTIL BOLOGNESE

—

Served with cooked spaghetti, this delicious lentil Bolognese sauce enhances this excellent low-fat
pasta dish for all vegetarians.

### INGREDIENTS

*1 tablespoon olive oil*
*1 onion, chopped*
*2 garlic cloves, crushed*
*2 carrots, coarsely grated*
*2 celery stalks, chopped*
*2/3 cup red lentils*
*14-ounce can chopped tomatoes*
*2 tablespoons tomato paste*
*scant 2 cups stock*
*1 tablespoon chopped fresh marjoram, or*
*1 teaspoon dried marjoram*
*1 pound dried spaghetti*
*salt and freshly ground black pepper*

### SERVES 6

**2** Add the lentils, tomatoes, tomato paste,
stock, marjoram and seasoning and stir
to mix.

**3** Bring the mixture to a boil, then
partially cover with a lid, reduce the heat
and simmer for about 20 minutes, until
thick and soft, stirring occasionally.

**4** Meanwhile, cook the pasta in a
large saucepan of boiling salted water,
according to the package instructions,
until tender or *al dente*. Drain well.

**5** Serve the cooked pasta on warmed
serving plates, with the lentil sauce
spooned on top.

**1** Heat the oil in a large saucepan, add
the onion, garlic, carrots and celery and
cook gently for about 5 minutes, until the
vegetables are soft, stirring occasionally.

### NUTRITIONAL NOTES
*Per portion:*

| | |
|---|---|
| Energy | 335cals |
| Total fat | 3.4g |
| Saturated fat | 0.4g |
| Cholesterol | 3.9mg |
| Fiber | 0g |

# TAGLIATELLE WITH HAZELNUT PESTO

Hazelnuts add a delicious flavor to this reduced-fat alternative to the classic Italian pesto sauce.
Serve with cooked pasta, such as tagliatelle or fettucine.

**2** Cook the tagliatelle in a large saucepan of boiling salted water, according to the package instructions, until tender or *al dente*, then drain well.

**3** Add the pesto sauce to the hot pasta, tossing together until well mixed. Sprinkle with pepper and serve hot.

### INGREDIENTS
*2 garlic cloves, crushed*
*1 cup fresh basil leaves*
*1/4 cup hazelnuts*
*7/8 cup low-fat cream cheese*
*8 ounces dried tagliatelle, or*
*1 pound fresh*
*salt and freshly ground black pepper*

### SERVES 4

**1** Place the garlic, basil, hazelnuts and cream cheese in a blender or food processor and blend to a thick paste. Set aside.

### NUTRITIONAL NOTES
*Per portion:*

| | |
|---|---|
| Energy | 227cals |
| Total fat | 4.7g |
| Saturated fat | 0.7g |
| Cholesterol | 2.1mg |
| Fiber | 1.7g |

# PASTA WITH TOMATO AND CHILI SAUCE

This is a specialty of Lazio. In Italian it is called *pasta all'arrabbiata*—the word *arrabbiata* means rabid or angry, and describes the heat that comes from the chile.

### INGREDIENTS

*1¼ pounds passata*
*2 garlic cloves, crushed*
*⅔ cup dry white wine*
*1 tablespoon sun-dried tomato paste*
*1 fresh red chile*
*11 ounces dried penne or tortiglioni*
*¼ cup finely chopped fresh
flat-leaf parsley*
*salt and freshly ground black pepper*
*½ ounce grated fresh Pecorino cheese,
to serve*

### SERVES 4

**3** Remove the chile from the sauce and add half the parsley. Add seasoning to taste. If you prefer a hotter taste, finely chop some or all of the chile and return it to the sauce.

**4** Drain the pasta and transfer it to a warmed serving bowl. Pour the sauce over the pasta and toss to mix. Serve immediately, sprinkled with a little grated Pecorino cheese and the remaining parsley.

### NUTRITIONAL NOTES
*Per portion:*

| | |
|---|---|
| Energy | 287cals |
| Total fat | 2.1g |
| Saturated fat | 0.7g |
| Cholesterol | 2.2mg |
| Fiber | 3g |

**1** Put the passata, garlic, wine, tomato paste and whole chile in a saucepan and bring to a boil. Cover, reduce the heat and simmer gently, stirring occasionally.

**2** Drop the pasta into a large saucepan of rapidly boiling salted water and simmer for 10–12 minutes or until tender or *al dente*.

# PENNE WITH ARTICHOKES

—

**Artichokes are a very popular vegetable in Italy, and are often used in sauces for pasta. This sauce is garlicky and richly flavored, perfect for a delicious light lunch or supper.**

### INGREDIENTS

*juice of 1/2–1 lemon*
*2 artichokes*
*1 tablespoon olive oil*
*1 small fennel bulb, thinly sliced, with*
*feathery tops reserved*
*1 onion, finely chopped*
*4 garlic cloves, finely chopped*
*1 handful of fresh flat-leaf parsley,*
*roughly chopped*
*14-ounce can chopped Italian*
*plum tomatoes*
*2/3 cup dry white wine*
*3 cups dried penne*
*2 teaspoons capers, chopped*
*salt and freshly ground black pepper*

### SERVES 6

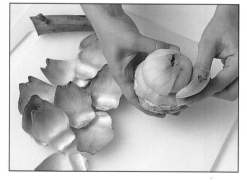

**1** Have ready a bowl of cold water to which you have added the juice of half a lemon. Cut off the artichoke stems, then discard the outer leaves until the pale inner leaves that are almost white at the base remain.

**2** Cut off the tops of these leaves so that the base remains intact. Cut the base in half lengthwise, then prise the hairy choke out of the center with the tip of the knife and discard. Cut the artichokes lengthwise into 1/4-inch slices, adding them immediately to the bowl of water.

**3** Bring a large saucepan of water to a boil. Add a good pinch of salt, then drain the artichokes and add them immediately to the water. Boil for 5 minutes, drain and set aside.

**4** Heat the oil in a large frying pan or saucepan and add the fennel, onion, garlic and parsley. Cook over low to medium heat, stirring frequently, for about 10 minutes, until the fennel has softened and is lightly colored.

**5** Add the tomatoes and wine, with salt and pepper to taste. Bring to a boil, stirring, then cover, reduce the heat and simmer for 10–15 minutes, stirring occasionally. Stir in the artichokes, replace the lid and simmer for another 10 minutes.

**6** Meanwhile, cook the pasta in a large saucepan of water, according to the package instructions. Drain, reserving a little cooking water. Stir the capers into the sauce, then adjust the seasoning and add the remaining lemon juice, if desired.

**7** Transfer the pasta to a warmed serving bowl, pour in the sauce and mix, adding a little cooking water if necessary. Serve, garnished with fennel fronds.

### NUTRITIONAL NOTES
*Per portion:*

| | |
|---|---|
| Energy | 269cals |
| Total fat | 3g |
| Saturated fat | 0.4g |
| Cholesterol | 0mg |
| Fiber | 2.7g |

# CHIFFERI RIGATI WITH EGGPLANT SAUCE

Full of flavor, this excellent Italian vegetarian sauce goes well with any short pasta shape, such as chifferi rigati or penne, to create an appetizing lunch or supper dish.

**2** Remove and discard the chile. Add the eggplant to the pan with the remaining parsley and all the basil. Pour in half the water. Crumble in the bouillon cube and stir until it is dissolved, then cover and cook, stirring frequently, for about 10 minutes.

**3** Add the tomatoes, wine, sugar, saffron and paprika, with salt and pepper to taste, then pour in the remaining water. Stir well, replace the lid and cook for another 30–40 minutes, stirring occasionally. Adjust the seasoning to taste.

**4** Meanwhile, cook the pasta in a large saucepan of boiling salted water, according to the package instructions, until tender or *al dente*. Drain well.

**5** Add the eggplant sauce to the cooked pasta, toss to ensure that it is thoroughly mixed and serve immediately.

### INGREDIENTS

*2 tablespoons olive oil*
*1 small fresh red chile*
*2 garlic cloves*
*2 handfuls of fresh flat-leaf parsley*
*1 pound eggplant, roughly chopped*
*1 handful of fresh basil leaves*
*scant 1 cup water*
*1 vegetable stock cube*
*8 ripe Italian plum tomatoes, skinned and*
*finely chopped*
*¹⁄₄ cup red wine*
*1 teaspoon sugar*
*1 envelope saffron powder*
*¹⁄₂ teaspoon ground paprika*
*1 pound dried short pasta such as chifferi*
*rigati or penne*
*salt and freshly ground black pepper*

**SERVES 6**

**1** Heat the oil in a large frying pan or saucepan and add the whole chile and whole garlic cloves. Roughly chop the parsley and add half to the pan. Smash the garlic cloves with a wooden spoon to release their juice, then cover the pan and cook the mixture over low to medium heat for about 10 minutes, stirring occasionally.

### NUTRITIONAL NOTES
*Per portion:*

| Energy | 300cals |
|---|---|
| Total fat | 3.6g |
| Saturated fat | 0.6g |
| Cholesterol | 0mg |
| Fiber | 4.1g |

# RIGATONI WITH WINTER TOMATO SAUCE

In winter, when fresh tomatoes are not at their best, this is the sauce the Italians make.
Try to use good-quality canned plum tomatoes from Italy.

### INGREDIENTS

*1 onion*

*1 carrot*

*1 celery stalk*

*1 tablespoon olive oil*

*1 garlic clove, thinly sliced*

*a few leaves each of fresh basil, thyme and*

*oregano or marjoram, plus extra to*

*garnish (optional)*

*2 14-ounce cans chopped Italian*

*plum tomatoes*

*1 tablespoon sun-dried tomato paste*

*1 teaspoon sugar*

*about 6 tablespoons dry red or white*

*wine (optional)*

*3 cups dried rigatoni*

*salt and freshly ground black pepper*

*1/2 ounce coarsely shaved fresh Parmesan*

*cheese, to serve (optional)*

### SERVES 4

**1** Chop the onion, carrot and celery finely, either in a food processor or by hand.

**2** Heat the oil in a medium saucepan, add the garlic slices and stir over very low heat for 1–2 minutes.

**3** Add the chopped vegetables and the fresh herbs. Cook over low heat, stirring frequently, for 5–7 minutes, until the vegetables have softened and have become lightly colored.

**4** Add the canned tomatoes, tomato paste and sugar, then stir in the wine, if using. Add salt and pepper to taste. Bring to a boil, stirring, then reduce the heat to a gentle simmer. Cook, uncovered, for about 45 minutes, stirring occasionally.

**5** Meanwhile, cook the pasta in a large saucepan of boiling salted water, according to the package instructions, until tender or *al dente*. Drain the pasta and transfer to a warmed bowl. Taste the sauce and adjust the seasoning. Pour the sauce on the pasta and toss well to mix. Serve immediately, with shavings of Parmesan passed separately, if using. If desired, garnish with extra chopped fresh herbs.

### NUTRITIONAL NOTES
*Per portion:*

| | |
|---|---|
| Energy | 351cals |
| Total fat | 4.4g |
| Saturated fat | 0.6g |
| Cholesterol | 0mg |
| Fiber | 4g |

# FUSILLI WITH TOMATO AND BALSAMIC VINEGAR

The intense, sweet-and-sour flavor of balsamic vinegar gives a pleasant kick to this sauce made
with canned tomatoes. It makes an appetizing low-fat pasta meal.

### INGREDIENTS

*2 14-ounce cans chopped Italian*
*plum tomatoes*
*2 pieces of drained sun-dried tomatoes in*
*olive oil, thinly sliced*
*2 garlic cloves, crushed*
*1 tablespoon olive oil*
*1 teaspoon sugar*
*3 cups dried fusilli*
*3 tablespoons balsamic vinegar*
*salt and freshly ground black pepper*
*1/2 ounce coarsely shaved*
*fresh Pecorino cheese and arugula salad,*
*to serve (optional)*

### SERVES 4

**1** Put the canned and sun-dried tomatoes
in a medium saucepan with the garlic,
olive oil and sugar. Add salt and pepper
to taste. Bring to a boil, stirring. Reduce
the heat and simmer for about
30 minutes, until reduced, stirring the
mixture occasionally.

**2** Meanwhile, cook the pasta in a
large saucepan of boiling salted water,
according to the package instructions,
until tender or *al dente*.

**3** Add the balsamic vinegar to the tomato
sauce and stir to mix evenly. Cook for
1–2 minutes, then remove from heat and
adjust the seasoning to taste.

**4** Drain the pasta and transfer to a
warmed bowl. Pour the sauce over the
cooked pasta and toss well to mix. Serve
immediately, with the arugula salad
and shaved Pecorino passed separately,
if using.

### VARIATION
The flavor of carrots goes well with
balsamic vinegar. Try adding some to
the saucepan with the tomatoes and
garlic in Step 1.

### NUTRITIONAL NOTES
*Per portion:*

| | |
|---|---|
| Energy | 360cals |
| Total fat | 4.5g |
| Saturated fat | 0.6g |
| Cholesterol | 0mg |
| Fiber | 4.1g |

# SPAGHETTI WITH FRESH TOMATO SAUCE

**This is the famous Neapolitan sauce from Italy that is made in summer when tomatoes are very ripe and sweet. Spaghetti is the traditional choice of pasta for a low-fat, flavorful Italian meal.**

### INGREDIENTS

*1½ pounds ripe Italian plum tomatoes*
*1 tablespoon olive oil*
*1 onion, finely chopped*
*12 ounces dried spaghetti*
*1 small handful of fresh basil leaves*
*salt and freshly ground black pepper*
*½ ounce coarsely shaved fresh Parmesan
cheese, to serve*

#### SERVES 4

**1** With a sharp knife, cut a cross in the bottom (flower) end of each tomato. Bring a medium saucepan of water to a boil and remove from heat. Plunge a few of the tomatoes into the water, let sit for 30 seconds or so, then lift them out with a slotted spoon. Repeat the process with the remaining tomatoes, then peel off and discard the skins and roughly chop the flesh. Set aside.

### NUTRITIONAL NOTES
*Per portion:*

| | |
|---|---|
| Energy | 330cals |
| Total fat | 5g |
| Saturated fat | 1.1g |
| Cholesterol | 2.2mg |
| Fiber | 4.05g |

**2** Heat the oil in a large saucepan, add the onion and cook over low heat, stirring frequently, for about 5 minutes, until softened and lightly colored. Add the tomatoes, with salt and pepper to taste. Bring to a gentle boil, then cover the pan, reduce the heat and simmer for 30–40 minutes, stirring occasionally, until thick.

**3** Meanwhile, cook the pasta in a large saucepan of boiling salted water, according to the package instructions, until tender or *al dente*. Shred the fresh basil leaves finely.

**4** Remove the sauce from heat, stir in the basil and adjust the seasoning to taste. Drain the pasta, transfer it to a warmed bowl, pour on the sauce and toss well to mix. Serve immediately, with a little shaved Parmesan passed separately.

# PASTA WITH CHICKPEA SAUCE

This is a delicious, and very speedy, low-fat Italian-style dish,
ideal for an appetizing lunch or supper.

### INGREDIENTS

*1 pound dried penne or other dried*
*pasta shapes*
*2 teaspoons olive oil*
*1 onion, thinly sliced*
*1 red bell pepper, deseeded and sliced*
*14-ounce can chopped tomatoes*
*15-ounce can chickpeas*
*2 tablespoons dry vermouth (optional)*
*1 teaspoon dried oregano*
*1 large bay leaf*
*2 tablespoons capers*
*salt and freshly ground black pepper*
*fresh oregano sprigs, to garnish*

### SERVES 6

**1** Cook the pasta in a large saucepan of
boiling salted water, according to the
package instructions, until tender or
*al dente*. Drain and keep hot. Meanwhile,
heat the olive oil in a large saucepan and
gently cook the sliced onion and pepper
for about 5 minutes, stirring occasionally,
until softened.

**2** Add the tomatoes, chickpeas with their
liquid, vermouth, if using, herbs and
capers and stir well to mix.

**3** Season to taste with salt and pepper
and bring to a boil, then reduce the heat
and simmer for about 10 minutes, stirring
occasionally. Remove and discard the bay
leaf. Add the hot pasta to the sauce, toss
to mix and serve hot, garnished with fresh
oregano sprigs.

### COOK'S TIP

Choose whatever pasta shapes desired,
although hollow shapes, such as penne
(quills) or shells are particularly good
with this sauce.

### NUTRITIONAL NOTES
*Per portion:*

| | |
|---|---|
| Energy | 372cals |
| Total fat | 4.9g |
| Saturated fat | 0.6g |
| Cholesterol | 0mg |
| Fiber | 6g |

# TAGLIATELLE WITH MUSHROOMS

—

**Freshly cooked tagliatelle is tossed with a flavorful mixed mushroom sauce to create this very tasty, low-fat pasta dish.**

**3** Remove the lid from the pan and boil until the liquid has reduced by half, stirring occasionally. Stir in the chopped fresh herbs and season to taste with salt and pepper.

**4** Meanwhile, cook the fresh pasta in a large saucepan of boiling, salted water for 2–5 minutes, until tender or *al dente.* Drain thoroughly, then toss the pasta lightly with the mushroom sauce. Serve, garnished with parsley and shavings of Parmesan cheese, if desired.

### INGREDIENTS

*1 small onion, finely chopped*
*2 garlic cloves, crushed*
*2/3 cup vegetable stock*
*8 ounces mixed fresh mushrooms, such as field, chestnut, oyster or chanterelle*
*1/4 cup white or red wine*
*2 teaspoons tomato paste*
*1 tablespoon soy sauce*
*1 teaspoon chopped fresh thyme*
*2 tablespoons chopped fresh parsley, plus extra to garnish*
*8 ounces fresh sun-dried tomato and herb tagliatelle*
*salt and freshly ground black pepper*
*1/2 ounce shaved fresh Parmesan cheese, to serve (optional)*

*SERVES 4*

**1** Put the onion and garlic in a saucepan with the vegetable stock, then cover and cook for 5 minutes or until tender, stirring occasionally.

**2** Add the mushrooms (quartered or sliced if large; left whole if small), wine, tomato paste and soy sauce. Cover and cook for 5 minutes, stirring occasionally.

### NUTRITIONAL NOTES
*Per portion:*

| | |
|---|---|
| Energy | 241cals |
| Total fat | 2.4g |
| Saturated fat | 0.7g |
| Cholesterol | 45mg |
| Fiber | 3g |

# MUSHROOM BOLOGNESE

—

**A quick—and exceedingly tasty—vegetarian version of the classic Italian dish. This dish is easy
to prepare and makes a very satisfying low-fat meal.**

### INGREDIENTS

*1 pound mushrooms*
*1 tablespoon olive oil*
*1 onion, chopped*
*1 garlic clove, crushed*
*1 tablespoon tomato paste*
*14-ounce can chopped tomatoes*
*3 tablespoons chopped fresh oregano*
*1 pound fresh pasta, such as spaghetti
or tagliatelle*
*salt and freshly ground black pepper*
*1/2 ounce shaved fresh Parmesan cheese,
to serve (optional)*

### SERVES 4

**3** Add the prepared mushrooms to the
pan and mix them gently with the olive
oil and crushed garlic. Cook over high
heat for 3–4 minutes, stirring the
mixture occasionally.

**5** Meanwhile, bring a large saucepan of
salted water to a boil. Cook the pasta
in the boiling water for 2–3 minutes or
according to the package instructions,
until tender or *al dente*.

**1** Trim the mushroom stems neatly, then
cut each mushroom into quarters. Set
them aside.

**4** Stir in the tomato paste, chopped
tomatoes and 1 tablespoon of the oregano.
Cover, reduce the heat, then cook for
about 5 minutes, stirring occasionally.

**6** Season the mushroom Bolognese sauce
with salt and pepper. Drain the pasta,
transfer to a bowl and add the mushroom
mixture. Toss to mix well. Serve in
individual bowls, topped with shavings
of fresh Parmesan, if using, and the
remaining chopped fresh oregano.

**2** Heat the olive oil in a large pan. Add
the onion and garlic and cook them for
2–3 minutes, stirring occasionally.

### COOK'S TIP

If you prefer to use dried pasta, make
this the first thing that you cook. It will
take 10–12 minutes to cook, during
which time you can make the
mushroom mixture. Use 12 ounces
dried pasta.

### NUTRITIONAL NOTES

*Per portion:*

| | |
|---|---|
| Energy | 404cals |
| Total fat | 4.9g |
| Saturated fat | 0.6g |
| Cholesterol | 0mg |
| Fiber | 5g |

# TAGLIATELLE WITH SPINACH GNOCCHI

---

**Italian-style gnocchi are extremely smooth and light and make a delicious accompaniment to this flavorful low-fat pasta dish.**

## INGREDIENTS

*1 pound mixed flavored
fresh tagliatelle
1/2 ounce shaved fresh Parmesan cheese,
to garnish (optional)*

### FOR THE SPINACH GNOCCHI

*1 pound frozen chopped spinach
1 small onion, finely chopped
1 garlic clove, crushed
1/4 teaspoon ground nutmeg
14 ounces low-fat cottage cheese
4 ounces dried white bread crumbs
3 ounces semolina or all-purpose flour
2 ounces grated fresh Parmesan cheese
3 egg whites*

### FOR THE TOMATO SAUCE

*1 onion, finely chopped
1 celery stalk, finely chopped
1 red bell pepper, deseeded and diced
1 garlic clove, crushed
2/3 cup vegetable stock
14-ounce can tomatoes
1 tablespoon tomato paste
2 teaspoons sugar
1 teaspoon dried oregano
salt and freshly ground black pepper*

### SERVES 6

**1** To make the tomato sauce, put the onion, celery, pepper and garlic into a nonstick saucepan. Add the stock, bring to a boil and cook for 5 minutes or until tender, stirring occasionally.

**2** Stir in the tomatoes, tomato paste, sugar and oregano. Season to taste, bring to a boil, then reduce the heat and simmer for 30 minutes, until thick, stirring occasionally. Keep hot.

**3** Meanwhile, make the gnocchi. Put the spinach, onion and garlic in a saucepan, cover and cook until the spinach is defrosted. Remove the lid for a minute or so, and increase the heat. Cook until the liquid has evaporated. Season with salt, pepper and nutmeg. Transfer to a bowl and let cool. Mix in the remaining gnocchi ingredients. Shape into about 30 ovals and refrigerate for 30 minutes.

**4** Cook the spinach gnocchi in a large saucepan of boiling salted water for about 5 minutes. Remove with a slotted spoon and drain. Keep hot. Meanwhile, cook the tagliatelle in a large saucepan of boiling salted water, according to the package instructions, until tender or *al dente*. Drain well. Transfer the pasta to serving plates, top with the gnocchi, the tomato sauce and shavings of Parmesan cheese, if using. Serve immediately.

## NUTRITIONAL NOTES
*Per portion:*

| | |
|---|---|
| Energy | 189cals |
| Total fat | 2g |
| Saturated fat | 0.8g |
| Cholesterol | 3.3mg |
| Fiber | 2.9g |

# RATATOUILLE PENNE CASSEROLE

Mixed Mediterranean vegetables and penne are tossed together and lightly
broiled to create this delicious and low-fat pasta meal.

**3** Put the eggplant, zucchini, pepper,
onion and remaining garlic into a
saucepan, with the stock. Bring to a boil,
cover and cook for about 10 minutes
until tender, stirring occasionally.
Remove the lid and boil until all the
stock has evaporated. Add the prepared
tomatoes and herbs and cook for another
3 minutes, stirring occasionally. Season
to taste with salt and pepper.

### INGREDIENTS

*1 small eggplant*
*2 zucchini, thickly sliced*
*7 ounces firm tofu, cubed*
*3 tablespoons dark soy sauce*
*2–3 garlic cloves, crushed*
*2 teaspoons sesame seeds*
*1 small red bell pepper, deseeded and sliced*
*1 onion, finely chopped*
*2/3 cup vegetable stock*
*3 firm ripe tomatoes, skinned, deseeded*
*and quartered*
*1 tablespoon chopped fresh mixed herbs*
*8 ounces dried penne*
*salt and freshly ground black pepper*
*crusty bread, to serve*

### SERVES 6

**1** Wash and cut the eggplant into
1-inch cubes. Put into a colander with the
zucchini, sprinkle with salt and let drain
for 30 minutes. Rinse thoroughly, drain
and set aside.

**2** Mix the tofu with the soy sauce,
1 crushed garlic clove and the sesame
seeds. Cover and let marinate for
30 minutes.

### NUTRITIONAL NOTES
*Per portion:*

| | |
|---|---|
| Energy | 208cals |
| Total fat | 3.7g |
| Saturated fat | 0.5g |
| Cholesterol | 0mg |
| Fiber | 3.9g |

**4** Meanwhile, cook the pasta in a
large saucepan of boiling salted water,
according to the package instructions,
until tender or *al dente*. Drain thoroughly.
Toss the pasta with the vegetable mixture,
the tofu and the marinade. Transfer to a
shallow 10-inch square ovenproof dish
and cook under a hot broiler until lightly
browned. Transfer the casserole to a
serving dish and serve immediately with
fresh crusty bread.

# BREADS

It's hard to beat the AROMA of freshly baked bread, and once you've mastered the basic techniques it's EASY to make your own BREAD. We bring you a selection of Italian breads ideal for breakfast, brunch or a picnic al fresco. Choose from traditional CIABATTA and Focaccia breads, Olive and Oregano Bread, Sun-dried TOMATO Breadsticks and, for a slightly sweet option, Italian CHOCOLATE Bread.

# CIABATTA

—

**This irregular-shaped Italian bread is so called because it looks like an old shoe or slipper. It is made with a wet dough flavored with olive oil, and is a great accompaniment to low-fat dishes.**

### INGREDIENTS
### FOR THE BIGA STARTER
*1/4-ounce envelope active dry yeast*
*scant 1 cup lukewarm water*
*3 cups unbleached all-purpose flour, plus extra for dusting*

### FOR THE DOUGH
*1/2 ounce active dry yeast*
*1 2/3 cups lukewarm water*
*1/4 cup lukewarm skim milk*
*5 cups unbleached white bread flour*
*2 teaspoons salt*
*3 tablespoons extra virgin olive oil*

*MAKES 3 LOAVES, SERVES 12*

**1** In a small bowl, mix the yeast for the biga starter with a little of the water. Sift the flour into a bowl. Gradually mix in the yeast mixture and enough of the remaining water to form a firm dough.

**2** Transfer the biga starter dough to a lightly floured surface and knead for about 5 minutes, until smooth. Return the dough to the bowl, cover with lightly oiled plastic wrap and let it sit in a warm place for 12–15 hours, or until the dough has risen and is starting to collapse.

**3** Sprinkle three baking sheets with flour and set aside. Mix the yeast for the dough with a little of the water until creamy, then mix in the remaining water. Add the yeast mixture to the biga and mix well. Mix in the milk, beating thoroughly with a wooden spoon. Mix in the flour by hand for 15 minutes, lifting the dough, to form a very wet mixture.

**4** Beat in the salt and olive oil. Cover with lightly oiled plastic wrap and let rise, in a warm place, for 1 1/2–2 hours or until doubled in bulk.

**5** Using a spoon, transfer one-third of the dough to each prepared baking sheet, trying to avoid punching it down in the process.

**6** Using floured hands, shape into long loaves, about 1 inch thick. Flatten slightly. Sprinkle with flour and let rise in a warm place for 30 minutes. Meanwhile, preheat the oven to 425°F. Bake the loaves for 25–30 minutes or until golden brown. Transfer to a wire rack to cool.

### NUTRITIONAL NOTES
*Per portion:*

| | |
|---|---|
| Energy | 268cals |
| Total fat | 3.7g |
| Saturated fat | 0.6g |
| Cholesterol | 0.4mg |
| Fiber | 2.2g |

# OLIVE OIL ROLLS

The Italians adore interesting and elaborately shaped rolls. This distinctively flavored bread
dough, enriched with olive oil, can be used for making rolls or shaped into one large loaf.

**4** For *filoncini* (finger rolls): flatten each
piece into an oval and roll to 9 inches
without changing the shape. Make it
2 inches wide at one end and 4 inches at
the other. Roll up from the wider end.
Stretch to 8–9 inches long. Cut in half.
Place on the baking sheets, well spaced.
Lightly brush with oil, cover with oiled
plastic wrap and let rise, in a warm place,
for 20–30 minutes.

### INGREDIENTS
*4 cups unbleached white bread flour*
*2 teaspoons salt*
*1/2 ounce active dry yeast*
*1 cup lukewarm water*
*1/4 cup extra virgin olive oil, plus*
*1 tablespoon extra for brushing*

### MAKES 16 ROLLS

**2** Transfer to a lightly floured surface
and punch down. Divide into 12 equal
pieces and shape into rolls as described
in Steps 3, 4 and 5.

**3** For *tavalli* (spiral rolls): roll each piece
into a strip about 12 inches long and
1½ inches wide. Twist into a loose spiral
and join the ends to make a circle. Place
on the baking sheets, well spaced. Lightly
brush with oil, cover with oiled plastic
wrap and let rise, in a warm place, for
20–30 minutes.

**1** Lightly oil three baking sheets and set
aside. Sift the flour and salt together in a
large bowl and make a well in the center.
In a bowl, mix the yeast with half the
water, then stir in the rest. Add to the
well with the oil and mix to form a dough.
Transfer to a lightly floured surface.
Knead for 8–10 minutes, until smooth
and elastic. Place in an oiled bowl, cover
with oiled plastic wrap and let rise, in a
warm place, for 1 hour or until almost
doubled in bulk.

### NUTRITIONAL NOTES
*Per portion:*

| | |
|---|---|
| Energy | 119cals |
| Total fat | 3.1g |
| Saturated fat | 0.4g |
| Cholesterol | 0mg |
| Fiber | 0.9g |

**5** For *carciofi* (artichoke-shaped rolls):
shape each piece into a ball and space
well apart on the baking sheets. Brush
with oil, cover with oiled plastic wrap and
let rise, in a warm place, for
20–30 minutes. Preheat the oven to
400°F. Using scissors, snip ¼-inch deep
cuts in a circle on the top of each roll,
then five larger horizontal cuts around the
sides. Bake all the rolls for 15 minutes.
Transfer to a wire rack to cool. Serve
warm or cold.

# TUSCANY BREAD

—

This bread from Tuscany is made without salt and probably originates from the days when salt was heavily taxed. To compensate for the lack of salt, serve with salty foods such as olives.

### INGREDIENTS
*5 cups unbleached all-purpose flour*
*1½ cups boiling water*
*½ ounce active dry yeast*
*¼ cup lukewarm water*

### MAKES 1 LOAF, SERVES 8

**1** First, make the starter. Sift 1½ cups of the flour into a large bowl. Pour on the boiling water, let sit for a couple of minutes, then mix well. Cover the bowl with a damp dish towel and set aside for 10 hours.

**2** Lightly flour a baking sheet and set aside. In a bowl, mix the yeast with the lukewarm water. Mix well into the starter.

**3** Gradually add the remaining flour and mix to form a dough. Transfer to a lightly floured surface and knead for 5–8 minutes, until smooth and elastic.

**4** Place in a lightly oiled bowl, cover with lightly oiled plastic wrap and let rise, in a warm place, for 1–1½ hours or until doubled in bulk.

### NUTRITIONAL NOTES
*Per portion:*

| | |
|---|---|
| Energy | 213cals |
| Total fat | 0.8g |
| Saturated fat | 0.1g |
| Cholesterol | 0mg |
| Fiber | 1.9g |

**5** Transfer the dough to a lightly floured surface, punch down, and shape into a round.

**6** Fold the sides of the round into the center and seal. Place seam-side up on the prepared baking sheet. Cover with oiled plastic wrap and let rise, in a warm place, for 30–45 minutes or until doubled in bulk.

**7** Flatten the loaf to about half its risen height and flip over. Cover with a large upturned bowl and let rise again, in a warm place, for 30 minutes.

**8** Meanwhile, preheat the oven to 425°F. Slash the top of the loaf, using a sharp knife, if desired. Bake for 30–35 minutes or until golden. Transfer to a wire rack to cool. Serve in slices or wedges.

# POLENTA BREAD

**Polenta is widely used in Italian cooking. Here it is combined with pine nuts to make a truly Italian bread with a fantastic flavor. Serve in slices topped with salad and low-fat cheese.**

### INGREDIENTS
*1/3 cup polenta*
*1 1/4 cups lukewarm water*
*1/2 ounce active dry yeast*
*1/2 teaspoon honey*
*2 cups unbleached white bread flour*
*2 tablespoons butter*
*2 tablespoons pine nuts*
*1 1/2 teaspoons salt*

### FOR THE TOPPING
*1 egg yolk*
*1 tablespoon water*
*1 tablespoon pine nuts*
*(optional)*

*MAKES 1 LOAF, SERVES 8*

**1** Lightly grease a baking sheet and set aside. Combine the polenta and 1 cup of the water in a saucepan and slowly bring to a boil, stirring continuously with a large wooden spoon. Reduce the heat and let simmer for 2–3 minutes, stirring occasionally. Remove from heat and set aside to cool for 10 minutes or until just warm.

**2** In a small bowl, mix the yeast with the remaining water and honey. Sift 1 cup of the flour into a large bowl. Gradually beat in the yeast mixture, then stir in the polenta mixture gradually to combine. Transfer to a lightly floured surface and knead for 5 minutes, until smooth and elastic. Cover the bowl with lightly oiled plastic wrap. Let the dough rise, in a warm place, for about 2 hours or until it has doubled in bulk.

**3** Meanwhile, melt the butter in a small saucepan, add the pine nuts and cook over medium heat, stirring, until pale golden. Remove the pan from heat and set aside to cool.

**4** Add the remaining flour and the salt to the polenta dough and mix to form a soft dough. Knead in the pine nuts. Transfer to a lightly floured surface and knead for 5 minutes, until smooth and elastic.

**5** Place in an oiled bowl, cover with plastic wrap and let rise, in a warm place, for 1 hour, until doubled in bulk.

### NUTRITIONAL NOTES
*Per portion:*

| | |
|---|---|
| Energy | 139cals |
| Total fat | 4.9g |
| Saturated fat | 1.7g |
| Cholesterol | 27.5mg |
| Fiber | 0.8g |

**6** Punch down the dough and transfer it to a lightly floured surface. Cut the dough into two equal pieces and roll each piece into a fat sausage about 15 inches long. Braid and place on the prepared baking sheet. Cover with lightly oiled plastic wrap and let rise, in a warm place, for 45 minutes. Preheat the oven to 400°F.

**7** Mix the egg yolk and water and brush onto the loaf. Sprinkle with pine nuts, if using, and bake for 30 minutes or until golden and hollow sounding. Transfer to a wire rack to cool.

# SICILIAN SCROLL

A wonderful pale yellow, crusty-topped loaf, enhanced with a nutty flavor from the sesame seeds. It's perfect for serving with low-fat cheese or cooked lean meats.

**3** Transfer the dough to a lightly floured surface. Knead for 8–10 minutes, until smooth and elastic. Place in a lightly oiled bowl, cover with lightly oiled plastic wrap and let rise, in a warm place, for 1–1½ hours or until the dough has doubled in bulk.

**4** Transfer to a lightly floured surface and punch down. Knead, then shape the dough into a fat roll about 20 inches long. Form into an "S" shape.

**5** Transfer to the prepared baking sheet, cover with oiled plastic wrap and let rise, in a warm place, for 30–45 minutes or until doubled in size.

### INGREDIENTS
*1 pound finely ground semolina*
*1 cup unbleached white bread flour*
*2 teaspoons salt*
*¾ ounce active dry yeast*
*generous 1½ cups lukewarm water*
*2 tablespoons extra virgin olive oil*
*2 tablespoons sesame seeds, for sprinkling*

MAKES 1 LOAF, SERVES 8

**1** Lightly grease a baking sheet and set aside. Combine the semolina, white bread flour and salt in a large bowl and make a well in the center.

**2** In a bowl, mix the yeast with half the water, then stir in the remaining water. Add the yeast to the center of the semolina mixture with the olive oil. Gradually incorporate the semolina and flour to form a firm dough.

**6** Meanwhile, preheat the oven to 425°F. Brush the top of the scroll with water and sprinkle with the sesame seeds. Bake for 10 minutes. Spray the inside of the oven with water twice during this time.

**7** Reduce the oven temperature to 400°F and bake for another 25–30 minutes or until golden. Transfer to a wire rack to cool. Serve in slices.

### NUTRITIONAL NOTES
*Per portion:*

| | |
|---|---|
| Energy | 197cals |
| Total fat | 4.1g |
| Saturated fat | 0.6g |
| Cholesterol | 0mg |
| Fiber | 0.5g |

# PROSCIUTTO LOAF

—

**This savory Italian bread from Parma is spiked with the local dried ham. Just a small amount
fills the loaf with delicious flavor and creates a great low-fat accompaniment or snack.**

### INGREDIENTS

*3 cups unbleached white bread flour*
*1¹/2 teaspoons salt*
*¹/2 ounce active dry yeast*
*1 cup lukewarm water*
*1¹/2 ounces prosciutto, torn into*
*small pieces*
*1 teaspoon ground black pepper*

### MAKES 1 LOAF, SERVES 6

**1** Lightly grease a baking sheet and set
aside. Sift the flour and salt into a bowl
and make a well in the center. In a small
bowl, mix the yeast with 2 tablespoons of
the water, then gradually mix in the rest.
Pour into the center of the flour.

**2** Gradually beat in most of the flour with
a wooden spoon to make a batter. Beat
gently at first and then more vigorously as
the batter thickens. When most of the
flour is incorporated, mix in the rest with
your hand to form a moist dough.

**3** Transfer to a lightly floured surface and
knead for 5 minutes, until smooth and
elastic. Place in an oiled bowl, cover with
lightly oiled plastic wrap and let rise, in a
warm place, for 1¹/2 hours or until
doubled in bulk.

**4** Transfer the dough to a lightly floured
surface, punch down and knead for
1 minute. Flatten into a round, then
sprinkle with half the prosciutto and
pepper. Fold in half and repeat with the
remaining ham and pepper. Roll up,
tucking in the sides.

**5** Place on the prepared baking sheet,
cover with oiled plastic wrap and let rise,
in a warm place, for 30 minutes. Transfer
to a lightly floured surface, roll into an
oval, fold in half and seal the edges.
Flatten and fold again. Seal and fold
again to make a long loaf.

**6** Roll into a stubby long loaf. Draw out
the edges by rolling the dough under the
palms of your hands. Place back on the
prepared baking sheet, cover with oiled
plastic wrap and let rise, in a warm place,
for 45 minutes or until the loaf has
doubled in bulk. Preheat the oven to
400°F.

**7** Slash the top of the loaf diagonally
three or four times, using a sharp knife,
and bake for 30 minutes or until
golden. Transfer to a wire rack to cool.
Serve in slices.

### NUTRITIONAL NOTES
*Per portion:*

| | |
|---|---|
| Energy | 200cals |
| Total fat | 1.6g |
| Saturated fat | 0.5g |
| Cholesterol | 3.3mg |
| Fiber | 1.7g |

# PROSCIUTTO AND PARMESAN BREAD

—

**This nourishing Italian bread is ideal served in slices and topped with grilled vegetables for a tasty, low-fat lunch or supper.**

### INGREDIENTS

*4 cups self-rising flour*
*1 teaspoon baking powder*
*1 teaspoon salt*
*1 teaspoon ground black pepper*
*3 ounces prosciutto, chopped*
*2 tablespoons grated fresh
Parmesan cheese*
*2 tablespoons chopped fresh parsley*
*3 tablespoons mustard*
*1 1/2 cups buttermilk*
*skim milk, to glaze*

*MAKES 1 LOAF, SERVES 8*

**3** Shape the dough into an oval loaf, brush with milk and sprinkle with the remaining cheese. Place the loaf on the prepared baking sheet.

### NUTRITIONAL NOTES
*Per portion:*

| | |
|---|---|
| Energy | 250cals |
| Total fat | 3.65g |
| Saturated fat | 1.30g |
| Cholesterol | 7.09mg |
| Fiber | 3.81g |

**4** Bake for 25–30 minutes or until golden brown. Transfer to a wire rack to cool. Serve in slices.

**1** Preheat the oven to 400°F. Flour a baking sheet and set aside. Place the flour in a bowl and sift in the baking powder and salt. Add the pepper and prosciutto. Set aside about 1 tablespoon of the grated Parmesan and stir the rest into the flour mixture. Stir in the parsley. Make a well in the center of the mixture.

**2** Combine the mustard and buttermilk in a bowl, pour into the flour mixture and quickly mix into a soft dough. Transfer the dough to a lightly floured surface and knead briefly.

# OLIVE AND HERB BREAD

Olive breads are popular all over the Mediterranean, especially in Italy. This delicious
olive bread is an ideal low-fat accompaniment to pasta dishes or salads.

### INGREDIENTS
*2 red onions, thinly sliced*
*2 tablespoons olive oil*
*1 1/2 cups pitted black or green olives*
*7 cups white bread flour*
*1 1/2 teaspoons salt*
*4 teaspoons active dry yeast*
*3 tablespoons roughly chopped fresh
parsley, cilantro or mint*
*2 cups hand-hot water*

### MAKES 2 LOAVES
### (EACH LOAF SERVES 10)

**1** Sauté the onions in the oil in a
saucepan until soft. Remove the pan from
heat and set aside. Roughly chop the
black or green olives and set aside.

**2** Put the flour, salt, yeast and parsley,
cilantro or mint in a large bowl with the
olives and onions and pour in the water.
Mix into a dough using a round-bladed
knife, adding a little more water if the
mixture feels dry.

### VARIATION
Shape the dough into 16 small rolls.
Slash the tops as above and reduce the
cooking time to 25 minutes.

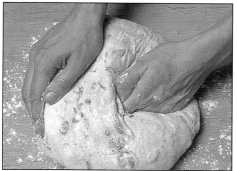

**3** Transfer to a lightly floured surface and
knead for about 10 minutes, until smooth
and elastic. Put in a clean bowl, cover
with plastic wrap and let sit in a warm
place until doubled in bulk.

**4** Preheat the oven to 425°F. Lightly
grease two baking sheets. Transfer the
dough to a lightly floured surface and cut
in half. Shape into two rounds. Place on
the prepared baking sheets, cover loosely
with lightly oiled plastic wrap and let sit
until doubled in bulk.

**5** Slash the tops of the loaves with a sharp
knife, then bake for about 40 minutes or
until they sound hollow when tapped
underneath. Transfer to a wire rack to
cool. Serve in slices.

### NUTRITIONAL NOTES
*Per portion:*

| | |
|---|---|
| Energy | 157cals |
| Total fat | 2.9g |
| Saturated fat | 0.41g |
| Cholesterol | 0mg |
| Fiber | 1.8g |

# OLIVE AND OREGANO BREAD

—

**This tasty Italian bread is an excellent low-fat accompaniment to all salads and is particularly good served warm.**

## INGREDIENTS

*1¼ cups warm water*
*1 teaspoon active dry yeast*
*pinch of sugar*
*1 tablespoon olive oil*
*1 onion, chopped*
*4 cups white bread flour, plus extra*
*for dusting*
*1 teaspoon salt*
*¼ teaspoon ground black pepper*
*½ cup pitted black olives,*
*roughly chopped*
*1 tablespoon black olive paste*
*1 tablespoon chopped*
*fresh oregano*
*1 tablespoon chopped*
*fresh parsley*

**MAKES 1 LOAF, SERVES 8**

**1** Put half the warm water in a bowl. Sprinkle the yeast on top. Add the sugar, mix well and set aside for 10 minutes.

## NUTRITIONAL NOTES

*Per portion:*

| | |
|---|---|
| Energy | 211cals |
| Total fat | 2.8g |
| Saturated fat | 0.4g |
| Cholesterol | 0mg |
| Fiber | 2g |

**2** Heat the oil in a frying pan and sauté the onion until golden brown, stirring occasionally. Remove the pan from heat and set aside.

**3** Sift the flour into a mixing bowl with the salt and pepper. Make a well in the center. Add the yeast mixture, the onions (with the oil), the olives, olive paste, oregano, parsley and remaining water. Gradually incorporate the flour and mix into a soft dough, adding a little extra water if necessary.

**4** Transfer the dough to a lightly floured surface and knead for 5 minutes, until smooth and elastic. Place in a mixing bowl, cover with a damp dish towel and let rise in a warm place for about 2 hours, until the dough has doubled in bulk. Lightly grease a baking sheet and set aside.

**5** Transfer the dough to a lightly floured surface and knead again for a few minutes. Shape into an 8-inch round and place on the prepared baking sheet. Using a sharp knife, make criss-cross cuts on top of the dough. Cover and set in a warm place for 30 minutes, until well risen. Preheat the oven to 425°F.

**6** Dust the loaf with a little flour. Bake for 10 minutes, then lower the oven temperature to 400°F. Bake for another 20 minutes or until the loaf sounds hollow when it is tapped underneath. Transfer to a wire rack to cool. Serve the bread warm or cold in slices or wedges.

# MIXED OLIVE BREAD

Mixed black and green olives and good-quality fruity olive oil combine to make this strongly flavored and irresistible Italian bread, ideal for a tasty low-fat snack.

### INGREDIENTS

*2¹/₂ cups unbleached white bread flour*
*¹/₂ cup whole-wheat flour*
*¹/₄-ounce envelope active dry yeast*
*¹/₂ teaspoon salt*
*scant 1 cup lukewarm water*
*1 tablespoon extra virgin olive oil, plus*
*1 tablespoon olive oil for brushing*
*2/3 cup mixed pitted black and green*
*olives, coarsely chopped*

***MAKES 1 LOAF, SERVES 8***

**1** Lightly grease a baking sheet and set aside. Mix the flours, yeast and salt in a bowl and make a well in the centre.

**2** Add the water and 1 tablespoon oil to the center of the flour and mix to form a soft dough. Knead the dough on a lightly floured surface for 8–10 minutes, until smooth and elastic. Place in a lightly oiled bowl, cover with oiled plastic wrap and let rise, in a warm place, for 1 hour or until doubled in bulk.

**3** Transfer the dough to a lightly floured surface and punch down. Flatten out and sprinkle on the olives. Knead to distribute the olives evenly throughout the dough. Let rest for 5 minutes, then shape into an oval loaf. Place on the prepared baking sheet.

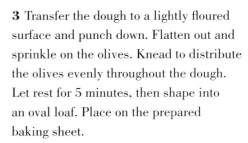

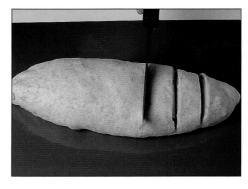

**4** Make six deep cuts in the top of the dough and gently push the sections over. Cover with oiled plastic wrap and let rise, in a warm place, for 30–45 minutes or until doubled in bulk.

**5** Meanwhile, preheat the oven to 400°F. Brush the bread with olive oil and bake for 35 minutes. Transfer to a wire rack to cool. Serve warm or cold in slices.

### NUTRITIONAL NOTES
*Per portion:*

| | |
|---|---|
| Energy | 165cals |
| Total fat | 3.5g |
| Saturated fat | 0.5g |
| Cholesterol | 0mg |
| Fiber | 2g |

# HAM AND TOMATO SCONES

—

These delicious home-baked scones make an ideal accompaniment for low-fat soup.
They are best eaten fresh on the day they are made, served either warm or cold.

### INGREDIENTS

*2 cups self-rising flour*
*1 teaspoon dry mustard*
*1 teaspoon paprika, plus extra*
*for sprinkling*
*1/2 teaspoon salt*
*2 tablespoons low-fat margarine*
*1 tablespoon chopped fresh basil*
*1 cup dry-packed sun-dried tomatoes,*
*soaked in warm water, drained and chopped*
*2 ounces cooked lean ham, chopped*
*6 tablespoons–1/2 cup skim milk, plus*
*extra for brushing*

*MAKES 12*

**1** Preheat the oven to 400°F. Flour a large baking sheet and set aside. Sift the flour, mustard, paprika and salt into a bowl. Rub in the margarine until the mixture resembles bread crumbs.

**2** Stir in the basil, sun-dried tomatoes and ham, and mix lightly. Pour in enough milk to mix into a soft dough.

**3** Transfer to a lightly floured surface, knead briefly and roll out to an 8 × 6-inch rectangle. Cut into 2-inch squares and arrange on the baking sheet.

**4** Brush the tops lightly with milk, sprinkle with paprika and bake for 12–15 minutes. Transfer to a wire rack to cool. Serve warm or cold.

### NUTRITIONAL NOTES
*Per portion:*

| | |
|---|---|
| Energy | 115cals |
| Total fat | 4.4g |
| Saturated fat | 1g |
| Cholesterol | 3.6mg |
| Fiber | 1g |

# ROSEMARY AND SEA SALT FOCACCIA

Focaccia is an appetizing Italian flat bread made with olive oil.
Here it is given added flavor with rosemary and coarse sea salt.

### INGREDIENTS
*3 cups all-purpose flour*
*1/2 teaspoon salt*
*2 teaspoons active dry yeast*
*1 cup lukewarm water*
*3 tablespoons olive oil*
*1 small red onion*
*leaves from 1 large fresh*
*rosemary sprig*
*1 teaspoon coarse sea salt*
*oil, for greasing*

### MAKES 1 LOAF, SERVES 8

**1** Sift the flour and salt into a mixing bowl. Stir in the yeast, then make a well in the middle of the dry ingredients.

**2** Pour in the water and 2 tablespoons of the oil. Mix well to make a dough, adding a little more water if the mixture seems too dry.

**3** Transfer the dough to a lightly floured surface and knead it for about 10 minutes, until smooth and elastic.

**4** Place the dough in a greased bowl, cover and let rise in a warm place for about 1 hour, until doubled in bulk. Punch down and knead the dough on a lightly floured surface for 2–3 minutes.

**5** Preheat the oven to 425°F and grease a baking sheet. Roll the dough to a circle 1/2-inch thick, transfer to the baking sheet and brush with remaining oil.

**6** Halve the onion and chop it into thin slices. Press the slices lightly onto the dough, with the rosemary and sea salt.

**7** Using a finger, make deep indentations in the dough. Cover the surface with oiled plastic wrap, then let rise in a warm place for 30 minutes. Remove and discard the plastic wrap and bake the loaf for 25–30 minutes, until golden. Transfer to a wire rack to cool. Serve in slices or wedges.

### COOK'S TIP
Use flavored olive oil, such as chili or herb oil, for extra flavor. Whole-wheat flour or a mixture of whole-wheat and white flour works well with this recipe.

### NUTRITIONAL NOTES
*Per portion:*

| | |
|---|---|
| Energy | 191cals |
| Total fat | 4.72g |
| Saturated fat | 0.68g |
| Cholesterol | 0mg |
| Fiber | 1.46g |

# SAFFRON FOCACCIA

A dazzling yellow bread with a distinctive flavor, this saffron focaccia
makes a tasty snack.

### INGREDIENTS
### FOR THE DOUGH
*pinch of saffron threads*
*2/3 cup boiling water*
*2 cups all-purpose flour*
*1/2 teaspoon salt*
*1 teaspoon active dry yeast*
*1 tablespoon olive oil*

### FOR THE TOPPING
*2 garlic cloves, sliced*
*1 red onion, cut into thin wedges*
*fresh rosemary sprigs*
*12 black olives, pitted and*
*coarsely chopped*
*1 tablespoon olive oil*

### MAKES 1 LOAF, SERVES 10

**1** Make the dough. In a bowl, infuse the
saffron in the boiling water. Let sit until
cooled to lukewarm.

**2** Place the flour, salt, yeast and olive oil
in a food processor. Turn the processor on
and gradually add the saffron and its
liquid until the dough forms a ball.

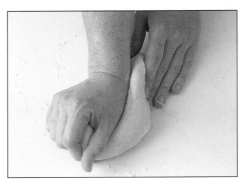

**3** Transfer the dough to a lightly
floured work surface and knead for
10–15 minutes, until smooth and elastic.
Place in a bowl, cover and let rise in a
warm place for 30–40 minutes, until
doubled in bulk. Lightly grease a baking
sheet and set aside.

**4** Punch down the risen dough on a
lightly floured surface and roll out into an
oval shape about 1/2 inch thick. Place on
the prepared baking sheet and let rise in
a warm place for 20–30 minutes.

**5** Preheat the oven to 400°F. Use your
fingers to press small indentations
in the dough.

**6** Cover the dough with the topping
ingredients, brush lightly with the olive
oil, and bake for about 25 minutes or
until it sounds hollow when tapped
underneath. Transfer to a wire rack
to cool. Serve the focaccia in slices
or wedges.

### VARIATION
You might like to experiment with
different topping ingredients for this
bread. Green olives and sun-dried
tomatoes are two others you could try.

### NUTRITIONAL NOTES
*Per portion:*

| | |
|---|---|
| Energy | 177cals |
| Total fat | 4.7g |
| Saturated fat | 0.7g |
| Cholesterol | 0mg |
| Fiber | 1.5g |

# ONION FOCACCIA

This typical Italian pizza-like flat bread is characterized by its soft dimpled surface. This focaccia is flavored with red onions and makes a tasty low-fat snack.

### INGREDIENTS
*6 cups white bread flour*
*¹/₂ teaspoon salt*
*¹/₂ teaspoon sugar*
*1 tablespoon active dry yeast*
*3 tablespoons extra virgin olive oil*
*scant 2 cups lukewarm water*

### TO FINISH
*2 red onions, thinly sliced*
*1 tablespoon extra virgin olive oil*
*1 tablespoon coarse salt*

### MAKES 2 LOAVES, SERVES 12

**1** Sift the flour, salt and sugar into a large bowl. Stir in the yeast, oil and water and mix into a dough using a round-bladed knife, adding a little extra water if the dough is dry.

**2** Transfer the dough to a lightly floured surface and knead for about 10 minutes, until smooth and elastic. Put the dough in a clean, lightly oiled bowl and cover with plastic wrap. Let rise in a warm place until doubled in bulk.

**3** Place two 10-inch plain metal flan rings on baking sheets. Oil the sides of the rings and the baking sheets.

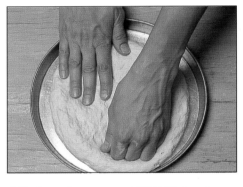

**4** Preheat the oven to 400°F. Halve the dough and roll each piece of dough into a 10-inch round. Press into the prepared flan rings, cover with a damp dish towel and let rise in a warm place for 30 minutes.

**5** Using a finger, make deep holes, about 1 inch apart, in the dough. Cover and set aside for another 20 minutes.

**6** To finish, sprinkle on the onions and drizzle on the oil. Sprinkle on the salt, then a little cold water, to stop a crust from forming.

**7** Bake for about 25 minutes, until golden, sprinkling with water again during cooking. Transfer to a wire rack to cool. Serve in slices or wedges.

### NUTRITIONAL NOTES
*Per portion:*

| | |
|---|---|
| Energy | 231cals |
| Total fat | 4.4g |
| Saturated fat | 0.6g |
| Cholesterol | 0mg |
| Fiber | 1.9g |

### COOK'S TIP
When buying onions, look for ones with dry, papery skins. To slice them, cut a slice from the top and remove the skin. Halve lengthwise and slice each half separately.

# SAFFRON AND BASIL BREADSTICKS

Saffron lends its delicate aroma and flavor, as well as rich yellow color, to these tasty breadsticks, ideal as a low-fat snack.

### INGREDIENTS
*generous pinch of saffron threads*
*2 tablespoons hot water*
*4 cups white bread flour*
*1 teaspoon salt*
*2 teaspoons active dry yeast*
*1 1/4 cups lukewarm water*
*3 tablespoons olive oil*
*3 tablespoons chopped fresh basil*

### MAKES 32

**3** Add the oil and basil and continue to mix to form a soft dough.

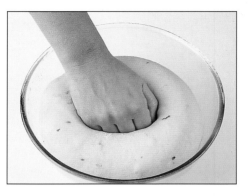

**6** Punch down and knead the dough on a lightly floured surface for 2–3 minutes.

**1** In a small bowl, infuse the saffron threads in the hot water for 10 minutes.

**2** Sift the flour and salt into a large mixing bowl. Stir in the yeast, then make a well in the center of the dry ingredients. Pour in the lukewarm water and saffron liquid and start to mix a little.

**4** Knead the dough on a lightly floured surface for about 10 minutes, until smooth and elastic.

**5** Place in a greased bowl, cover with plastic wrap and let rise in a warm place for about 1 hour, until the dough has doubled in bulk.

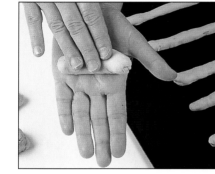

**7** Preheat the oven to 425°F. Lightly grease two baking sheets and set aside. Divide the dough into 32 even pieces and shape into long sticks. Place them well apart on the prepared baking sheets, then leave them for another 15–20 minutes, until they become puffy. Bake for about 15 minutes, until crisp and golden. Transfer to a wire rack to cool. Serve warm or cold.

### COOK'S TIP
Use powdered saffron if saffron threads are not available. Turmeric is an inexpensive alternative: it imparts a lovely gold color, but its flavor is not as delicate.

### NUTRITIONAL NOTES
*Per portion:*

| | |
|---|---|
| Energy | 59cals |
| Total fat | 1.3g |
| Saturated fat | 1.17g |
| Cholesterol | 0mg |
| Fiber | 0.4g |

# SUN-DRIED TOMATO BREADSTICKS

Once you've tried this delicious and simple recipe you'll never buy manufactured breadsticks
again. Serve with a low-fat dip or with low-fat cheese to end a meal.

### INGREDIENTS
*2 cups all-purpose flour*
*1/2 teaspoon salt*
*1 1/2 teaspoons active dry yeast*
*1 teaspoon honey*
*1 teaspoon olive oil*
*2/3 cup warm water*
*6 sun-dried tomato halves in olive oil,*
*drained and chopped*
*1 tablespoon skim milk*
*2 teaspoons poppy seeds*

### MAKES 16

**1** Place the flour, salt and yeast in a food
processor. Add the honey and olive oil
and, with the processor running, gradually
pour in the water (you may not need to
add it all, as flours vary). Stop adding
water as soon as the dough starts to stick
together. Process for another 1 minute.
Transfer the dough to a lightly floured
surface. Knead for 3–4 minutes, until
smooth and elastic.

### NUTRITIONAL NOTES
*Per portion:*

| Energy | 54cals |
|---|---|
| Total fat | 0.8g |
| Saturated fat | 0.1g |
| Cholesterol | 0.02mg |
| Fiber | 0.5g |

**2** Once the dough is very smooth, knead
in the chopped sun-dried tomatoes.
Form the dough into a large ball and
place in a lightly oiled bowl. Let rest
for 5 minutes. Lightly oil a baking sheet
and set aside. Preheat the oven to 300°F.

**3** Divide the dough into 16 equal pieces
and roll each piece into an 11 × 1/2-inch
long stick. Place on the prepared baking
sheet and let rise in a warm place for
15 minutes.

**4** Brush the sticks with milk and sprinkle
with poppy seeds. Bake for 30 minutes.
Place on a wire rack to cool.

# CHOCOLATE BREAD
—

**This slightly sweet chocolate bread from Italy is often served with a little creamy mascarpone as a special dessert. The dark chocolate pieces add texture.**

**3** Transfer the dough to a lightly floured surface and punch down. Knead in the chocolate, then cover with oiled plastic wrap. Let rest for 5 minutes.

**4** Shape the dough into a round and place in the prepared pan. Cover with lightly oiled plastic wrap and let rise, in a warm place, for 45 minutes or until doubled in bulk.

## INGREDIENTS

*3 cups unbleached white bread flour*
*1 1/2 tablespoons unsweetened*
*cocoa powder*
*1/2 teaspoon salt*
*2 tablespoons sugar*
*1/2 ounce active dry yeast*
*1 cup lukewarm water*
*2 tablespoons butter, softened*
*3 ounces semi-sweet chocolate,*
*coarsely chopped*
*1 tablespoon melted butter, for brushing*

*MAKES 1 LOAF, SERVES 12*

**1** Lightly grease a 6-inch deep round cake pan. Set aside. Sift the flour, cocoa and salt together in a large bowl. Stir in the sugar. Make a well in the center.

**2** Mix the yeast with 1/4 cup of the water, then stir in the remaining water. Add to the center of the flour mixture and mix into a dough. Knead in the butter, then turn out and knead on a lightly floured surface until smooth and elastic. Place in an oiled bowl, cover with plastic wrap and let rise, in a warm place, for 1 hour or until doubled in bulk.

**5** Preheat the oven to 425°F. Bake for 10 minutes, then reduce the oven temperature to 375°F and bake for another 25–30 minutes. Brush the hot bread with melted butter and transfer to a wire rack to cool. Serve in slices.

### VARIATION
You can also bake this in one large or two small rounds on a baking sheet.

## NUTRITIONAL NOTES
*Per portion:*

| | |
|---|---|
| Energy | 154cals |
| Total fat | 4.8g |
| Saturated fat | 2.8g |
| Cholesterol | 7.4mg |
| Fiber | 1.0g |

# DESSERTS
## AND
# BAKED GOODS

*Desserts provide the flavorful* FINALÉ *to
a meal, and we include a collection of
delectable* HOT *and cold Italian
desserts, all of which are* LOW *in fat!
Choose from delights such as classic*
ZABAGLIONE, *Broiled Nectarines
with Ricotta,* SORBETS, *including*
MANGO *and Lime and Watermelon,
Chocolate* AMARETTI *and Biscotti.*

# ZABAGLIONE

—

A much-loved, simple and very delicious Italian dessert traditionally made with Marsala,
an Italian fortified wine, although Madeira is a good alternative.

### INGREDIENTS
*4 egg yolks*
*¹/4 cup sugar*
*¹/4 cup Marsala or Madeira*
*amaretti cookies, to serve (optional)*

### SERVES 6

**1** Place the egg yolks and sugar in a
large, clean, heatproof bowl and beat with
an electric beater until the mixture is pale
and thick and forms fluffy peaks when the
beaters are lifted.

**2** Gradually add the Marsala or Madeira,
beating well after each addition (at this
stage the mixture will be quite runny).

### VARIATION
If you don't have any Marsala or
Madeira, you could use a medium-
sweet sherry or a dessert wine.

**3** Now place the bowl over a pan of gently
simmering water and continue to beat for
at least 5–7 minutes, until the mixture
becomes thick and mousse-like; when the
beaters are lifted, they should leave a
thick trail on the surface of the mixture.

**4** Pour into six warmed, stemmed small
glasses and serve immediately with the
amaretti cookies for dipping, if desired.

### NUTRITIONAL NOTES
*Per portion:*

| | |
|---|---:|
| Energy | 93cals |
| Total fat | 4.1g |
| Saturated fat | 1.2g |
| Cholesterol | 150.9mg |
| Fiber | 0g |

# STUFFED PEACHES WITH ALMOND LIQUEUR

—

Together amaretti cookies and Amaretto liqueur have an intense almond flavor, and make a natural partner for peaches in this exquisite Italian low-fat dessert.

**2** Put the amaretti cookies in a bowl and crush them finely with the end of a rolling pin. Set aside.

**3** Cream the low-fat margarine and sugar together in a separate bowl until smooth. Stir in the reserved chopped peach flesh, the egg yolk and half the liqueur with the amaretti crumbs. Mix well. Lightly grease an ovenproof dish that is just large enough to hold the peach halves in a single layer.

### INGREDIENTS
*4 ripe but firm peaches*
*1/2 cup amaretti cookies*
*2 tablespoons low-fat margarine*
*2 tablespoons sugar*
*1 egg yolk*
*1/4 cup Amaretto liqueur*
*a little low-fat margarine, for greasing*
*1 cup dry white wine*
*8 tiny sprigs of fresh basil, to decorate*

*SERVES 4*

**1** Preheat the oven to 350°F. Cut the peaches in half and remove and discard the pits. With a spoon, scrape out some of the flesh from each peach half, slightly enlarging the hollow left by the pit. Chop this flesh and set it aside. Set the peach halves aside.

**4** Stand the peach halves in the dish and spoon the amaretti stuffing into them. Mix the remaining liqueur with the wine, pour over the peaches and bake for 25 minutes or until the peaches feel tender. Decorate with basil sprigs and serve immediately, with a little low-fat ice cream, if desired.

### NUTRITIONAL NOTES
*Per portion:*

| | |
|---|---|
| Energy | 232cals |
| Total fat | 5g |
| Saturated fat | 1.37g |
| Cholesterol | 54.7mg |
| Fiber | 1.9g |

# BROILED NECTARINES WITH RICOTTA

**This tasty Italian dessert is quick and easy to make at any time of year—use canned peach halves if fresh nectarines or peaches are not available.**

### INGREDIENTS

*4 ripe nectarines or peaches*
*1 tablespoon light brown sugar*
*1/2 cup low-fat ricotta cheese*
*1/2 teaspoon ground star anise*

### SERVES 4

**2** Arrange the halved nectarines or peaches, cut-side up, in a wide flame-proof dish or on a baking sheet.

**3** Stir the sugar into the ricotta. Using a teaspoon, spoon the mixture into the hollow of each nectarine or peach half.

**1** Cut the nectarines or peaches in half and remove and discard the pits.

### COOK'S TIP

Star anise has a warm, rich flavor—if you can't get it, try ground cloves or ground allspice instead.

**4** Sprinkle with the star anise. Place the nectarines or peaches under a medium hot broiler for 6–8 minutes, or until they are hot and bubbling. Serve warm.

### NUTRITIONAL NOTES
*Per portion:*

| | |
|---|---|
| Energy | 83cals |
| Total fat | 2g |
| Saturated fat | 1.3g |
| Cholesterol | 7.17mg |
| Fiber | 1.7g |

# BROILED NECTARINES WITH AMARETTO

Amaretto, the sweet almond-flavored liqueur from Italy, adds a touch of luxury
to these delicious low-fat broiled nectarines.

**INGREDIENTS**

*6 ripe nectarines*

*2 tablespoons honey*

*1/4 cup Amaretto*

*low-fat crème fraîche, to serve (optional)*

**SERVES 4**

### NUTRITIONAL NOTES

*Per portion:*

| | |
|---|---|
| Energy | 150cals |
| Total fat | 0.2g |
| Saturated fat | 0g |
| Cholesterol | 0mg |
| Fiber | 2.7g |

**1** Cut the nectarines in half by running a small sharp knife down the side of each fruit from top to bottom, pushing the knife right through to the pit. Gently ease the nectarine apart and remove and discard the pit. Try not to handle the fruit too much, as nectarines bruise easily.

**2** Place the nectarines cut side up in an ovenproof dish and drizzle 1/2 teaspoon honey and 1 teaspoon Amaretto on each nectarine half. Preheat the broiler until very hot and then broil the fruit until slightly charred. Serve warm with a little low-fat crème fraîche, if desired.

# STRAWBERRY CONCHIGLIE SALAD

This is a divinely decadent Italian low-fat dessert, laced with liqueur and luscious raspberry sauce, for the whole family to enjoy.

## INGREDIENTS

*1¹/2 cups dried conchiglie*
*a little salt*
*8 ounces fresh or frozen raspberries,*
*thawed if frozen*
*1–2 tablespoons sugar*
*lemon juice*
*1 pound small fresh strawberries*
*¹/2 ounce sliced almonds*
*3 tablespoons kirsch*

**SERVES 4**

**1** Cook the pasta in a large saucepan of boiling lightly salted water, according to the package instructions, until tender or *al dente*. Drain well and set aside to cool.

**2** Purée the raspberries in a blender or food processor and press through a sieve to remove the seeds. Discard the seeds.

**3** Add the sugar to the raspberry purée, then place in a saucepan and simmer for 5–6 minutes, stirring occasionally. Add lemon juice to taste. Remove the pan from heat and set aside to cool.

**4** Hull the strawberries and halve if necessary. Toss with the pasta and transfer to a serving bowl.

**5** Spread the almonds out on a baking sheet and toast under a hot broiler until golden. Set aside to cool.

**6** Stir the kirsch into the raspberry sauce and pour over the pasta salad. Sprinkle on the toasted almonds and serve.

### COOK'S TIP
Like all berries, strawberries and raspberries should be used as soon as possible after they are picked. Wash them very gently and use immediately.

### VARIATION
You might like to try making sweet pasta salads with other types of berries, such as blackberries and loganberries.

### NUTRITIONAL NOTES
*Per portion:*

| | |
|---|---|
| Energy | 203cals |
| Total fat | 1.8g |
| Saturated fat | 0.2g |
| Cholesterol | 0mg |
| Fiber | 3.4g |

# FRESH FIG, APPLE AND DATE DESSERT

Sweet Mediterranean figs and dates combine especially well with crisp apples to create this appetizing low-fat dessert. A hint of almond serves to unite the flavors.

### INGREDIENTS
*6 large apples*
*juice of 1/2 lemon*
*6 ounces fresh dates*
*1 ounce white marzipan*
*1 teaspoon orange flower water*
*1/4 cup low-fat yogurt*
*4 ripe green or purple fresh figs*
*4 whole almonds, toasted*

### SERVES 4

**1** Core the apples. Slice them thinly, then cut into thin matchsticks. Put into a bowl, sprinkle with lemon juice to keep them white and set aside.

**2** Remove and discard the pits from the dates and cut the flesh into thin strips, then combine with the apple slices. Toss to mix.

**3** In a small bowl, soften the marzipan with the orange flower water and combine this with the yogurt. Mix well.

**4** Pile the mixed apples and dates into the center of four plates. Remove and discard the stem from each of the figs and cut the fruit into quarters without cutting right through the base. Squeeze the base with the thumb and forefinger of each hand to open up the fruit.

**5** Place a fig in the center of each apple and date salad, spoon in some yogurt filling and decorate each portion with a toasted almond. Serve.

### COOK'S TIPS
• Figs are at their best right off the tree when they are perfectly ripe. Bear in mind that ripe figs are extremely delicate and do not travel well, so take great care not to squash them on the way home. If you buy underripe figs, they can be kept at room temperature for a day or two until the skin softens, but they will never develop the fine flavor of tree-ripened figs. Ripe figs should be eaten on the day they are bought.
• When choosing fresh dates, select those that are fat and shiny, with skins that are golden and smooth. You may wish to remove the skin by squeezing the stem end. Most figs, however, have thin skins that are edible.

### NUTRITIONAL NOTES
*Per portion:*

| | |
|---|---|
| Energy | 178cals |
| Total fat | 2.3g |
| Saturated fat | 0.2g |
| Cholesterol | 0.5mg |
| Fiber | 4.4g |

### VARIATION
For a true Mediterranean touch, use fresh fig or grape leaves, if available, to decorate the serving plates for this dessert.

# FIGS WITH RICOTTA CREAM

—

**Fresh, ripe figs are full of natural sweetness and need little adornment. This simple Italian recipe makes the most of their intense flavor and creates a mouthwatering low-fat dessert.**

## INGREDIENTS

*4 ripe, fresh figs*
*1/2 cup low-fat ricotta or cottage cheese*
*3 tablespoons low-fat crème fraîche*
*1 tablespoon honey*
*1/2 teaspoon vanilla extract*
*freshly grated nutmeg, to decorate*

### SERVES 4

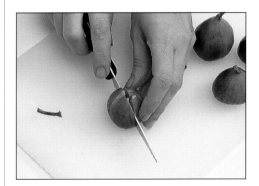

**1** Trim the stems from the figs. Make four cuts through each fig from the stem end, cutting them almost through but leaving them joined at the base.

**2** Place the figs on serving plates and open them out.

**3** In a bowl, combine the ricotta or cottage cheese, crème fraîche, honey and vanilla.

### NUTRITIONAL NOTES
*Per portion:*

| | |
|---|---|
| Energy | 55cals |
| Total fat | 2g |
| Saturated fat | 1.2g |
| Cholesterol | 6.7mg |
| Fiber | 0g |

**4** Spoon a little ricotta cream onto each plate and sprinkle with grated nutmeg to decorate. Serve.

# MANGO AND LIME SORBET IN LIME SHELLS

—

**This richly flavored virtually fat-free sorbet looks pretty served in the lime shells,
but is also good served in scoops for a more traditional presentation.**

### INGREDIENTS
*4 large limes*
*1 ripe mango*
*1¹/₂ teaspoons powdered gelatin*
*2 egg whites*
*1 tablespoon sugar*
*pared lime zest strips,*
*to decorate*

### SERVES 4

### NUTRITIONAL NOTES
*Per portion:*

| | |
|---|---|
| Energy | 50.5cals |
| Total fat | 0.09g |
| Saturated fat | 0.3g |
| Cholesterol | 0mg |
| Fiber | 1g |

**2** Peel, halve, pit and chop the mango,
then purée the flesh in a blender or food
processor with 2 tablespoons of the lime
juice. Set aside. Dissolve the gelatin in
3 tablespoons of lime juice in a small bowl
placed over a saucepan of simmering
water, then stir it into the mango mixture.

**3** Whisk the egg whites in a bowl until
they hold soft peaks. Whisk in the sugar,
then quickly fold the egg white mixture
into the mango mixture. Spoon the
mixture into the lime shells. (Any leftover
sorbet that will not fit in can be frozen in
small ramekins.)

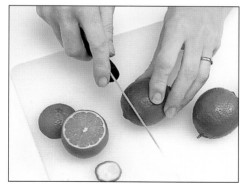

**1** Cut a thick slice from the top of each
of the limes, and then cut a thin slice
from the bottom end so that the limes will
stand upright. Squeeze out the juice, then
use a small sharp knife to remove all the
white membrane from the centers.
Discard the membranes. Set the lime
shells aside.

**4** Wrap the lime shells in plastic wrap
and put in the freezer until the sorbet is
firm. Before serving, let the lime shells
stand at room temperature for about
10 minutes; decorate them with strips of
pared lime zest and serve.

# BAKED FRUIT COMPOTE

—

**Mixed dried fruits, combined with fruit juice and spices, then baked, make a nutritious and warming Italian-style winter dessert.**

### INGREDIENTS

*2/3 cup dried figs*
*1/2 cup dried apricots*
*1/2 cup dried apple rings*
*1/4 cup prunes*
*1/2 cup dried pears*
*1/2 cup dried peaches*
*1 1/4 cups unsweetened apple juice*
*1 1/4 cups unsweetened orange juice*
*6 cloves*
*1 cinnamon stick*
*toasted sliced almonds,*
*to decorate (optional)*

### SERVES 6

**1** Preheat the oven to 350°F. Place the figs, apricots, apple rings, prunes, pears and peaches in a shallow ovenproof dish and stir to mix.

**2** Combine the apple and orange juices and pour over the fruit. Add the cloves and cinnamon stick and stir gently to mix.

**3** Bake for about 30 minutes until the fruit mixture is hot, stirring once or twice during cooking. Remove from the oven, set aside and let soak for 20 minutes, then remove and discard the cloves and cinnamon stick.

**4** Spoon into serving bowls and serve warm or cold, decorated with toasted sliced almonds, if desired.

### NUTRITIONAL NOTES
*Per portion:*

| | |
|---|---|
| Energy | 174cals |
| Total fat | 0.8g |
| Saturated fat | 0.05g |
| Cholesterol | 0mg |
| Fiber | 5.16g |

# MANGO FROZEN YOGURT

—

**Serve this delicious mango frozen yogurt in scoops for a popular and low-fat family dessert.**

### INGREDIENTS

*1 pound ripe mango flesh, chopped*
*1 1/4 cups low-fat peach or apricot yogurt*
*2/3 cup low-fat plain yogurt*
*2–4 tablespoons sugar*
*fresh mint sprigs, to decorate*

### SERVES 6

**1** Place the mango flesh in a blender or food processor and blend until smooth. Transfer to a bowl. Add the yogurts and mix thoroughly.

**2** Add enough of the sugar to sweeten to taste and stir to mix. Pour into a shallow, plastic container. Cover and freeze for 1 1/2–2 hours, until it is mushy in consistency. Transfer the mixture to a chilled bowl and beat until smooth.

**3** Return the mixture to the plastic container, cover and freeze until firm. Transfer to the refrigerator about 30 minutes before serving to let it soften a little. Serve in scoops, decorated with fresh mint sprigs.

### NUTRITIONAL NOTES
*Per portion:*

| | |
|---|---|
| Energy | 155cals |
| Total fat | 2.9g |
| Saturated fat | 1.7g |
| Cholesterol | 6.5mg |
| Fiber | 2.17g |

# LEMON GRANITA

**Nothing is more refreshing on a hot summer's day than an Italian fat-free fresh lemon granita. Try making a lime version as well.**

INGREDIENTS

*2 cups water*

*¹/2 cup sugar*

*2 large lemons*

SERVES 4

### NUTRITIONAL NOTES
*Per portion:*

| | |
|---|---|
| Energy | 114cals |
| Total fat | 0g |
| Saturated fat | 0g |
| Cholesterol | 0mg |
| Fiber | 0g |

**1** In a large saucepan, heat the water and the sugar together over low heat until the sugar dissolves. Bring to a boil, stirring occasionally. Remove the pan from heat and set aside to cool.

**2** Finely grate the zest from 1 lemon, then squeeze the juice from both. Stir the grated lemon zest and juice into the sugar syrup. Pour it into a shallow plastic container or freezer tray, and freeze until it is solid.

**3** Plunge the bottom of the frozen container or tray in very hot water for a few seconds. Turn the frozen mixture out into a bowl and chop it into large chunks.

**4** Place the mixture in a blender or food processor fitted with metal blades, and process until it forms small crystals. Spoon the granita into serving glasses and serve immediately.

# COFFEE GRANITA

**Espresso coffee adds a delicious flavor to this appetizing fat-free Italian-style dessert.**

INGREDIENTS

*2 cups water*

*¹/2 cup sugar*

*1 cup very strong espresso coffee, cooled*

SERVES 4

**1** Heat the water and sugar together in a saucepan until the sugar dissolves. Bring to a boil, stirring occasionally. Remove the pan from heat and set aside to cool.

**2** Stir the cooled coffee and the sugar syrup together. Pour the mixture into a shallow, plastic container and freeze until solid. Plunge the bottom of the frozen container in very hot water for a few seconds. Turn the frozen mixture out into a bowl and chop it into large chunks.

**3** Place the mixture in a blender or food processor fitted with metal blades, and process until it forms small crystals. Spoon the granita into tall serving glasses and serve.

### COOK'S TIP
If not served immediately, the granita can be frozen again.

### NUTRITIONAL NOTES
*Per portion:*

| | |
|---|---|
| Energy | 115cals |
| Total fat | 0g |
| Saturated fat | 0g |
| Cholesterol | 0mg |
| Fiber | 0g |

# WATERMELON SORBET

A slice of this refreshing Italian fruit sorbet is the perfect way to cool down on a hot sunny day.
It also makes an excellent summer appetizer.

## INGREDIENTS

*1/2 small watermelon, weighing about*
*21/4 pounds*
*1/2 cup sugar*
*1/4 cup cranberry juice or water*
*2 tablespoons lemon juice*
*fresh mint sprigs, to decorate*

### SERVES 6

**1** Cut the watermelon into six equal-sized wedges. Scoop out the pink flesh from each wedge, discarding the seeds but reserving the shell.

**2** Line a freezerproof bowl, about the same size as the melon, with plastic wrap. Arrange the melon skins in the bowl to re-form the shell, fitting them together snugly so that there are no gaps. Put in the freezer.

**3** Put the sugar and cranberry juice or water in a saucepan and stir over low heat until the sugar dissolves. Bring to a boil, then reduce the heat and simmer for 5 minutes. Remove the pan from heat and set aside to cool.

**4** Put the melon flesh and lemon juice in a blender or food processor and blend into a smooth purée. Pour into a bowl, stir in the sugar syrup, then pour into a freezer-proof container. Freeze the mixture for 3–3½ hours or until slushy.

**5** Transfer the sorbet to a chilled freezerproof bowl and whisk well to break up the ice crystals. Return to the freezer for another 30 minutes. Whisk again, then transfer to the melon shell and freeze until solid.

**6** Remove the sorbet from the freezer and let stand at room temperature for 15 minutes. Take the melon out of the bowl and cut into wedges with a warmed sharp knife. Serve decorated with fresh mint sprigs.

## NUTRITIONAL NOTES

*Per portion:*

| | |
|---|---|
| Energy | 101cals |
| Total fat | 0.5g |
| Saturated fat | 0.2g |
| Cholesterol | 0mg |
| Fiber | 0.2g |

## COOK'S TIP

If preferred, this pretty pink sorbet can be served scooped into balls. Do this before the mixture is completely frozen, and re-freeze the balls on a baking sheet, ready to serve.

# ICED ORANGES

—

**The ultimate virtually fat-free treat—these delectable orange sorbets served in fruit shells create a light and refreshing flavorful dessert.**

### INGREDIENTS

*2/3 cup sugar*
*juice of 1 lemon*
*14 oranges*
*8 fresh bay leaves, to decorate*

### SERVES 8

**1** Put the sugar in a heavy saucepan. Add half the lemon juice, then add 1/2 cup water. Cook over low heat until the sugar has dissolved, stirring. Bring to a boil and boil for 2–3 minutes, until the syrup is clear. Remove the pan from heat and set aside.

**2** Slice the tops off eight of the oranges to make "hats." Scoop out the flesh of the oranges and reserve. Freeze the empty orange shells and "hats" until needed.

**3** Finely grate the zest of the remaining oranges and stir into the syrup. Squeeze the juice from the oranges, and from the reserved flesh. There should be about 3 cups of juice. Squeeze another orange or add store-bought unsweetened orange juice, if necessary, to make up to the correct quantity.

**4** Stir the orange juice and remaining lemon juice with 6 tablespoons water into the syrup. Taste, adding more lemon juice or sugar as desired. Pour the mixture into a shallow freezerproof container and freeze for 3 hours.

**5** Transfer the orange sorbet mixture in a chilled bowl and whisk thoroughly to break up the ice crystals. Return to the container and freeze for another 4 hours, until firm, but not solid.

**6** Pack the frozen mixture into the hollowed-out orange shells, mounding it up, and set the "hats" on top. Freeze the filled sorbet shells until ready to serve. Just before serving, push a skewer into the tops of the "hats" and push in a bay leaf, to decorate.

### NUTRITIONAL NOTES

*Per portion:*

| | |
|---|---|
| Energy | 139cals |
| Total fat | 0.17g |
| Saturated fat | 0g |
| Cholesterol | 0mg |
| Fiber | 3g |

# ITALIAN FRUIT SALAD AND ICE CREAM

**If you visit Italy in the summer, you will find little sidewalk fruit stands selling small dishes of macerated fruit, which are delectable on their own, but also wonderful with low-fat ice cream.**

### INGREDIENTS

*8 cups mixed ripe fruit, such as
strawberries, raspberries, loganberries, red
currants, blueberries, peaches, apricots,
plums and melons
juice of 6–8 oranges
juice of 1 lemon
1 tablespoon pear and apple concentrate
¼ cup low-fat sour cream
2 tablespoons orange-flavored
liqueur (optional)
fresh mint sprigs, to decorate*

### SERVES 6

**1** Prepare the fruit according to type. Cut it into reasonably small pieces, but not so small that the mixture becomes a mush.

**2** Put the fruit in a serving bowl and pour in enough orange juice to cover. Add the lemon juice, stir gently to mix, cover and chill in the refrigerator for 2 hours.

**3** Set half the macerated fruit aside to serve as it is. Purée the remainder in a blender or food processor. Pour the purée into a bowl.

**4** Gently warm the pear and apple concentrate in a small saucepan and stir it into the fruit purée. Whip the sour cream and fold it in to the fruit purée, then add the liqueur, if using.

**5** Churn the mixture in an ice cream maker. Alternatively, place in a shallow freezerproof container and freeze it until ice crystals form around the edge. Beat the mixture in a chilled bowl until smooth. Repeat the process once or twice, then freeze until firm. Soften slightly in the refrigerator before serving in scoops. Decorate with mint sprigs and serve with the macerated fruit.

### NUTRITIONAL NOTES
*Per portion:*

| | |
|---|---|
| Energy | 60cals |
| Total fat | 0.2g |
| Saturated fat | 0.01g |
| Cholesterol | 0.1mg |
| Fiber | 3.2g |

# NECTARINE AMARETTO CAKE

Try this delicious Italian-style cake served with a little low-fat sour cream for dessert, or serve it
solo for an afternoon treat. The syrup makes it deliciously moist but not soggy.

## INGREDIENTS

*3 eggs, separated*
*generous 3/4 cup sugar*
*finely grated zest and juice of 1 lemon*
*1/3 cup semolina*
*1/3 cup ground almonds*
*1/4 cup all-purpose flour*
*2 nectarines or peaches, halved and pitted*
*1/4 cup apricot glaze (see Cook's Tip)*

## FOR THE SYRUP

*6 tablespoons sugar*
*6 tablespoons water*
*2 tablespoons Amaretto liqueur*

### SERVES 10

**1** Preheat the oven to 350°F. Lightly
grease an 8-inch round loose-based cake
pan. Beat the egg yolks, sugar, lemon zest
and juice in a bowl until thick, pale
and creamy.

**2** Fold in the semolina, almonds and flour.

**3** Whisk the egg whites in a separate
bowl until fairly stiff. Using a metal
spoon, stir a generous spoonful of the
whisked egg whites into the semolina
mixture to lighten it, then fold in the
remaining egg whites. Spoon the mixture
into the prepared cake pan and then level
the surface.

**4** Bake for 30–35 minutes until the
center of the cake springs back when
lightly pressed. Remove the cake from the
oven and carefully loosen around the
edge with a knife. Prick the top of the
cake all over with a skewer and let cool
slightly in the pan.

**5** Meanwhile, make the syrup. Heat the
sugar and water in a small saucepan,
stirring until dissolved, then boil without
stirring for 2 minutes. Stir in the
Amaretto liqueur, then drizzle the syrup
slowly on top of the cake.

**6** Remove the cake from the pan and place
it on a serving plate. Slice the nectarines
or peaches, arrange them on top of the
cake and brush with the warm apricot
glaze. Serve warm or cold in slices.

## COOK'S TIP

To make apricot glaze, place a few
spoonfuls of apricot jam in a small
saucepan along with a squeeze of
lemon juice. Heat the jam, stirring, until
it is melted and runny. Pour the melted
jam through a wire sieve set over a bowl
and stir the jam with a wooden spoon to
help it go through. Discard the contents
of the sieve. Keep the strained glaze
warm and use as required.

## NUTRITIONAL NOTES
### *Per portion:*

| | |
|---|---|
| Energy | 165cals |
| Total fat | 1.8g |
| Saturated fat | 0.5g |
| Cholesterol | 57mg |
| Fiber | 0.4g |

# CHOCOLATE AMARETTI

**These mouthwatering Italian chocolate amaretti are delicious served on their own or with low-fat sorbet, mousse or zabaglione.**

### INGREDIENTS

*1 cup blanched whole almonds*
*1/2 cup sugar*
*1 tablespoon unsweetened cocoa powder*
*2 tablespoons confectioners' sugar*
*2 egg whites*
*pinch of cream of tartar*
*1 teaspoon almond extract*
*1/2 ounce sliced almonds, to decorate*

### MAKES ABOUT 24

**1** Preheat the oven to 350°F. Place the whole almonds on a small baking sheet and bake for 10–12 minutes, stirring occasionally, until the almonds are golden brown. Remove from the oven and set aside to cool to room temperature. Reduce the oven temperature to 325°F.

**2** Line a large baking sheet with nonstick baking parchment or aluminum foil and set aside. In a blender or food processor with a metal blade, process the toasted almonds with 1/4 cup sugar until the almonds are finely ground but not oily. Transfer to a medium bowl and sift in the cocoa powder and confectioners' sugar; stir to mix. Set aside.

**3** In a mixing bowl, beat the egg whites and cream of tartar together, using an electric mixer, until stiff peaks form. Sprinkle in the remaining 1/4 cup sugar, a tablespoon at a time, beating well after each addition, and continue beating until the egg whites are glossy and stiff. Beat in the almond extract.

**4** Sprinkle the almond-sugar mixture onto the whisked egg whites and gently fold them in until just blended. Spoon the mixture into a large piping bag with a plain 1/2-inch nozzle. Pipe the mixture into 1 1/2-inch rounds about 1 inch apart on the prepared baking sheet. Press a sliced almond into the center of each one.

**5** Bake the amaretti for 12–15 minutes or until they appear crisp. Place the baking sheets on a wire rack and let cool for 10 minutes. With a metal spatula, remove the amaretti and place on a wire rack, then let cool completely. When cool, store in an airtight container.

### NUTRITIONAL NOTES
*Per portion:*

| | |
|---|---|
| Energy | 58cals |
| Total fat | 3.7g |
| Saturated fat | 0.4g |
| Cholesterol | 0mg |
| Fiber | 0.6g |

# APRICOT AND ALMOND BARS

—

These moist apricot and almond bars are an irresistible low-fat snack
or treat for all to enjoy.

**2** Transfer the mixture to the prepared pan, spread to the edges and sprinkle with the almonds.

**3** Bake for 30–35 minutes or until the center of the cake springs back when lightly pressed. Turn out onto a wire rack and let cool. Remove and discard the paper, place the cake on a board and cut it into 18 slices with a sharp knife. Store in an airtight container.

### INGREDIENTS

*2 cups self-rising flour*
*2/3 cup light brown sugar*
*1/3 cup semolina*
*1 cup dried apricots, chopped*
*2 eggs*
*2 tablespoons malt extract*
*2 tablespoons honey*
*1/4 cup skim milk*
*1/4 cup sunflower oil*
*few drops of almond extract*
*2 tablespoons sliced almonds*

*MAKES 18*

**1** Preheat the oven to 325°F. Lightly grease and line an 11 × 7-inch shallow baking pan and set aside. Sift the flour into a bowl and add the sugar, semolina, dried apricots, eggs, malt extract, honey, milk, oil and almond extract. Mix well until smooth.

### NUTRITIONAL NOTES
*Per portion:*

| | |
|---|---|
| Energy | 153cals |
| Total fat | 4.56g |
| Saturated fat | 0.61g |
| Cholesterol | 21.5mg |
| Fiber | 1.27g |

# BISCOTTI
—

**These delicious Italian cookies are part-baked, sliced to reveal a feast of mixed nuts and then baked again until crisp and golden. They're perfect for rounding off a low-fat Italian meal.**

### INGREDIENTS

*1/4 cup unsalted butter, softened*
*1/2 cup sugar*
*1 1/2 cups self-rising flour*
*1/4 teaspoon salt*
*2 teaspoons baking powder*
*1 teaspoon ground coriander*
*finely grated zest of 1 lemon*
*1/2 cup polenta*
*1 egg, lightly beaten*
*2 teaspoons brandy or orange-
flavored liqueur*
*1/2 cup unblanched almonds*
*1/2 cup pistachios*

### MAKES 24

**1** Preheat the oven to 325°F. Lightly grease a baking sheet and set aside. Cream together the butter and sugar in a bowl.

**2** Sift the flour, salt, baking powder and coriander onto the creamed mixture in the bowl. Add the lemon zest, polenta, egg and brandy or liqueur and combine to make a soft dough.

### COOK'S TIP

Use a sharp, serrated knife to slice the cooled cookies in Step 4, otherwise they will crumble.

**3** Add the nuts and mix until evenly combined. Halve the mixture. Shape each half of the dough into a flat sausage about 9 inches long and 2 1/2 inches wide. Place on the prepared baking sheet. Bake for about 30 minutes, until risen and just firm. Remove from the oven and set aside to cool on a wire rack.

### NUTRITIONAL NOTES
*Per portion:*

| | |
|---|---|
| Energy | 94cals |
| Total fat | 4.2g |
| Saturated fat | 1.2g |
| Cholesterol | 12.6mg |
| Fiber | 0.2g |

**4** When cool, cut each sausage diagonally into 12 thin slices. Return to the baking sheet and bake for another 10 minutes, until crisp.

**5** Transfer the biscotti to a wire rack to cool completely. Store in an airtight container for up to one week.

# INDEX

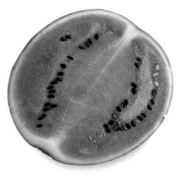